SKYLINE

Nino Migliori

WALLS
time gesture sign

19 June -10 September 2004
Rocca Sforzesca
Dozza (Bologna)

Curated by
Andrea Albertini
Nino Migliori

Coordination
Giuseppe Villirillo

Layout
Antonella Minzoni by Publimago

Translation
Helen Claudia Doyle

© **Damiani Editore 2004**
Via Zanardi, 376
Tel. +39.051.6350805
Fax +39.0516347188
Bologna 40131
Italy
www.damianieditore.it
info@damianieditore.it

© Authors for the text
© Nino Migliori for pictures

This book is distribuited by:

ITALIA

Consorzio Distributori Associati scrl
Monte San Pietro (Bologna) Italy
Tel. +39 051 969312

FRANCE

Critiques Livres SAS,
93172 Bagnolet Cedex,
tel: 33 (0)1 43 60 39 10

UK

Art Data
12 Bell Industrial Estate
50 Cunnington Street
London W4 5HB
Telephone: +44 (0) 208 747 1061

EUROPE

IDEA BOOKS
Nieuwe Herengracht 11
1011 rk Amsterdam Netherlands
Tel. +31 20 622 6154

USA

Distributed Art Publishers, inc.
155 sixth avenue second floor
New York City 10013.1507
Tel. +1 212 627 1999

Thanks to:
Cesare Biancini
GAM, Bologna
Roberta e Franco Calarota
Romano Cenni
Silvano Conti
Giorgio Domenichini
Enoteca Regionale
Daniela Facchinato
Ilford
Scuola Alberghiera Castel San Pietro
Keith de Lellis
Silvia Pesci
Vanda e Vincenzo Piccinini
Pro-Loco, Dozza
Angela Tassinari

WALLS · TIME GESTURE SIGN

NINO MIGLIORI

CURATED BY MARILENA PASQUALI

WALLS

DAMIANI

Nino Migliori may not even be aware that a fine photograph of his was among the handful of artworks surrounding the Bolognese painter Morandi in his home in Via Fondazza. The image was found slipped in between the pages of Henry Cartier-Bresson book (the only volume on photography in Morandi's library). This 1958 black and white print depicted – and it comes as no surprise – a breached piece of wall weathered by time and the elements. The tattered fragment of plasterwork has a great deal in common with the canvases by several European and American artists of that period, ranging from Burri to Tàpies and from Dubuffet to Fautrier, to name but a few. Theirs was an investigation into the formless and an exploration of matter, perhaps consciously considering Leonardo da Vinci's thoughts on the patterns emerging from the random unevenness of plasterwork, his reflections in an era marked by appreciation of a precise hand setting out limitations and boundaries, a hand guided by a geometric mind. And so we deemed it fitting, as the first step in our foundation, to give space to what Marilena Pasquali has been suggesting for some time: a review of walls. Not in the sense of paintings, as found in the hill village of Dozza (now famous for the artworks on its walls), but rather as chance has placed them directly before our eyes. Of course, our eyes would probably never even have noticed them, and we would not have been aware of those walls, if painters had not celebrated them. Indeed this is, and always has been, a valuable part of the painter's role – that of opening our eyes and drawing our attention to a thousand and one aspects of the visible world that might otherwise have gone unseen. And our choice of having Nino Migliori begin this journey of discovery is not a casual one. Migliori is in fact a photographer and as such very aware of being heir to a millennium-old tradition. A tradition that started right back in the Lascaux caves and forged its way forward to Monet's water lilies, and beyond; one that was permanently severed by the onslaught of the industrial civilization, where what had been the usual role of painting was replaced by photography, cinema and later television. He is well aware that Picasso and Pollock are not the rightful heirs to Fidia and Raffaello. Instead, those such as Daguerre, Nadar and the Lumière brothers are; those that still today reveal the face of the world, of our civilization, and of our barbarities. Migliori is sensitive to the magnetic force that the new art world exerts on everything around him. This spurs him to use the camera in an unusual fashion, and not solely to reproduce what is visible. The light-sensitive film and photographic paper are his palette and canvas. They are his tools for exploration, yielding unexpected results, where imagination is set free and dallies with the objectiveness of the camera lens, often enticing it far away from the fields most suited to the camera, and surprising the onlooker.

Eugenio Riccòmini
Chairman
Foundation Dozza Città d'Arte

Plato asserts in his Timaeus that the 'gentle fire' that warms the human body flows out through the eyes in a smooth and dense stream of light. Thus a tangible bridge is established between the observer and the observed thing, and over this bridge the impulses of light that emanate from the object travel to the eyes and thereby to the soul

Rudolf Arnheim, 1954[1]

If we accept the definition that photography is writing in light, and considering that I have always striven to do something similar to writing using light, then I may define myself as a photographer

Nino Migliori, 1997[2]

Arturo Carlo Quintavalle laid the most solid foundations for interpreting Nino Migliori's work on walls in his landmark essay written in 1977[3] . It is fundamental reading for anyone wishing to thoroughly explore a topic that has undoubtedly been crucial and constructive for the whole body of work by this Bolognese photographer, who has been acclaimed as among the discipline's leading exponents – not only at an Italian level – for some decades.

Migliori's exploration of walls extended for some thirty years[4], from the early 1950s to the late 1970s, and was so rich in interest and potential visual and expressive stimuli that it acted as a conducting theme for all his work, yielding coherent and continual development. Setting out from initial attention for surface elements and the expressive opportunities of matter itself, the young photographer, breathing the Informal air, turned his gaze to the subject during the full ripeness of his photography, opting to capture marks and gestures of expression residing in the wall and which have it speak with the language of protest, of irony, of love and even of dreams.

Quintavalle analyses the various stages of this body of work, thoroughly and passionately, in his almost endless research. He particularly looks into the underlying theoretical reasoning and psychological-perception impulses, pivoting his attention around the time element, and especially the concept of duration, emphasising Migliori's own words that "the central point lies in the image's duration"[5] .

But is Migliori's sense of time truly so 'profoundly new and revolutionary', and if so, why? I believe that a likely, and of course affirmative, answer may be found in his extraordinary ability to give memory a body and even a face, 'freezing' a fragment of reality, extracting it from the passing of time, trapping it in apparent timelessness and lastly delivering it to eternity. Yet, at the exact moment when Migliori 'saves' a snippet of life that has struck his keen artistic sensitivity, he also recognises its end, its disappearance as a real entity, as an object, replacing it with the equally intense – and perhaps more fascinating – reality of the image.

Attracted and enthralled by the stratification of human time, by what exists now and in an instant shall no longer be (or at least shall not be the same), the photographer entrusts an image, his image, to the time of his work. This work then becomes the sole reality, the inaccurate and disturbing transposition of what once was and that has ceased to exist. The very human difficulty in accepting death can be perceived amongst this. It is almost as if identifying and picking out excerpts of everyday life – what we may call 'phenomenon' – and transforming them into icons could also protect their 'saviour', ensuring irreplaceable scope for presence, duration and life through the work.

Of course this does not exclusively apply to Migliori and his *Walls*, but there is no doubt that his relentless, 30-year-long investigation of these testimonies of life provides one of the most authentic and convincing examples of the almost mediumistic ability (once known as the divine spark of creation) that makes artists unique and endows them with the gift of defeating time.

Not only Migliori's sharp sense of the ephemeral but also the way he approaches it, his way of 'building' the image (and I use this word deliberately to underline the importance of the photographer's intervention, its influence and determining force), set him among the leading post-war exponents. They were the first to be capable of recognising and interpreting the unease and the sense of existential anguish that the renewed awareness of the presence of Evil in the world had brought to all through the horrors of the war and its endless aftermath of global and personal insecurity. Quintavalle wrote that "the timescale of his works is 'high-pitched' and his chronology is in perfect parallel, if not preceding, much of what was being developed in painting" (he is of course referring to Mimmo Rotella's *Décollages*, Tàpies' new materiality, and the many Informal experiments ranging from Pollock's dripping to the dissolving assaults on form by the geographically closer Vasco Bendini).

The dates of Migliori's *Walls* are interesting not only for when the subject was embarked upon but also for when his expedition was concluded. He abandoned the topic in the mid 1970s, when writing on walls and using them as image support had become the artistic practice of the *Writers* and American graffiti artists (most of the *Murales*, with varying degrees of political or artistic content, emerged in these years). However, there is one large and essential conceptual difference between the *Writer*'s or the graffiti artist's work and that of the photographer: the former execute their work, their performance, on the wall, within the body of the wall itself; the later observes the wall, extracting his image from it, to make it his own.

Is it perhaps when writing and painting on walls officially became part of the artistic language that Migliori ceased creating images from the wall? Is it perhaps that he was not interested in creating a work from an intentional work, one that was not spontaneous but planned, and linguistically leaning towards the artistic? We shall leave the answer to the artist – and Migliori should forgive me if I find it so natural to use this term for him, as I consider him such. However, I feel one thing is certain: the first New York and West Coast Writers were spontaneous and authentic spokesmen for the needs and requests of a marginalized group (and as such were of interest to the photographer). Yet, once they became a school and were welcomed by the market ('embedded'), when they began to identify with a more or less codified language that would become genre and then manner, then they definitely left Migliori's field of interest and exploration. The *Muro dei drogati* ('Addicts' Wall') images, taken in Genoa in 1977, are some of the last in his long cycle. Here we can see the distinction between the spontaneous matter interpreted and recreated by the photographer on the one hand and, on the other, the encounter between two precise artistic intentions. But making an image of an artistic image is not what Migliori was seeking in these urban walls. Other experiments of his[6] would later follow this direction – but not in that period, because then walls were for him predominantly an account of spontaneous life and memory.

Migliori nurtures the wall and is 'curious' about it, doing so with his natural expressive spontaneity and exuberant manner[7]. As he himself underlines, his is a linguistic, gestural and semiological dialogue that calls in an entirely personal method – a method very precise and distinct in its refusal of genres, confines and categories, so that it may favour two stages of the creative process: perception and restitution, in what Arnheim defines as "vision as active exploration"[8] . Perception, in that it is awareness of the sensorial experience, is instinctive, immediate and very sensitive in Migliori because, as with all true artists, he is first and foremost an 'eye' penetrated and brought to life by light – that 'gentle fire' identified by Plato. However, perception alone is not enough: restitution is the other vital ingredient, this being the ability to translate visual stimuli, sensorial leads and emotional intimations into an independent image.

Thus a dual process is seen: from reality, from the character of the wall with its constantly changing matter, its gestures of expression and its writing, to the photographer's reality and character. He reads and interprets every detail like an unfaithful translator aware of becoming the sole author, and perhaps sole protagonist, of that reflection of himself that is the image. This process can of course proliferate, accumulating mark upon mark and gesture upon gesture, in a chain of erasures, additions, reinstatements and fusion between layers – a process that will find an end only with the final and total destruction of the wall. What counts is that the sole static point in this whole process of change is constituted by the photographer's eye, and that the sole work is his photograph.

Migliori's is therefore an essentially gestalt approach – one of shapes and the relationship between them, one of similarities and associations, and of spatial organisation and orientation. He defines this space with clarity, excluding any visual intrusion outside of the portion of wall portrayed, barring any contextualisation or frame. As has been perceptively observed once again by Quintavalle, Migliori photographs the wall, taking it as a surface to be engraved (and the light does this here, without the need for nibs or etchings) since, as a photographer, he wants to see how the 'film' – the plasterwork – reacts to the mark and the action of photographing.

However, the wall for him is also a page to choose from, for coordinating and recording the marks and expression of others. A page of writing that on closer inspection is little other than his own writing, watermarked with his own history as a man and artist. He intervenes like a director making active use of the actors present for a work: many pairs of hands are involved but the result nonetheless bears his unmistakeable imprint. Or like an orchestra conductor performing his music through skilled musicians, whose every movement and expression is directed by him.

There are a few more important observations that I should like to share before taking a closer look Migliori's *Walls*, which are arranged into three core groups according to execution date and critical convention. Nevertheless, careful analysis of the individual photographs and their interrelation reveals that the divisions are not actually so clear-cut and that Nino's investigations into memory chronologically overlap with those into gestural expression and those where the photographer discovers a particularly provocative mark. And here I have taken the liberty of emphasising a few terms in bold that I hold to be key words for interpreting Migliori's work.

Firstly I feel I should underline the close, essential and contradictory relationship established between Nino's constantly receptive (but apprehensive and almost ravenous) gaze and **chance**. There is no need here to go into the vexing question of cause and chance. However, it is appropriate to remember how this photographer, this artist, is able to capture an occasion – even the most unexpected or fortuitous one – and make it his own, imparting order to what comes and goes, not unlike a creator converting chaos into cosmos. This act of transformation and appropriation takes place through the tool of **recognition**, which is fundamentally the relationship with the **visible** (a word very dear not only to painters but also to photographers, I believe), this being with the phenomenon, the manifestation of reality, its optical and sensorial appearance.

The **depth** of Migliori's *Walls* should also be underlined, a depth found in the wealth of layers and presences making walls a boundless source of amazement and narration. That there is much beyond the surface may be strongly sensed, that something is pushing to emerge, coveting a spot in the limelight. And Nino cannot help but be the first to be fascinated by this opportunity to go beyond appearances, to bring out the **unsaid**, the **unseen**, and to give it visibility.

The **figure/background relationship** should be considered alongside the question of depth. Migliori's images in fact require careful attention because, due to their funambulatory metamorphic capacity, this relationship is frequently inverted and what should remain in the shadows instead basks in the sunlight, like in a Cinderella tale. Then, upon further investigation, it emerges that everything is figure in Nino's *Walls*, everything is the **central star** with equal rights, since this choice was made by the photographer beforehand in terms of cut and frame; thus everything in the image is acknowledged, nothing of what he has decided to include is left mute.

Lastly, we come to a topic touched on by the artist many a time: **landscape**. Migliori expanded on this subject in a text published in 1993 to mark the 45th Venice Biennial[9] : "Landscape is everything to me, not only the documentation of what I see. It is in my mind before it is in the objects surrounding me. It is what you see, what enthrals you, what inspires you. It is not merely the naturalistic aspect of producing a copy, it is the picture postcard, it is the reappraisal of customs, it is the paving, and the road we follow, changing from area to area, from climate to climate, going from mud to gravel, and from gravel to the tarmacked motorway".

And so, looking at his *Walls*, I am naturally led to place them – also conceptually – alongside what may be seen as their alter ego and what is also their stage, their everyday dimension: the street. Both are meeting places, whether intentional or by chance, and as such are strongly marked by Man's presence. They put themselves forward as the opposite (salvific and necessary) of those horrifying, dehumanised non-places studied by modern sociology to denounce their danger: airports, supermarkets, motorways, and everything designed and built to flatten differences, taking with it Mankind's humanity.

By contrast – and thankfully, I should like to add – Migliori's *Walls* are human places, as well as inner landscapes, uniting these in a single act coming from the heart and mind before it comes from the gaze and hand. It is the process of identification between Man and nature, between Man and his environment, that permits only the former to recognise and love what surrounds him, to make it his dwelling place and to transform it into a stage for his every hazardous adventure, for every return to the path, for every new beginning.

There is no type of wall that attracts Migliori more than another along this common path that he follows with and through his images. Certainly the elect – the wall that freezes his gaze in a sudden burst of inspiration, alluring him to the challenge of photographing – must be a wall with a 'past', with intense marks. However, what truly matters to him is (to use a rather appropriate expression taken from the parallel worlds of psychology and pedagogy)[10] 'giving the clouds a name', moving forth through analogies, echoes and reminders, and 'inventing' the wall in the original sense of the Latin invenio, meaning 'to find'.

In the early 1950s, his attention focused on the traces of time, on the neglected memory that the wall preserves and displays, on the city's oblivious and blotted out face[11] . Everything attracted him. One example is a piece of wall puffed with matter, becoming 'figure' during the gradual process of shedding its plaster (a 1950 black and white photograph particularly comes to mind, one depicting the nightmarish face of a threatening phantom, surfacing through subtraction). Another is in the obsessively and densely engraved surfaces where every scratch, every mark added (or erased), contributes to heightening the impression of a wave-like rhythm, as if it were the musical score of the whole. Or the image where colour plays the leading role – often an aggressive one – as in the 1950 green wall where the bright ground that should alleviate, instead accentuates the violent air of a black stain that seems to still be running, like blood on a wall after a firing-squad execution (yet, with its rusty studs embedded in the green, the fragment could also be seen as an urban metaphor for the wood of the Cross). Or the wall displaying a clear white mark on the black silky-smooth skin, or the first writings, or the first drawings (a man holding balloons, the loosely sketched faunlike face, the outlines of two children holding hands as in a paper ring-a-ring o'roses cut out with scissors) where Nino's love for Paul Klee's constantly changing figures is clearly evident, and Migliori is, like Klee, fascinated by children's drawings, as a framework for every visual thought and an endless source of discovery for creativity and imagination. Or the surfaces encrusted with mould or knobbled with outgrowths, and those corroded and riddled with holes in the crumbling plasterwork, which are certainly among the most 'Informal' of Migliori's works – achieved through an adding and subtracting process that, in a complex interweaving of solids and voids, unites the pattern of cracks, holes, and abrasions with a weft of craters, swellings and explosions of matter.

Yet there is still more, because the surface 'eaten' by a black shadow invading like blazing leprosy (and here the mind cannot but turn to Migliori's *off-camera* experiments and *Pyrograms* from the same period) is also the image of a time often not conceded. Likewise for the figures embodying simple contracted lyricism that emerge, that stand out from their background to the point of becoming icons, such as the 'king' and 'queen' discovered in the early 1950s by Migliori on a Bolognese red wall in Via Fondazza. He later gave this image to the artist Giorgio Morandi during one of their meetings when, going beyond all the barriers of age, cultural differences and aesthetic leanings, the elderly master and the young photographer used to discuss photography, cinema and painting – in other words, images.

The photographer then moved on to expand on his research into gestural expression and "torn posters", this being in the 1950s and the early '70s, when he returned to this topic. Of the entire *Walls* body of work, it is perhaps the most tumultuous period, since it involves the urban suburbs and is therefore the most desperate. Whether the photos are black and white or colour makes little difference, what counts is the meeting/clashing of the shrill colours assaulting our gaze, almost the sensation of the overloud tearing of paper assailing our inner ear with no prospect of protection. Visual and auditory provocation loom in the photo, like concrete and tangible proof of the inanity of every advertising message and the emptiness of every media promise revealing nonsensical stuttering, indifferent repetition, and fundamental falseness and uselessness.

However, going beyond the political-social content, what is questioned is the language, Man's ability to exchange words for communicating and – the peak of utopia – even perhaps for understanding each other. In this tower of Babel of lost letters, unfinished words and slurred sentences that are feverishly overlain and then swallowed and erased by each other, a sensation of precariousness, unease and senselessness is the unopposed ruler. Perhaps what remains, what instead takes on identity and power in this drift of destructive gestures, is in fact emptiness, the fragment of free space, the new form that is created in the gaps between the no longer meaningful forms.

Sometimes in Migliori's *Walls*, these scrambled, trampled rejected mass images manage to transform themselves to become something unique. Four of his photos strike me in particular in this respect, and all are joined by the same magic: that gaze that succeeds in cracking the cocoon of rejected words to then turn intact to the casual passer-by and to the hunter-photographer, in a game of deferments and imperious demands for attention, with the visual dimension of a panopticon, where it is no longer clear who is the observer and who is observed, but which never fails to create the opportunity for dialogue. The first two of the four show the huge winking eyes of cartoon characters from the period as they pierce the layers of paper to stare us directly in the face. Moshe Dayan's single eye and its imperious gaze projecting from the shadows of an incomprehensible poster steal the attention in the third. The fourth features the gaze of a fully aware, and nevertheless untroubled, Antonio Gramsci emerging from the blood red of human stupidity and brutality.

At the onset of the 1970s, the focus of Migliori's experiments began, with a strongly motivated approach, to switch to the writings on walls and to the marks made by humans (and loaded with meaning), marks made by individuals leaving their imprint on a city to speak of themselves, to establish territory and compare with others. The sense of solitude leaving a lump in the throat as found in the "torn posters" is absent in these works. Instead, the onlooker seems to be witnessing and taking part in a debate with many participants, or in a chorus where the various forms of individuality challenge, chase, court and reject each other.

Nino is the director and interpreter of everything: of the political messages that are full blown manifestos of marks and symbols, where colour plays a vital role and the heavy white of the crossings-out allowing a new round to begin reigns in importance; of the writing deciphered into thirty ideograms in the complex *In immagin abile - Lessico distratto* from 1975; of the huge and even solemn icons of *PACE GUERRA E POI PACE* ('peace') and *EUROPA LIBERA* ('a free Europe') that have become authentic visual models of inalienable demands for many of us, and which are even more topical and urgent today.

Migliori finds the images of others, making them him own, throughout the built environment and especially on the burning red of many walls in his native Bologna. They range from the rough blurred ones such as the rudimentary outlines scored by inexpert hands – a woman's profile, a bearded silhouette, a prophetic 'electoral' alarm that thirty years on is once again about to ring – to the unsettling symbols of terror – the extremist five-pointed star branded into the black flesh of the wall, a dark dagger that is both a cross and an airplane plummeting to the ground, leaving black trails of death in its wake, or the horned "devils" (grotesque puppets, long-eared masks with fanatical eyes) – speaking of suffering and squalor but also of unbridled creativity and an innate ability to jeeringly lighten hardships in life.

And lastly, like gems in the dirt, Migliori encounters images of tenderness: the words of love 'Ti Amo' repeated and enlarged in obsessive expression as a cry of liberation; a 'despairing Indian' speaking didactically of politics, using the walls like a primary school blackboard, only to acknowledge inconsolably that it is exclusively and always all about love; or the tormented disclosure "My name's Daniela. My dad's died", which is so concise and all-encompassing in its innocent distress.

The artist is touched, but this does not detract his attention from cleansing the form that is his task to forge – like the placing of a signature – isolating and extracting it from the context.

There is an unusual match to finish on, one perhaps unique for its poetic aura and sharpness of image, where its aesthetic nature meets a spontaneous mark that almost seems to be a work in itself, just waiting for Migliori to capture it with his expert gaze and to offer it up to us as a gift: the *Fiore del muro rosa* ('flower on a pink wall') emerges from the spontaneous combination of the six-holed cup-shaped form opened in the wall and the creativity of its anonymous maker – certainly one with a young spirit.

And today Migliori gives us this gift, with that same intact youth.

Marilena Pasquali

---

1) *Rudolf Arnheim, Arte e percezione visiva (Milan: Feltrinelli, 1984), p. 56.*

2) *Paolo Barbaro, "Conversazione con Nino Migliori", in Luci e Tracce (Cavezzo, 1997).*

3) *Arturo Carlo Quintavalle, "Muri", in the exhibition catalogue Antonio Migliori, Parma, Salone dei Contrafforti, 1977, p. 30-33.*

4) *Ibid., p. 30. "I photographed walls as I was interested in Man. They are the only record of his history from the Altamira caves to the graffiti or paintings on the walls in Pompei. Man loses his inhibitions before a wall; using a coin or a key to scratch with, or a piece of chalk or a spray can, he may set free his subconscious and his gestural expressiveness, and is himself. The reason for exploring walls, the stains, the formlessness, the mould, the damp and the marks resides here. Walls where a succession of signs of intervention has been left by dozens of people exert a particular fascination for me, in that they record the passing of the world. Morandi was very alert to photography, he was very keen on my walls and even kept one or two of my images in his studio, such as the one shot in Via Fondazza showing a pair of informal figures he called the king and the queen. He was the one who spoke to me of Brassaï, making me really see Brassaï. He also had books on Cartier-Bresson, Bishof, and Capa, but Morandi's favourite was Bresson. We would discuss these photos at length. We spoke about Brassaï,'s line of exploration, his book on "Graffiti" (I only caught a glimpse of it), which in essence is research into a topic that stood outside of his photography, and instead entirely fitted with Bresson and his concept of the captured image. Brassaï's is a study of Paris, one carefully looking into signs and graphic marks in particular, and therefore into the history of Paris. I feel that the dialogue I have developed is a different one. As far as technique is concerned, it is very simple: I start off with black and white negative or colour slide film and I tend to go in very close to isolate a single detail. Very seldom, in extremely few cases, do I choose the whole. I have always strived to draw the scene out from its surroundings."*

5) *Ibid., p. 31.*

6) *I remember Segnificazione, his extremely interesting study of a Guercino engraving, which read as 'unfaithful' translator for its writing details. The work was presented at the memorable Franco Solmi exhibition, Metafisica del Quotidiano, held in Bologna at the Galleria d'Arte Moderna in summer 1978.*

7) *I owe this fitting definition to Claretta Stefanelli Spatzer, who put forward this interesting comparison between the off-camera photography of Luigi Veronesi (which she defined as 'Apollonian'), and that of Nino Migliori ('Dionysian').*

8) *Rudolf Arnheim, op. cit., p.55.*

9) *Cf. Arturo Carlo Quintavalle, Muri di carta, Fotografia e paesaggio dopo le avanguardie (Milan: Electa, 1993), p91*

10) *Migliori is undoubtedly a master in educating the younger generation on images, and for some years now he has devoted much of his time to furthering awareness of photography in schools and education institutes, collaborating with schools, colleges and university faculties, as well as education councillors, for this purpose.*

11) *It is worth while quoting another enlightening reflection by Quintavalle (op. cit., 1977, p. 32) in relation to this point: "The idea that the plasterwork is graffitied, florid with mould, running with blurred colours, puffed with damp or powdery from the scorching summer sun, and that it is layered with torn or faded posters is all part of urban history, or rather of the perception of the city (the italics are mine, author's note). No one has done this to date, but a day will come when half of urban planners' studies of cities and the urban environment as communication tools will be based on paving surfaces, plasterwork, flaky walls and graffiti". I add that anyone who intends to do this will not be able to ignore Nino Migliori's work*

"I decided to focus on *Walls* as I was interested in Man. They are the only record of his history from the Altamira caves to the graffiti or paintings on the walls in Pompei. Man loses his inhibitions before a wall; using a coin or a key to scratch with, or a piece of chalk or a spray can, he may set free his subconscious and his gestural expressiveness, and is himself". This statement by Migliori, taken from the 1977 essay by A. C. Quintavalle[1] , is valuable in enabling us to concisely grasp exactly what this photographer's core stimulus has been on the topic. Indeed, we find a rich repertoire of images where the documentary process inherent in the concept of reporter coverage is moulded to a new need: one of freezing and extolling the worth of a whole complex of human action that, by nature, is prone to transience and functional irrelevance. These actions may also be deciphered as models of psychological reaction to the dissipating and often oppressive environment of the metropolis.

Thus, Migliori's approach is not one of Dadaist extraction and restitution, as it has defined by some. Neither is he interested in abstracting details that could take on prominence in a compositional order, in a Cavalli-like Formalism. Instead, "the photographer closes in on the wall as if it were a great blackboard upon which nature and Man have left their marks – marks belonging to 'time' above all "[2].

And here we come to the topic of time, which is not evoked as sampling the instant. To the contrary, the mould, the peeling surfaces, the erasings or corrections to previous writings bring a sense of wear, of creeping and relentless disintegration. Much later, in 1976, Migliori went on to express this disintegration also in relation to himself – in his renowned series of self-portraits where his facial features gradually give way to the contours of a skull.

These images often avoid lengthy calculation: the wall is not inspected for the primary purpose of deriving an informal or abstract composition, or one with 'new wording'. Instead, the images restrict themselves to recording the progressive sedimentation of written or graphic signs inferring anonymous human presence, in a form not dissimilar – from an ethological standpoint – to the biological traces intentionally left by some animal species for the purposes of marking territory.

It should here be pointed out that the number of photographers interested in this topic, at least on an intermittent basis, was great enough to stir the curiosity of the prominent academic, Umberto Eco, who in fact published a brief essay on the subject in 1961[3]. We instead shall specifically look at the Frenchman Brassaï and the American Aaron Siskind in our analysis of works by other photographers on the same topic.

Let us start with Brassaï. He had already created his famous series *Graffiti parisiens* as early on as the 1930s and the reason for him often being named as a reference for Migliori's work – even if subconsciously – is evident: there are in fact precise parallels, but yet again analysis should not come to a halt at a level simply comprising the grammar of vision.

Firstly, the existence of a 'history of writings' may be perceived by examining a broader range of images portraying the same subject. This 'history' – first identified by Quintavalle[4] – is well suited to recognising the chronology of techniques, themes and impulses of various types. For example, we would not, within this framework, expect sprayed writings or certain types of political slogans in a picture by the French photographer, yet this induces us to further broaden our observation horizons.

Whilst reflecting on the respective bodies of work as a whole, we may recall that "Brassaï's language mirrors Bresson's as well as the Bergsonian idealism of the French culture: the photographer should be an invisible witness to the event, should capture the image and convey it to others, and the image should be narration"[5]. His is therefore a discourse on the city, on relevant or irrelevant everyday events, and on characters and views depicted with undeceived irony but nevertheless not lacking in a tinge of nostalgia. In short, it is an account immediately striving to be history, as it is aware of drawing attention to the fleeting elements of a swiftly changing city.

As may be supposed, Migliori's cultural context is somewhat different, as is his underlying attitude to photography. It should first be emphasised that his decision to keep this project open for many years was seen alongside a gradual shifting of the core of his primary interest – something not to be found in the French photographer. More recent statements by Migliori himself on the matter clarify that the entire body of work "may be divided into two or three periods. I was initially driven by my curiosity for the marks on walls, then my interest moved to the stains and moulds, the informal reread by means of the wall, to finish off with the topic of the writings on walls. I consider the wall as a ground to writing, to communication and to gestural expression in this period"[6]. These divisions are flexible, since he himself confirms that he has "always dealt with walls with a rather instinctive approach", without forcing himself to "undertake pre-established courses"[7].

If, on the other hand, this body of work is taken within a more general context – one comprising Migliori's parallel research in the dark room – his persistent investigation into the possibilities and shapes of writing in the photographic ambit stands out. We may, from this point of view, place this exploration of other writings (ideographic, gestural or alphabetical) in the threshold area between the two worlds of *in-* and *off-camera* – an area found alongside, and sometimes overlapping with, the previous investigation. In fact, many negatives created with the camera then went on to be a visual pretext for a series of subsequent processes occurring under the enlarger.

Differently to Brassaï, who explored walls only at a precise moment in his career, the New Yorker Aaron Siskind's choice to use the lens to isolate minimal portions of reality has with time become an unmistakeable stylistic hallmark.

A brief exploration of this photographer's career should be embarked upon in this case, in order to fully understand the meaning of the above. Siskind started out in the 1930s, carrying out photo coverage for the Film & Photo League; *Harlem document* and several other works particularly stand out in this period for their extremely elegant images, showing that "even during his most intense photo-reporting phase, Siskind never lost sight of the importance of composition"[8] .

However, dissatisfaction with this type of activity emerged a few years later, in spring 1944, when the photographer reached a new-found resoluteness that would mark the course of all his subsequent output. Indeed, Siskind realised that "for the first time in my life, subject matter (...) has ceased to be of primary importance. Instead, I found myself involved in the relationships of these objects, so much so that these pictures turned out to be deeply moving and personal experiences"[9] . Others of the photographer's statements of a similarly expressionist nature are also interesting, such as "the interior drama is the meaning of the exterior event"[10] , or the one defining a concept of photography as "shifted from what the world looks like to what we feel about the world and what we want the world to mean"[11]. This underpinning attitude would in fact lead him to move nearer to the world of *action painting* – at the time flourishing there in his native New York – through a series of rather close, if not always easy, relationships with its main exponents[12] . The theme of the wall (rendered primarily with strongly contrasting black and white tones) soon became increasingly frequent – culminating in it being practically exclusive – as an answer to the presumable need to capture and preserve, on a two-dimensional surface, certain fragments of his own psychic projections. This conclusion is confirmed by other affirmations by the artist, where he admits that "these photographs are psychological in character"[13], inasmuch as "the reason I'm making pictures is out of a necessity to order the world, which is really ordering myself"[14] .

In introducing a comparison with Informalism in painting, which shall be picked up in more detail later, we may immediately point out that whilst a constant quest for instinctive spontaneity is found in Abstract Expressionism and whilst the work's completeness of form generally derives from the repeated practice of psychic automatism that tends to quash pictorial technique (or rather to make it 'transparent'), the contrary occurs in Siskind's specific case. Here, the extreme technical perfection inverts this relationship, concentrating expression into tiny iconic crystals, which are both sublime and fascinating in their coolness. This may easily be explained through his impeccable shooting methods – strongly marked by the investigative quality acquired in the 1930s during his years training as photo-reporter. Despite appearances, these methods place his process perfectly within the Bauhaus objectifying approach, as outlined above. In fact, it should not be forgotten that he also taught at and later headed the Photography Department founded in 1944 by Moholy-Nagy at Chicago's Institute of Design.

The walls by this American photographer consequently constitute the fruit of reporting activity that evolved into research into himself and a quest for his innermost being through the subject shown. From this stance, Migliori has very little in common. However, we are examining two bodies of work that are often very alike externally, and although they are to be found within very different artistic paths, they share some aspects of a general concept of photography taken as – to use Siskind's words once again – the "transformation or transfiguration"[15] of real objects and events.

If instead we assess these bodies of work using a broader perspective, one involving the directions developed in the visual arts during the 1950s, it is indeed impossible to ignore the striking similarities these photos share, on a visual plane, with some Informalism images – so much so as to see them included in art exhibitions focusing on this[16].

So the matter lies, once again, within the acceptability margin of the debate that has accompanied the history of photography since its origins, and which the critics in this case have focused on Italian artists such as Burri and Schifano, on Rotella's *Décollages* or on Wols, Dubuffet, Twombly and Tàpies.

If the meaning of the two entities prevailing here – the mark and the matter – is examined parallelly from both pictorial and photographic standpoints, we are able to make certain observations that assist us in defining a more precise position. This should be without overlooking that Migliori set out on this quest totally independently, even before the creation of several of the informal works that his many images might be compared to and, in any case, without his direct awareness of the movement's leading exponents.

Firstly, it may be noted that the technique Migliori uses in this case is the one conventionally handed down, the one that entails camera use. Here transgressions beyond the overturning of the traditional figure/background relationship – or rather the merging of their matter – are not brought in. Introduction of a different critical statute for these works would not appear justifiable in this context; we could therefore turn to the same considerations that apply for comparison between a 19th century photographic landscape and a similar oil painting from the same period. However, our investigation follows a different direction. Moving forth, analysis of the mark in the informal language implicates the artist in a particularly strong relationship. This process in fact emerges as an intimately personal and private entity, one that at times is oriented towards the past in a sense of regression to childhood or illness. This is contemporary to these photographs taking on another's imprint, when stripped bare of any potential protection. It is not by chance that the marks made in a painting are destined to a more secluded life, such as within the rooms of the artist's studio or a gallery where it is displayed only to a select public. The marks are public in Migliori's images and at the mercy of all; only rarely are they reserved for art connoisseurs. Furthermore, these marks are not usually made with artistic purposes in mind. Quite the contrary: going beyond the loose similarities, the marks are seldom connected with the level of awareness that is generally reached by the professional artist. If impermanence may be interpreted as an intermediary term between the act producing the graffiti and the action itself of photographing – in that both these operations deal with structurally fragile matter (the plasterwork and the light-sensitive film) prone to decomposition – then the physical matter of the painting and, as a consequence, the memory preserved within it both face the challenge of time with far less uncertainty. Upon further examination of this second term, it is most clear that matter is simply represented in two dimensions in photography and often two tonalities – black and white – whilst pictorial matter is real and three-dimensional to a point where the dividing line with sculpture is often crossed. Matter is part of a functional whole in a photographic print, since the case of the walls always involves buildings performing their purposes independently of the mould or writing that may be found on them: as the mere biological or cultural superficial features that they are, these elements transform the underlying structure only in the eyes of the observer studying or admiring them. By contrast, not only formless, burnt, confused matter but also the primigenial, germinal and palingenesian type in any case prove to be non-functional, outside of the expressive context that they are located within. Finally, the size or overall physicality of much pictorial intervention – and which often presents empathic overtones evoked by the colours chosen – generate a powerful impact on perception, one that cannot be replaced by any photographic paper or support.

Lastly – and in reference to something touched on by Migliori himself, as contained in the statement in the opening paragraph of this text – we believe this body of work should also be read in a psychoanalytic key, although we are aware that the photographer (upon his own admittance) was not familiar with that context of introspective quest at the time. Writings and graffiti certainly constitute for their creators an "instant of releasing angst, passion or lust"[17], whilst at the same time "if you photograph a wall with a history, a wall where many have left the mark of their presence, you bring a highly revolutionary process to that urban environment, because you place the accent exactly on what has been removed, on the 'old' – in short, on everything that cannot be sold, passed off, or revered as 'antique' [18]". An explanation for the great acclaim that these photographs have met with may be found exactly in this approach, one embodying a sensitivity widespread in the post-war period.

Flavio Eugenio Marelli

[1] A.C. Quintavalle, *Antonio Migliori*, exhibition catalogue, C.S.A.C. Photograpic Department (Parma, 1977).

[2] See A. Colombo, "Nino Migliori", in *Progresso fotografico* (November 1977), p. 55.

[3] See U. Eco, "Di foto fatte sui muri", in *Il Verri*, no. 4 (Milan, 1961).

[4] See A.C. Quintavalle (edited by), *Enciclopedia pratica per fotografare* (Milan: Fabbri, 1979), pp. 1434 and

[5] *Ibid.*, p. 1432.

[6] See P. Barbaro, C. Cavatorta, N. Migliori, *Luci e tracce* (Cavezzo: Assessorato alla Cultura di Cavezzo, 1997) p. 9.

[7] *Ibid.*

[8] See L. Ballerini, "Le meraviglie del mondo screziato, o la canzone d'amore di Aaron Siskind", in *Aaron Siskind. Cinquant'anni di fotografia 1931 - 1981*, ed. G. Scimè (Milan: Selezione d'Immagini, 1984), p. 13.

[9] See J. Green, *American Photography. A critical history 1945 to the present* (New York: Harry N. Abrams Inc., 1984), p. 53.

[10] *Ibid.*

[11] *Ibid.*, p. 55.

[12] Regarding this topic, we in fact learn from James Enyeart, Head of the Center for Creative Photography at the University of Arizona, that although Aaron Siskind's first photographic book was partly financed by the sale of a Franz Kline painting presented by Harold Rosenberg (art critic and movement supporter), the photographer's work was nevertheless only partially accepted by the artists (see G. Scimè, 1984, p. 7)

[13] See J. Green, 1984, p. 53.

[14] *Ibid.*, p. 55.

[15] *Ibid.*

[16] See the exhibition on *L'informale in Italia*, curated by Renato Barilli and Franco Solmi, held at the Galleria d'Arte Moderna in Bologna in 1983, where a section concentrating on 'Informal photography' included images by Nino Migliori, Paolo Monti, Emilio Vedova and Luca Patella.

[17] See "Migliori al Diaframma", in *Progresso fotografico* (Milan, April 1974), p. 8.

[18] See A. C. Quintavalle 1977, p. 31.

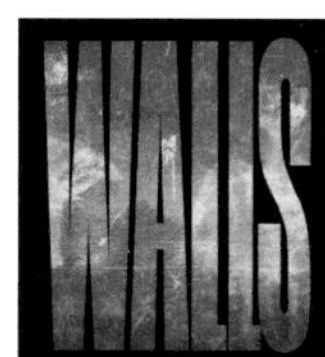

TABLE OF CONTENTS

SOMMARIO

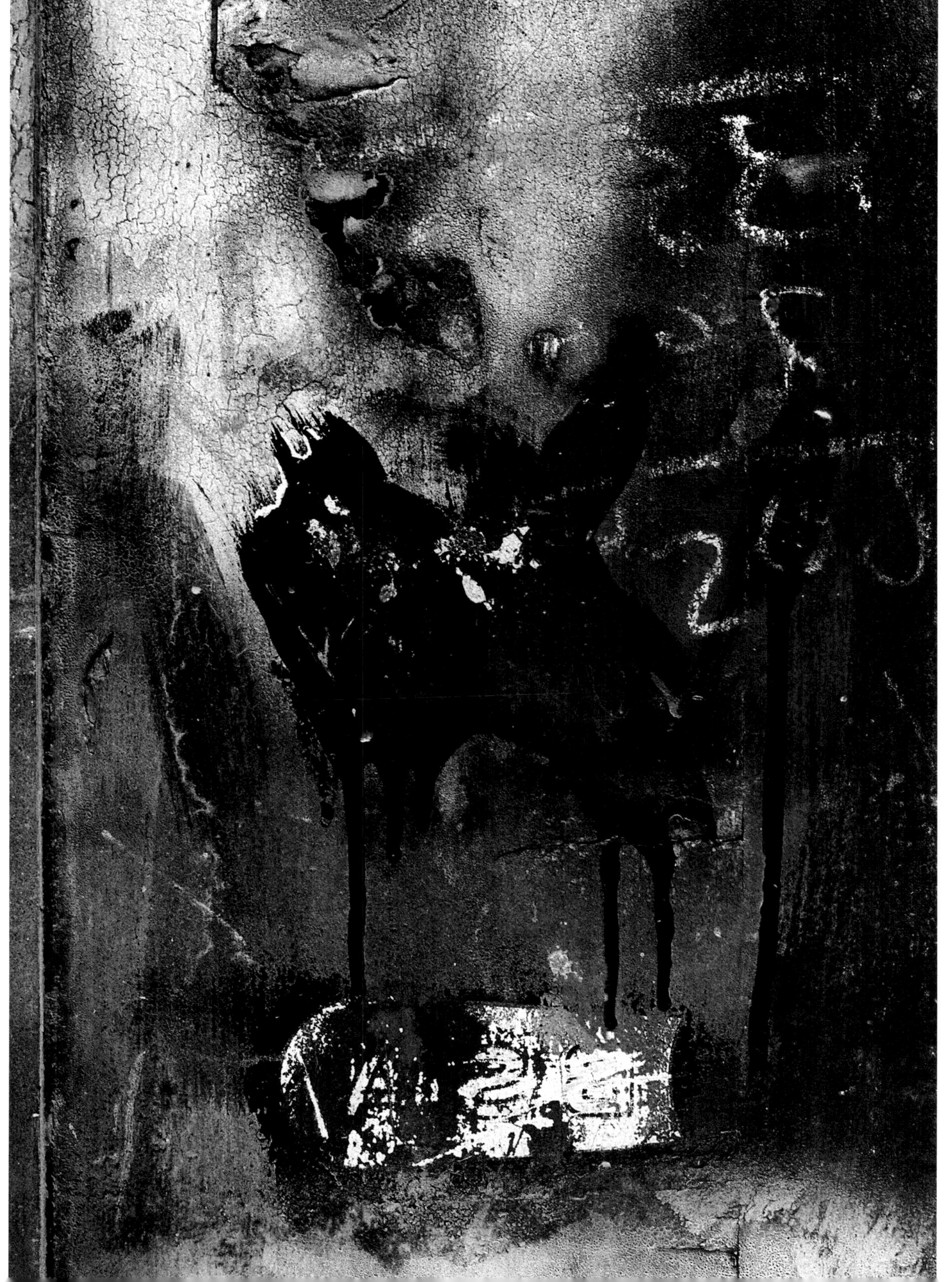

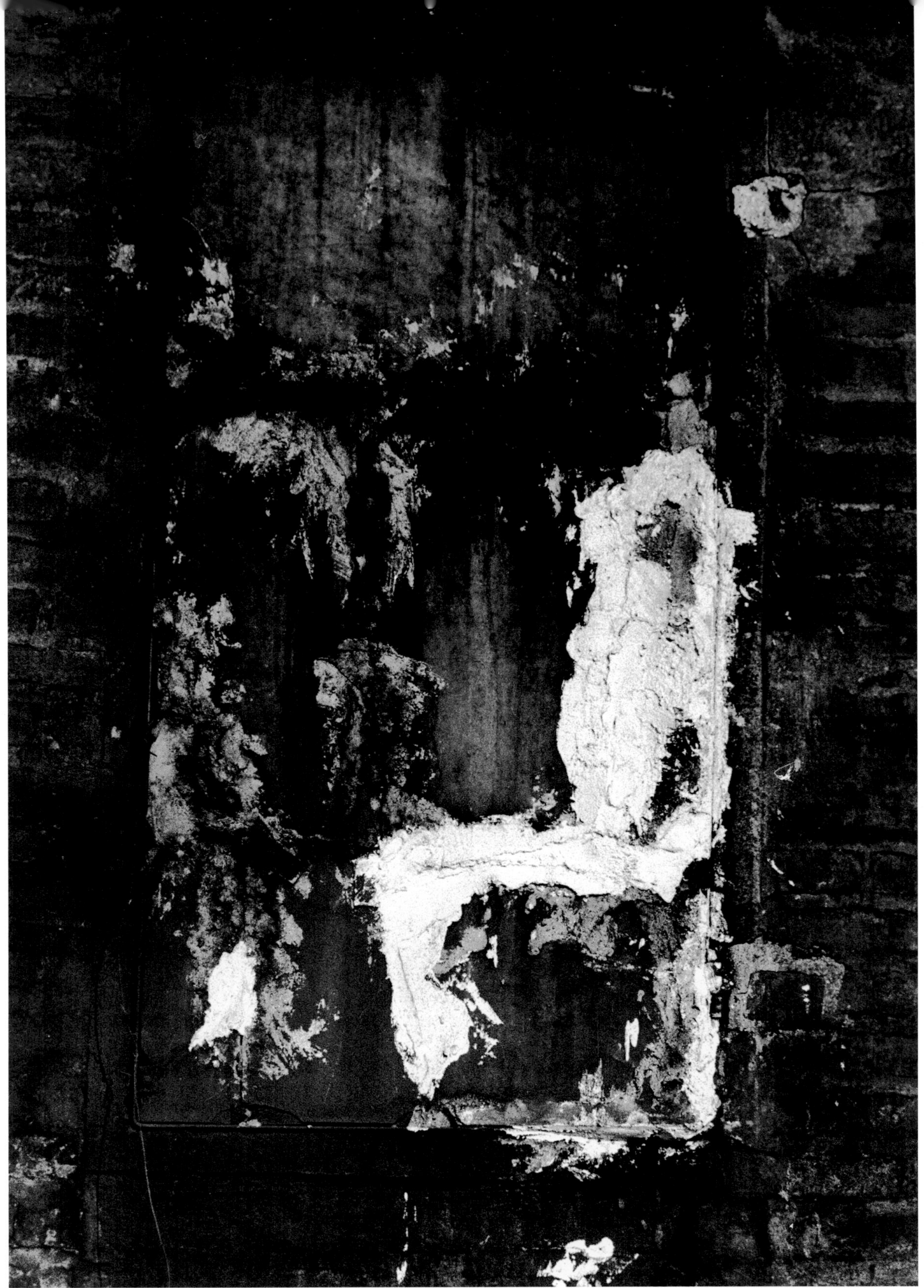

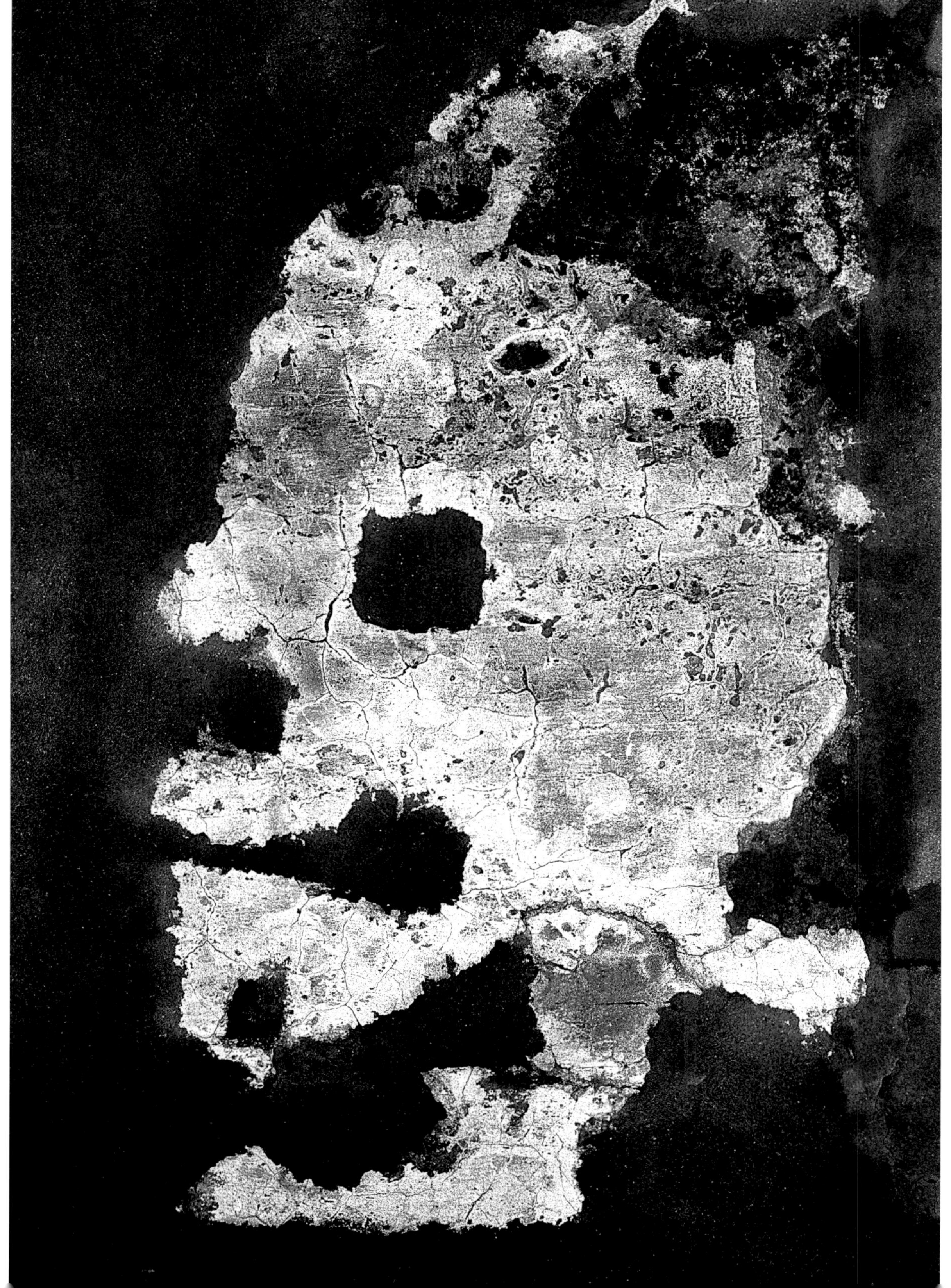

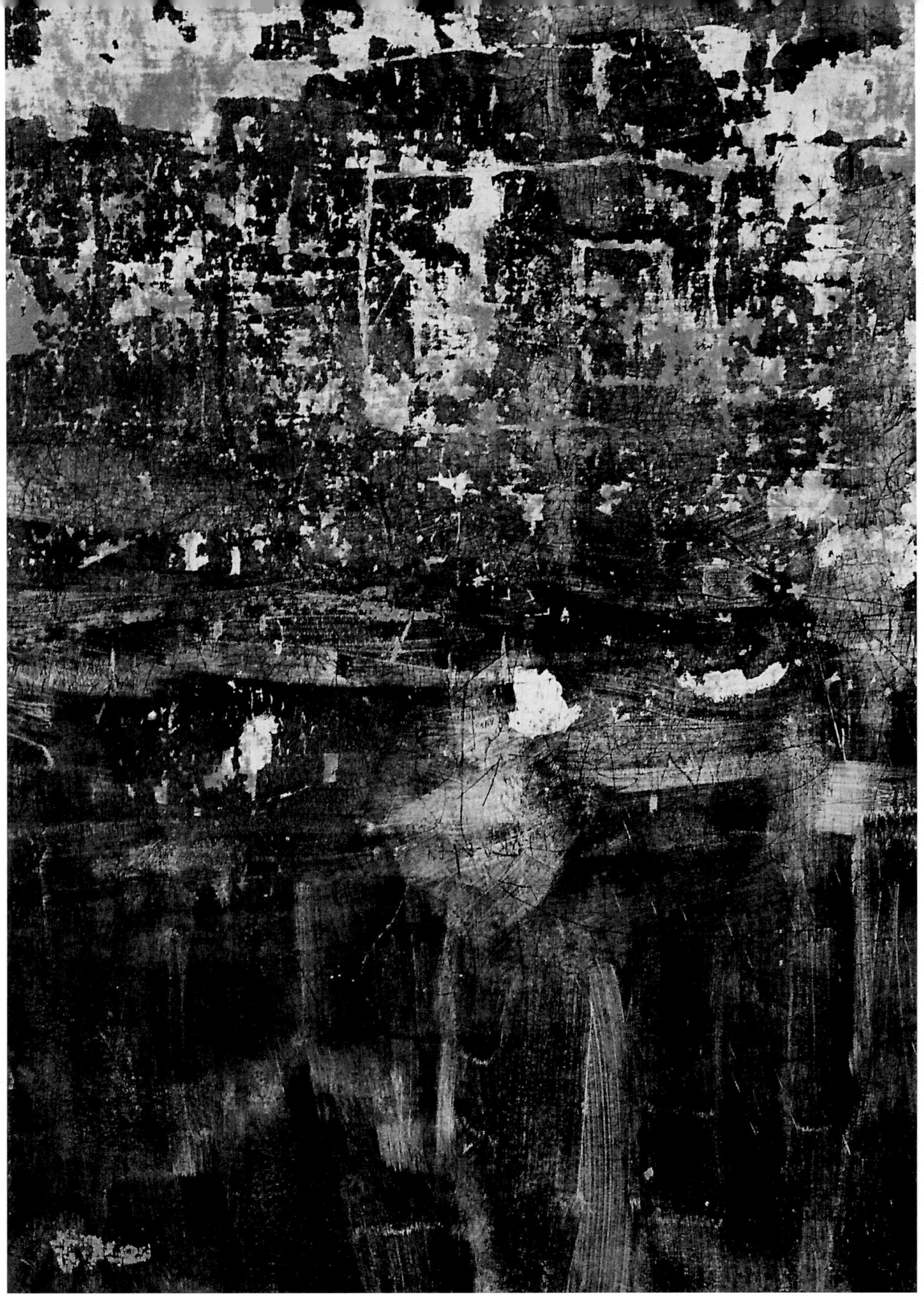

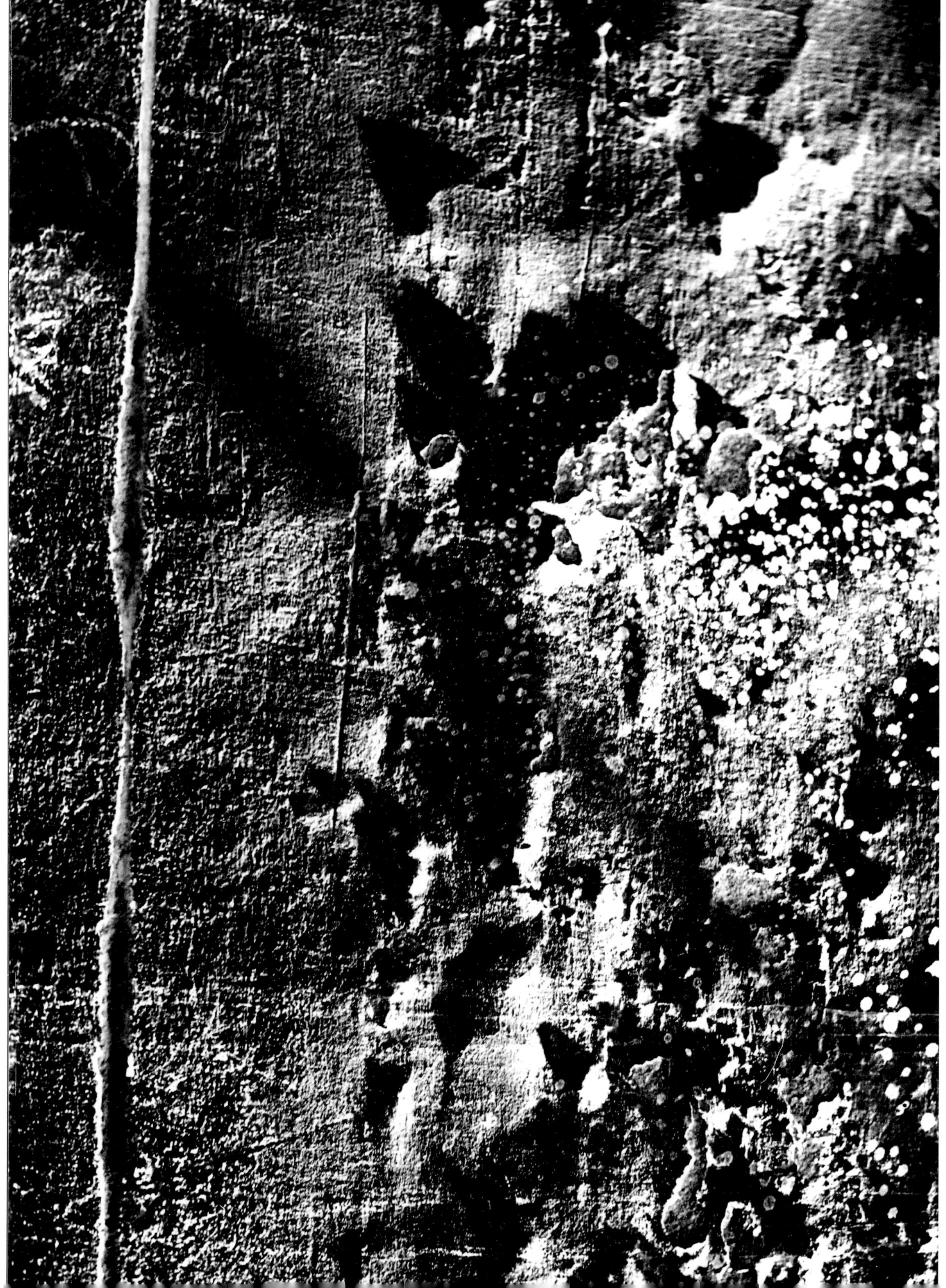

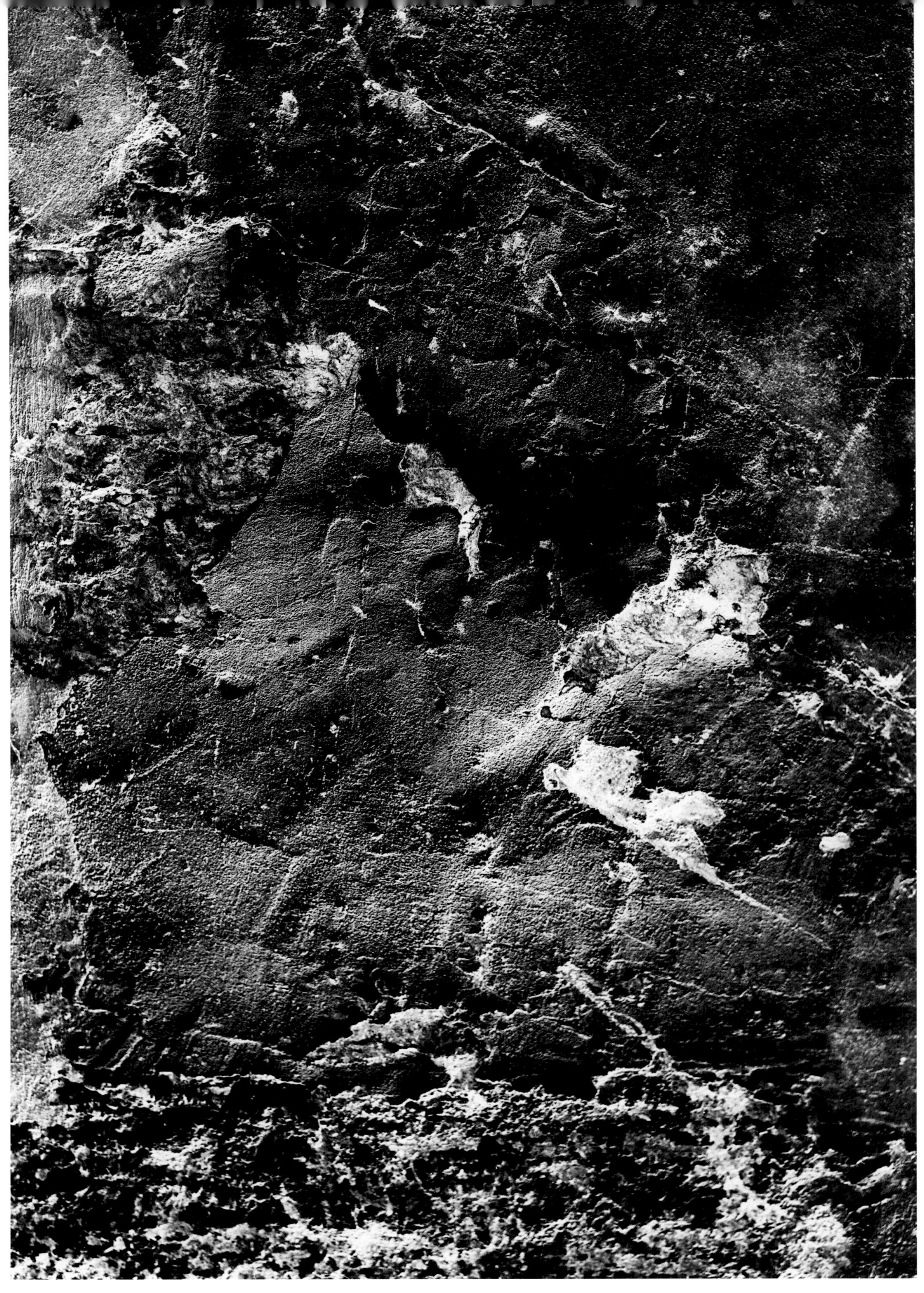

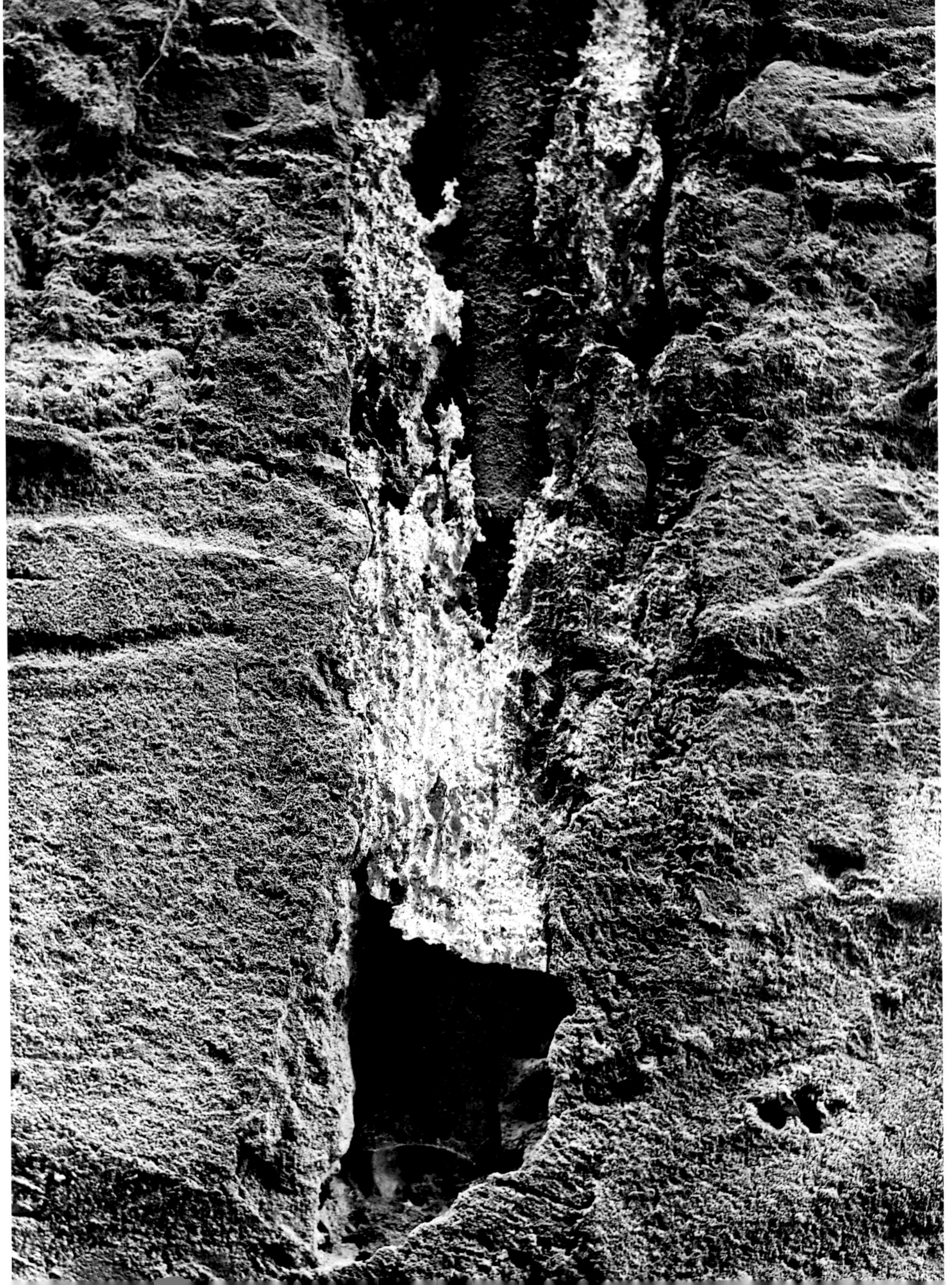

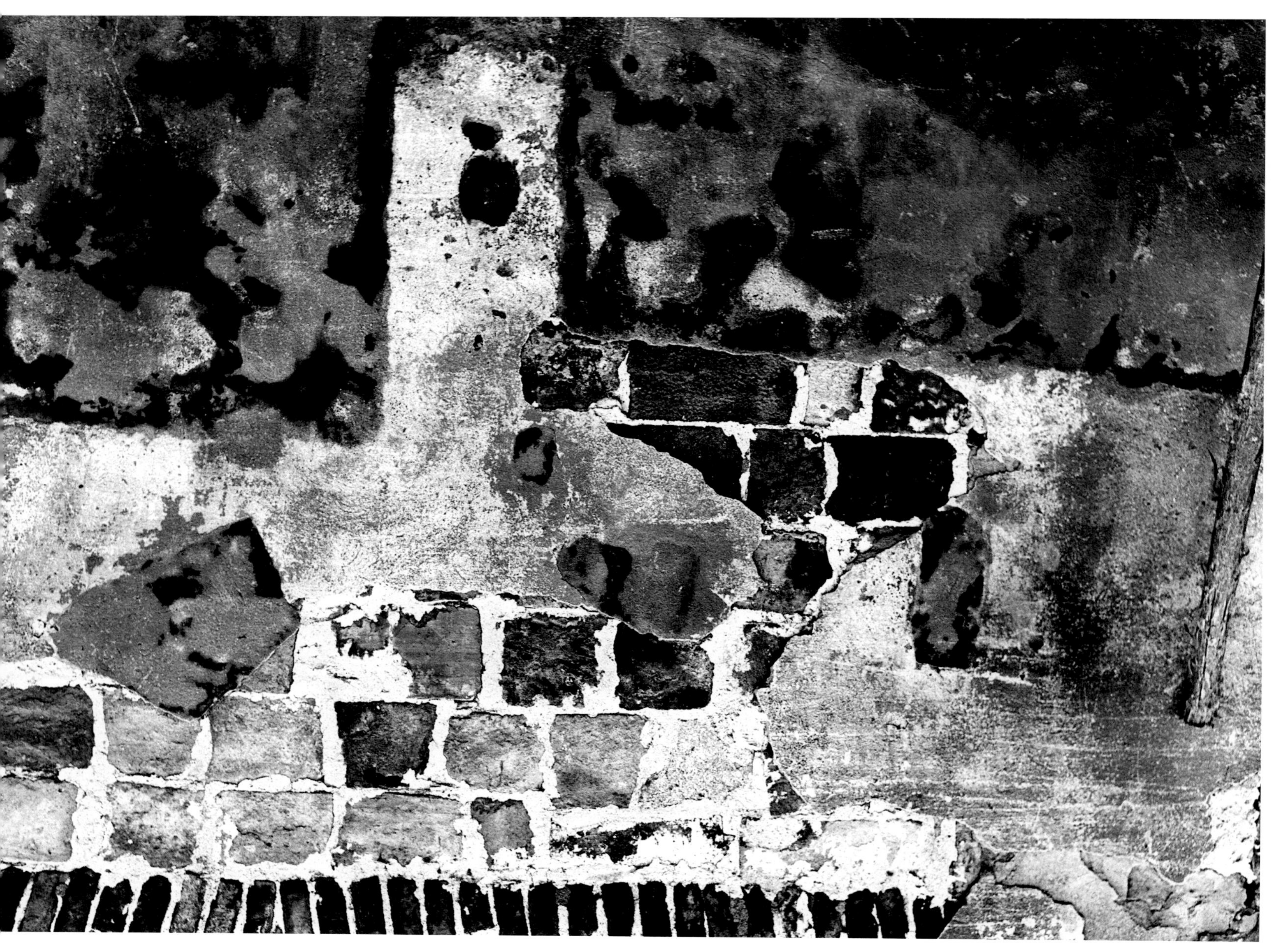

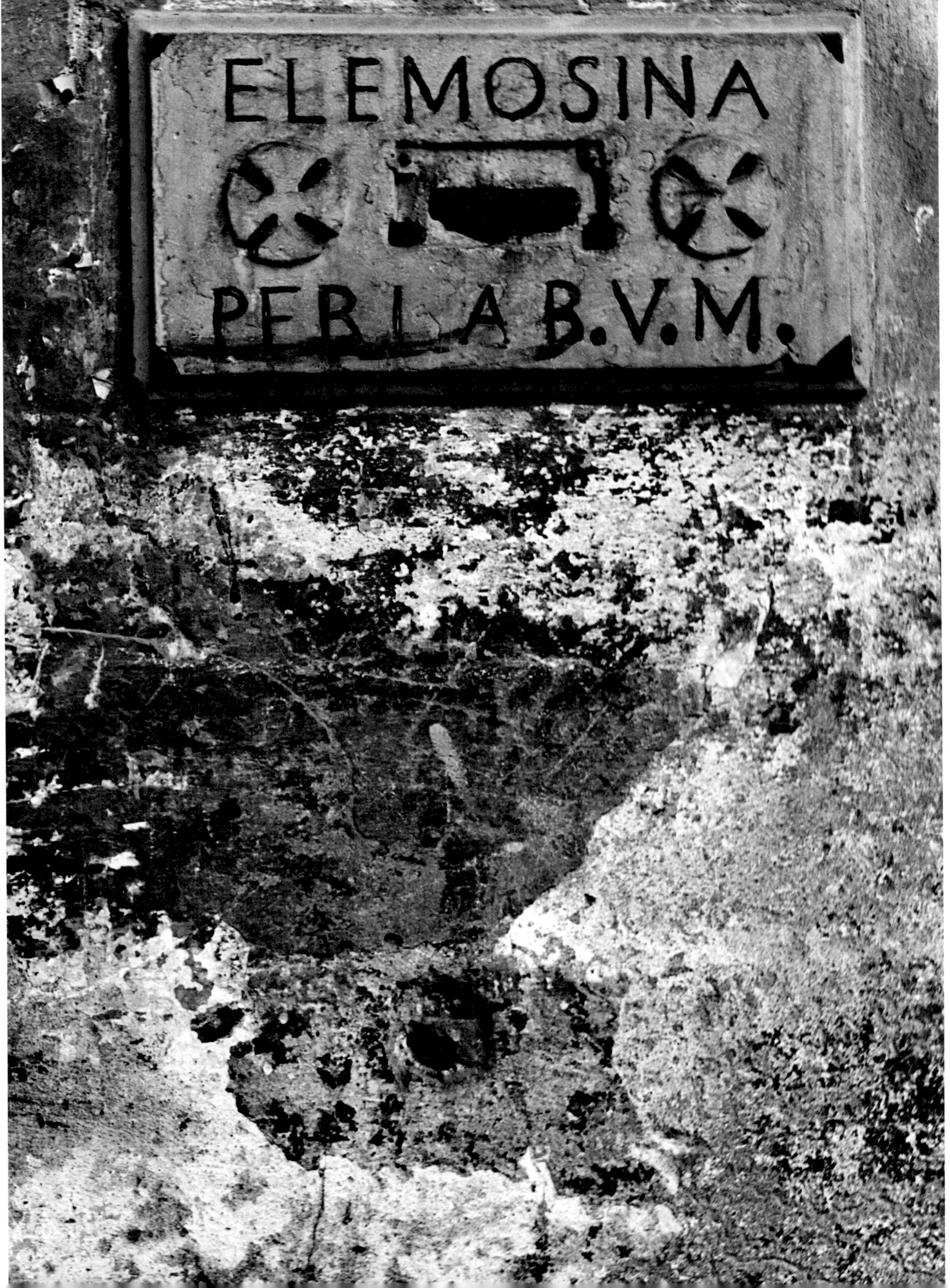
ELEMOSINA
PER LA B.V.M.

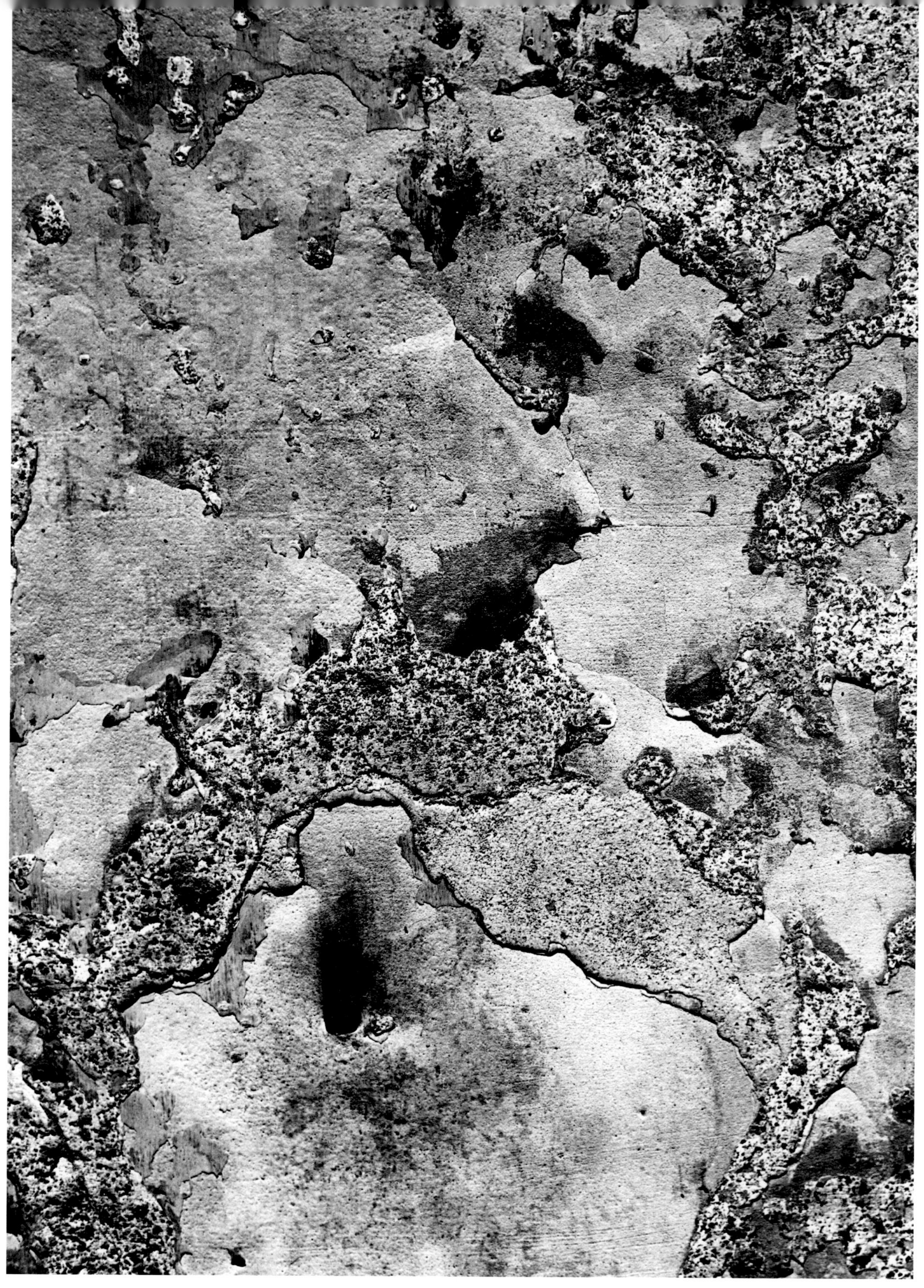

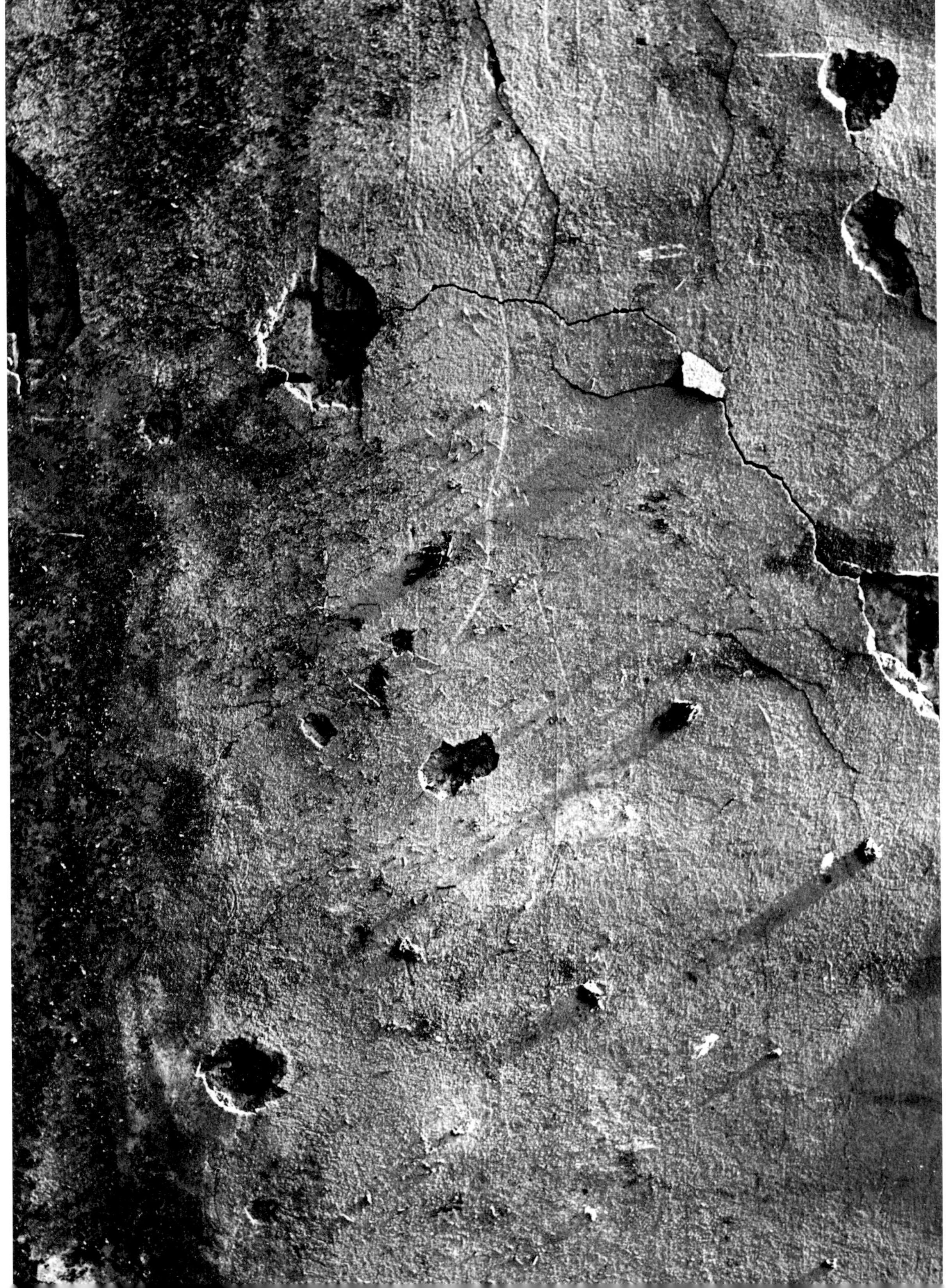

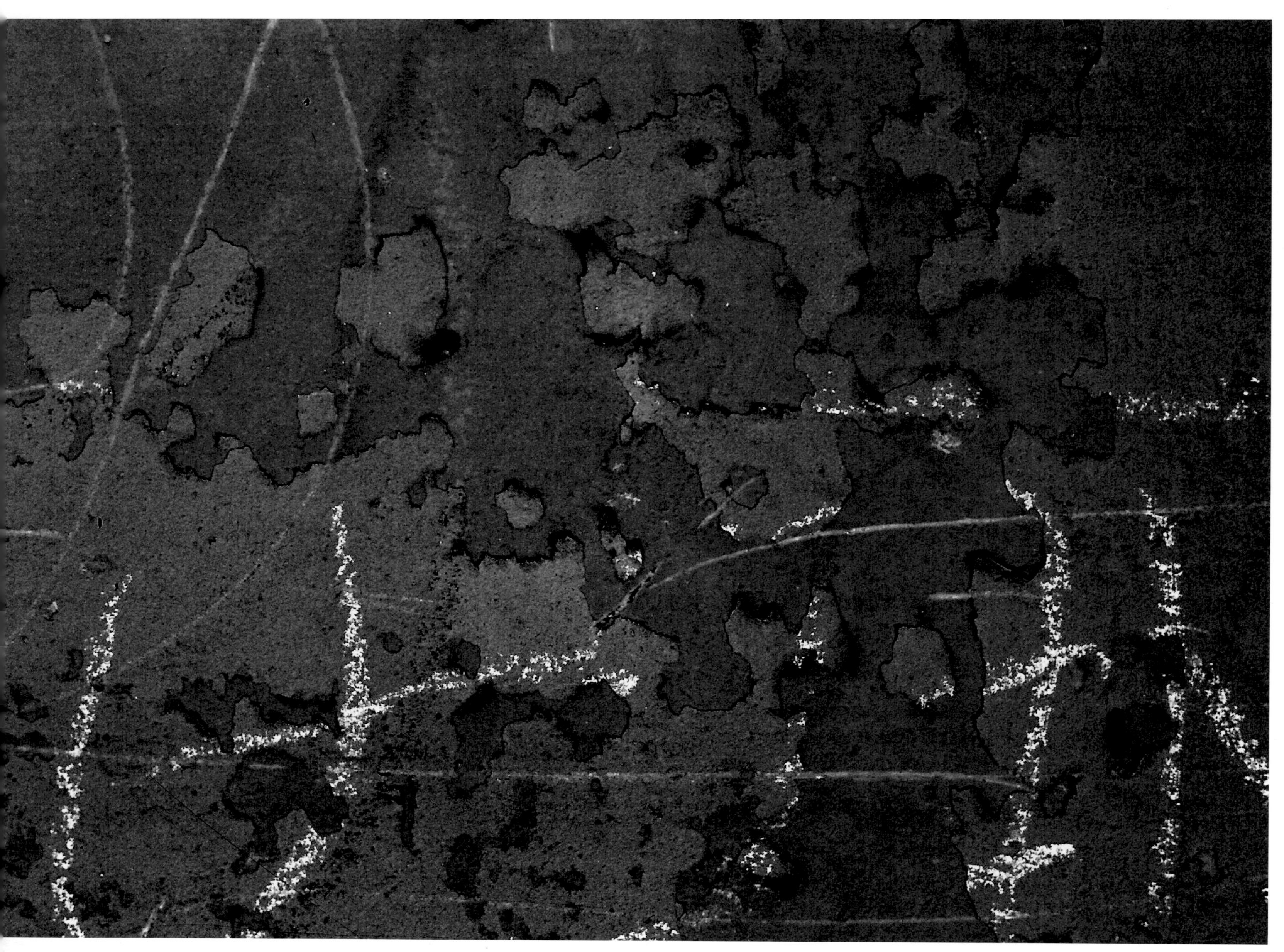

da "MURI" 1950-1954

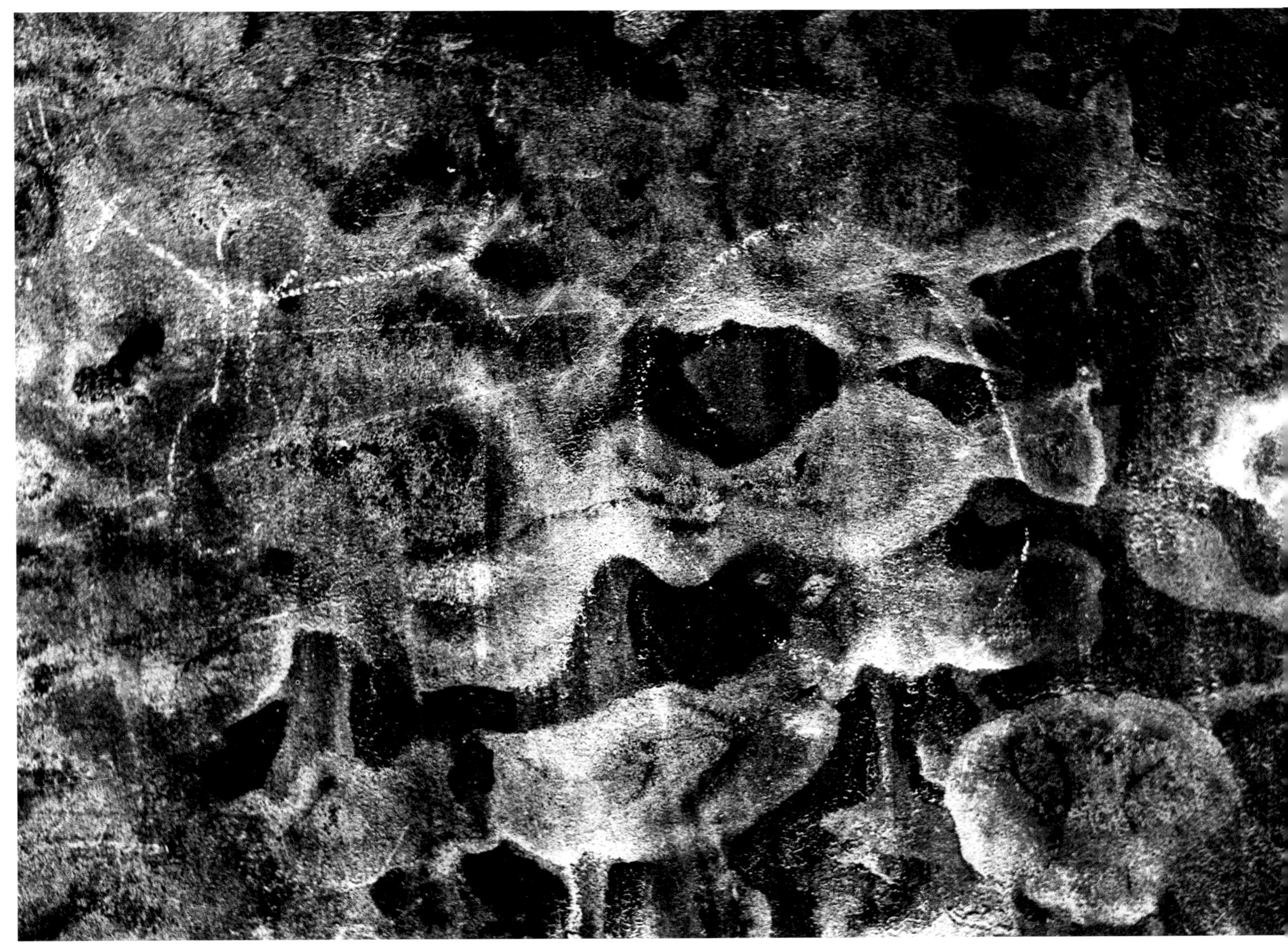

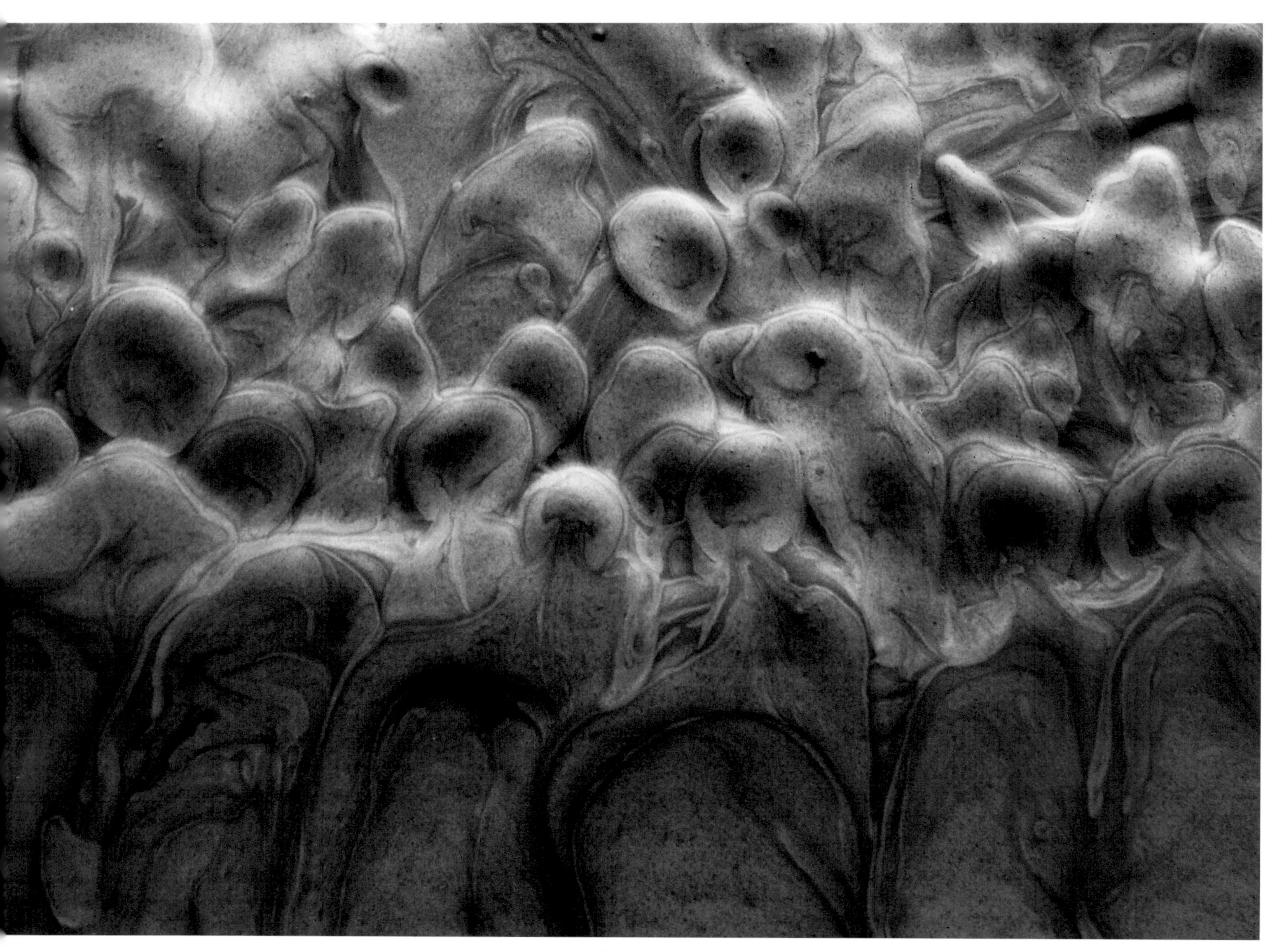

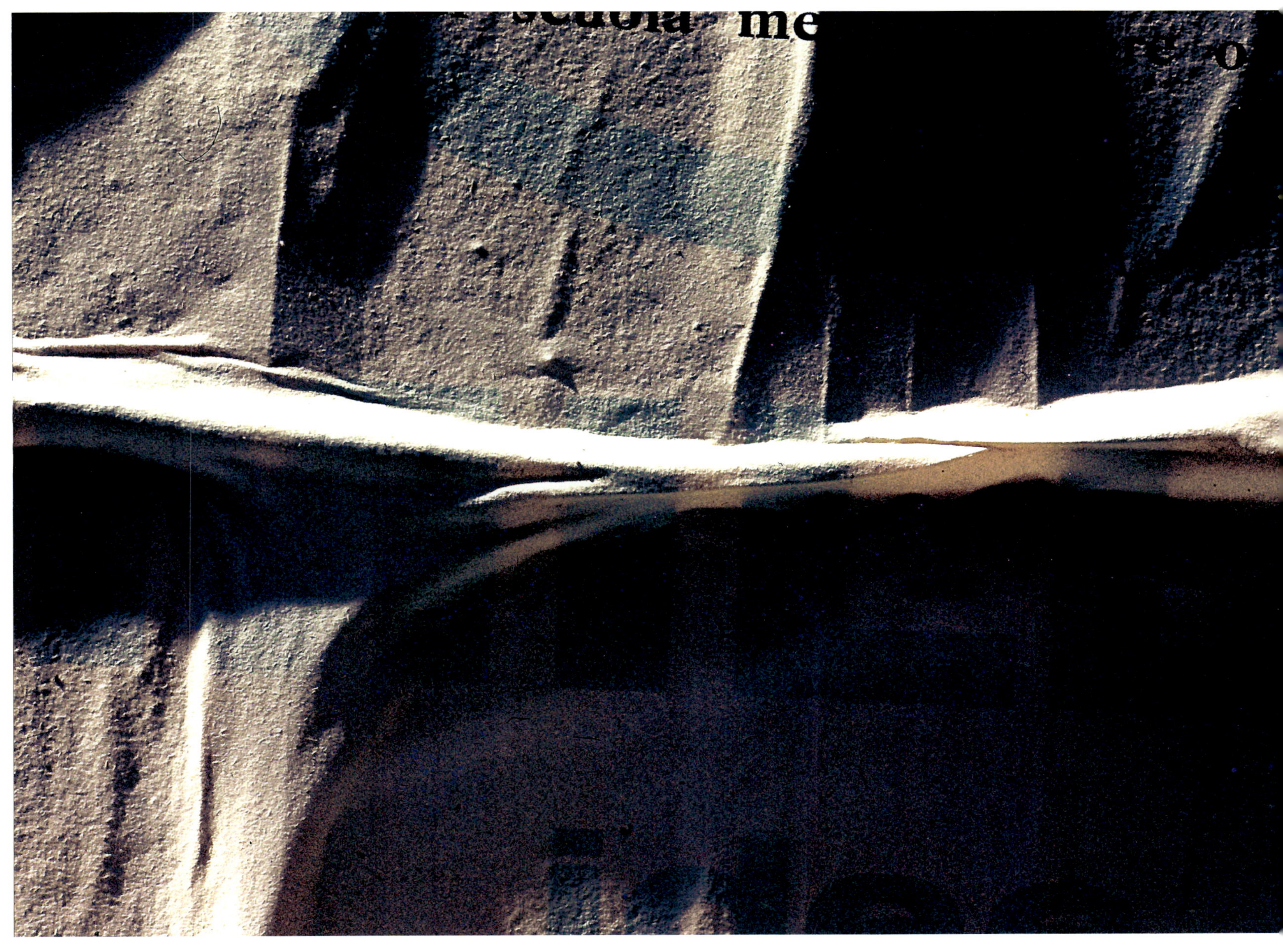

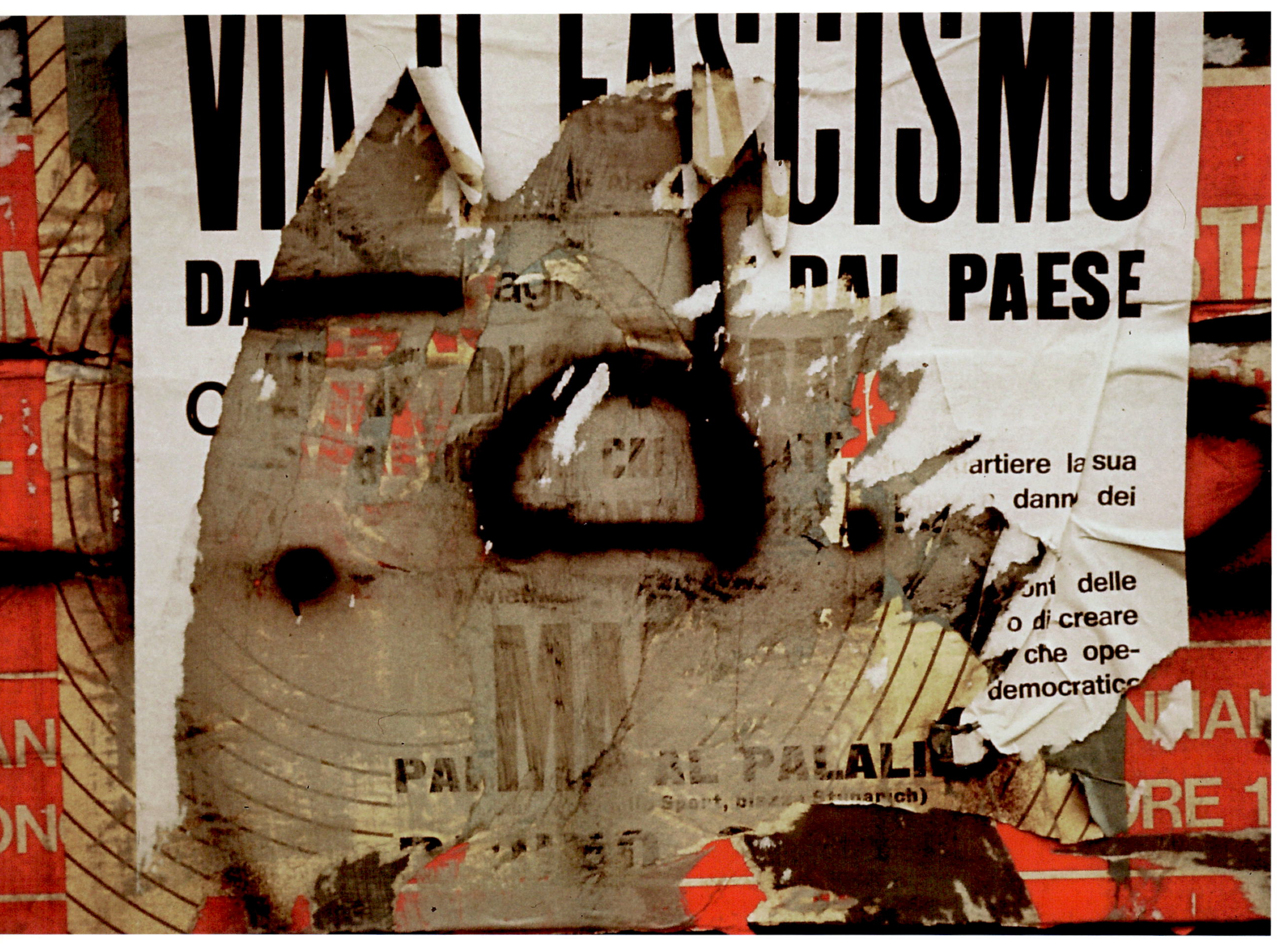
VIA IL FASCISMO
DA ... DAL PAESE
PAESE
artiere la sua
danni dei
ni delle
o di creare
che ope-
democratico
PAL ... AL PALALID
Sport, piazza Steinarich)

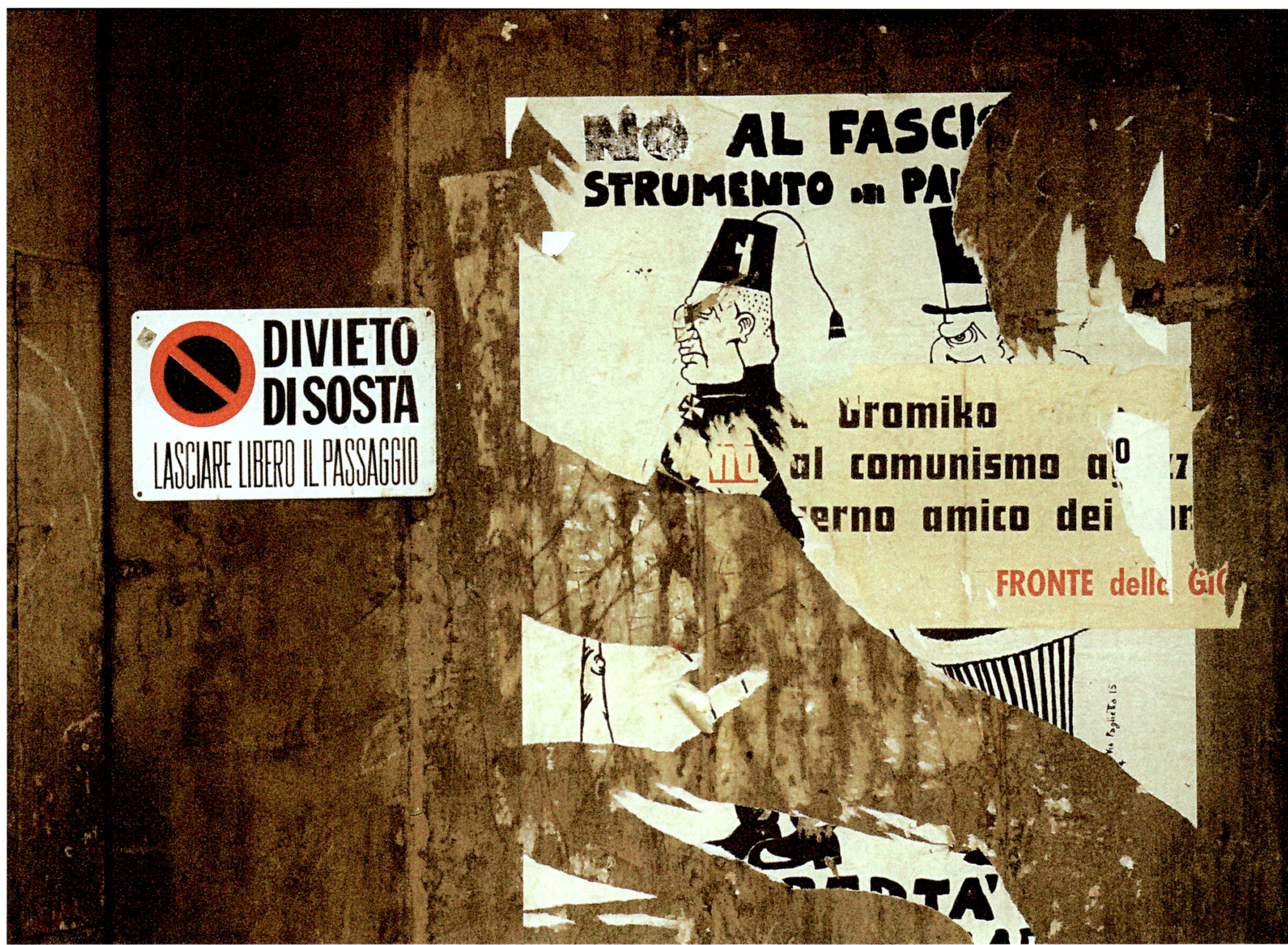
NO AL FASCI
STRUMENTO di PA
Gromiko
al comunismo a
erno amico dei
FRONTE della GIO
DIVIETO
DI SOSTA
LASCIARE LIBERO IL PASSAGGIO

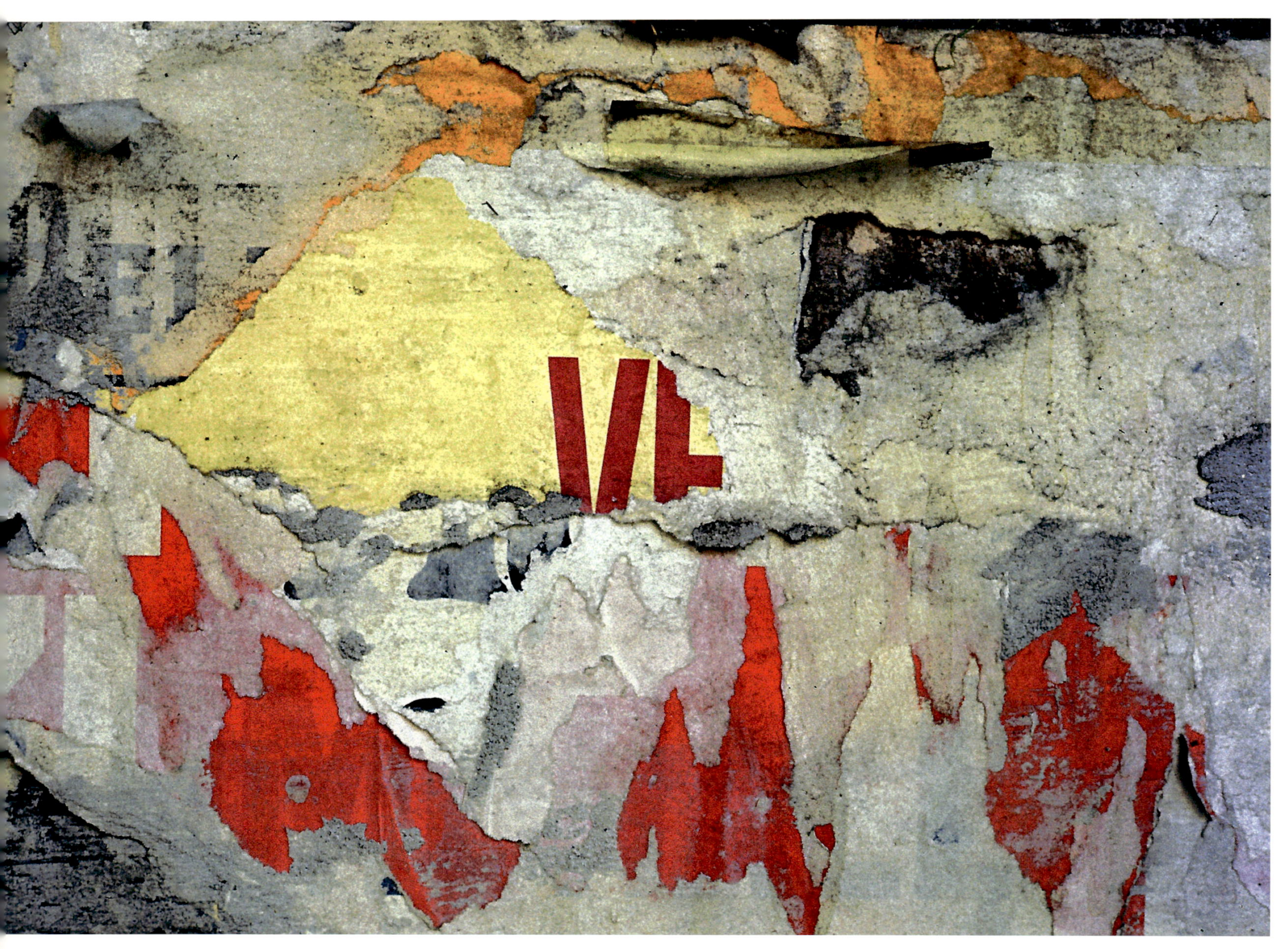

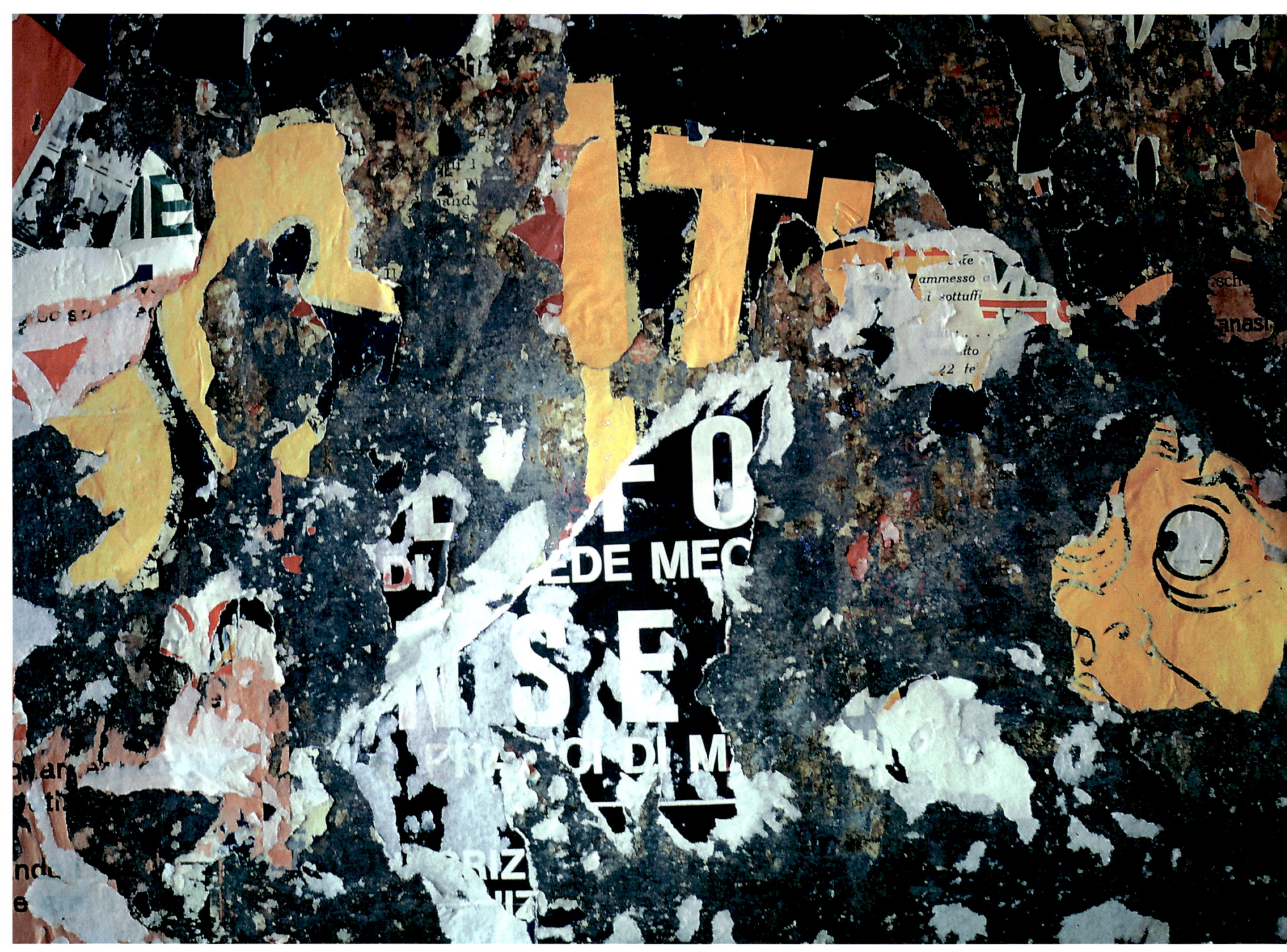

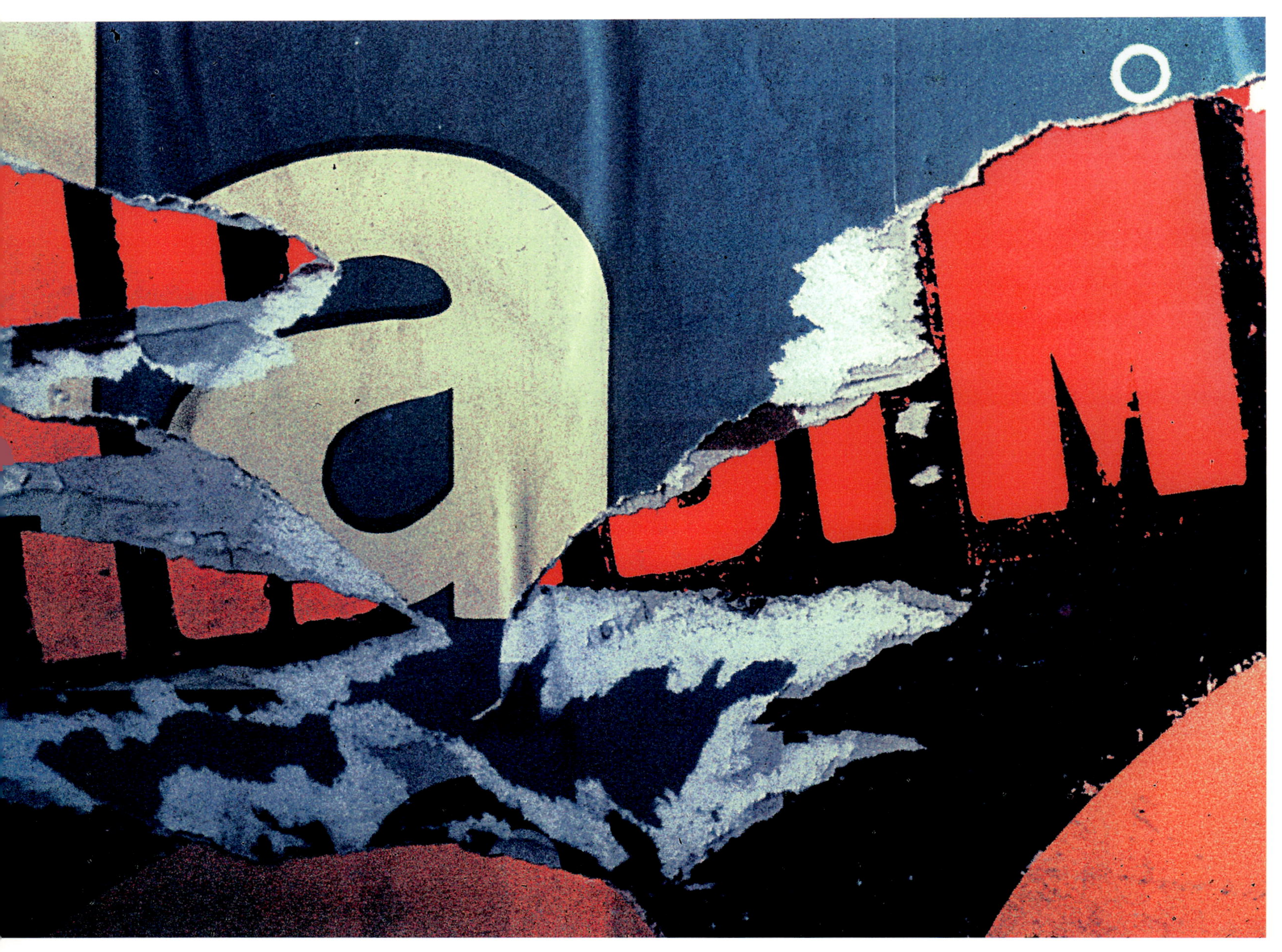

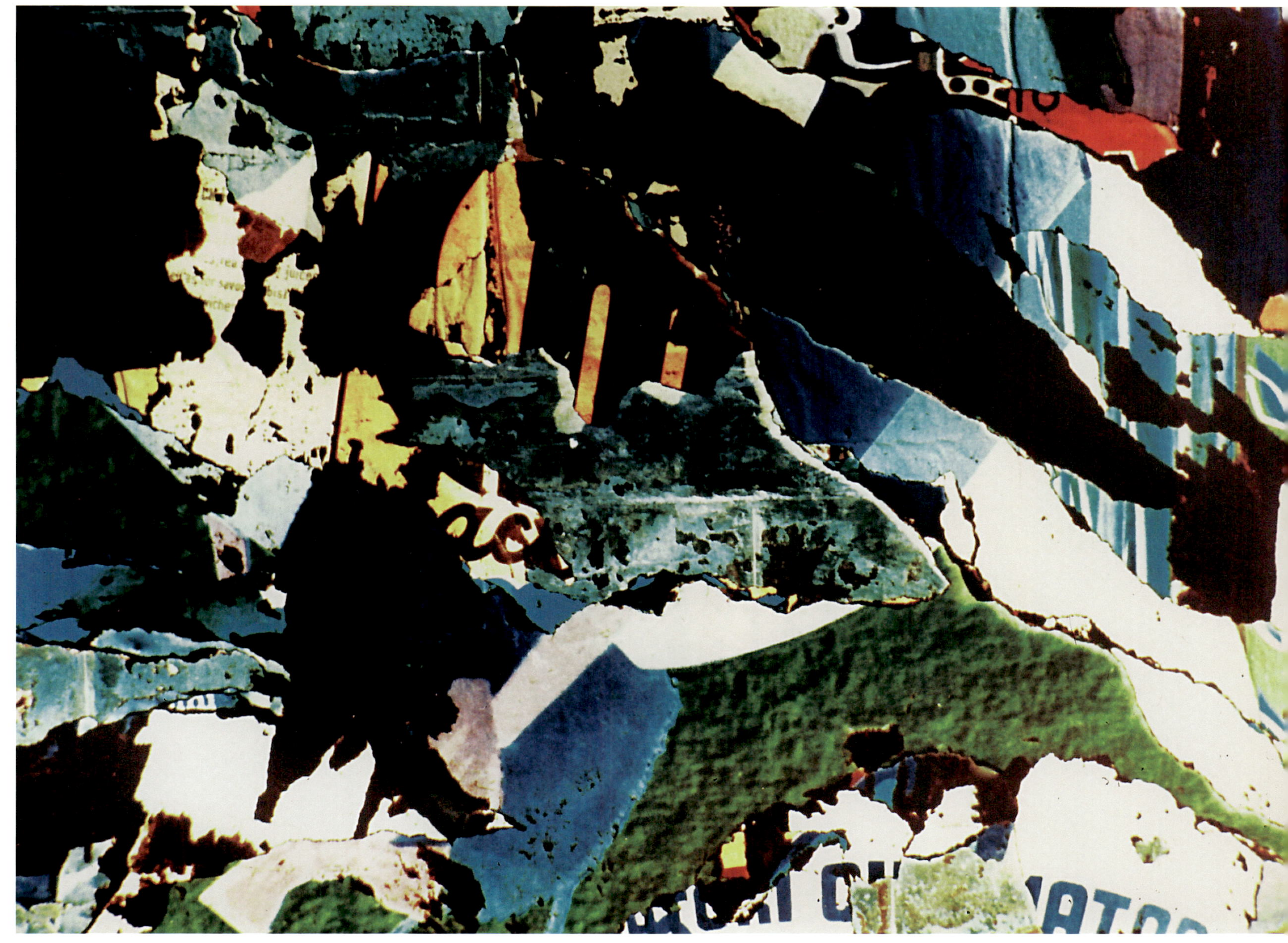

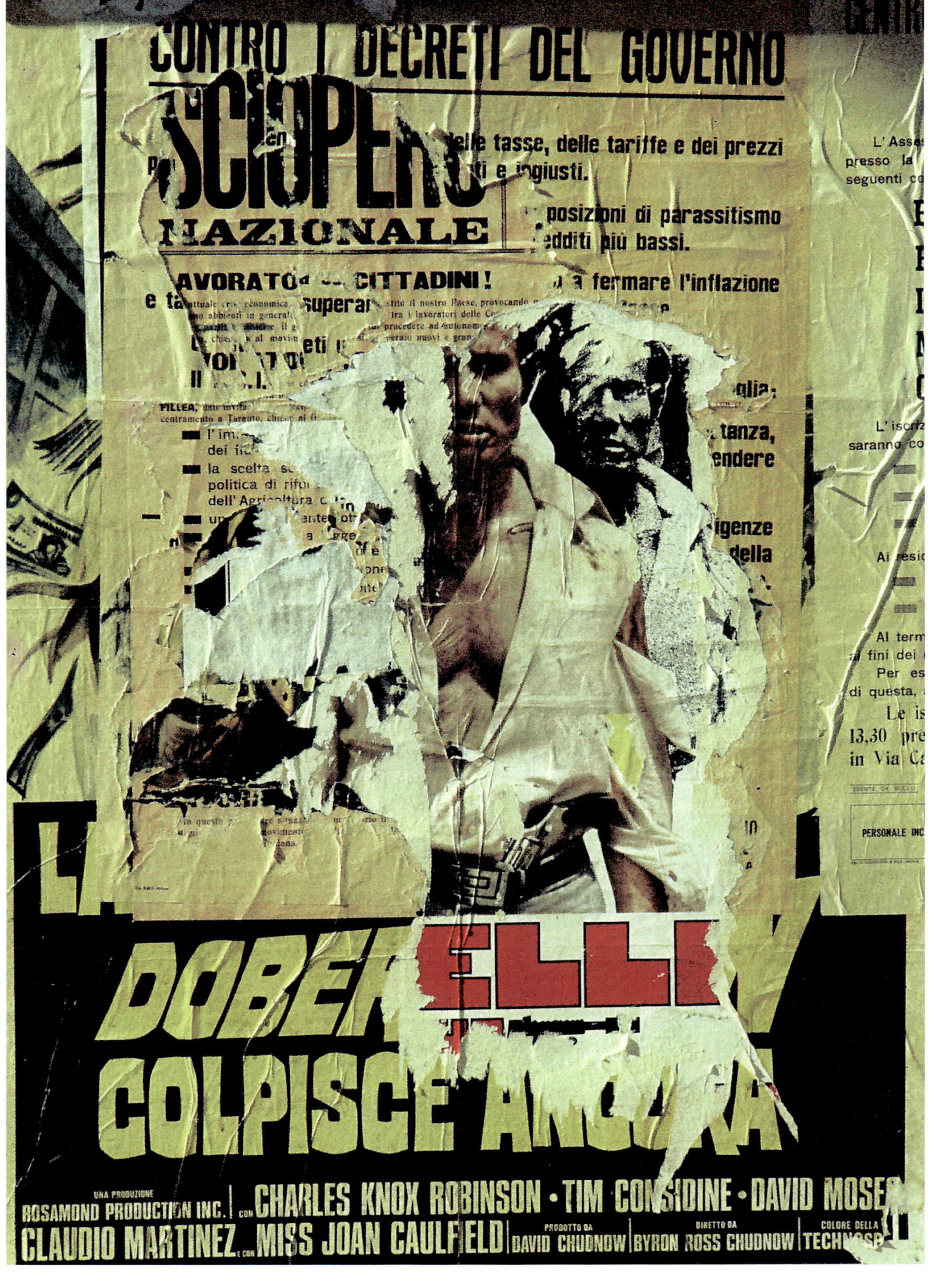
CONTRO I DECRETI DEL GOVERNO
SCIOPERO
NAZIONALE
delle tasse, delle tariffe e dei prezzi
ti e ingiusti.
posizioni di parassitismo
edditi più bassi.
LAVORATORI E CITTADINI!
a fermare l'inflazione
DOBERMAN
COLPISCE ANCORA
UNA PRODUZIONE
ROSAMOND PRODUCTION INC.
CHARLES KNOX ROBINSON · TIM CONSIDINE · DAVID MOSES
con
CLAUDIO MARTINEZ e con MISS JOAN CAULFIELD
PRODOTTO DA
DAVID CHUDNOW
DIRETTO DA
BYRON ROSS CHUDNOW
COLORE DELLA
TECHNICOLOR

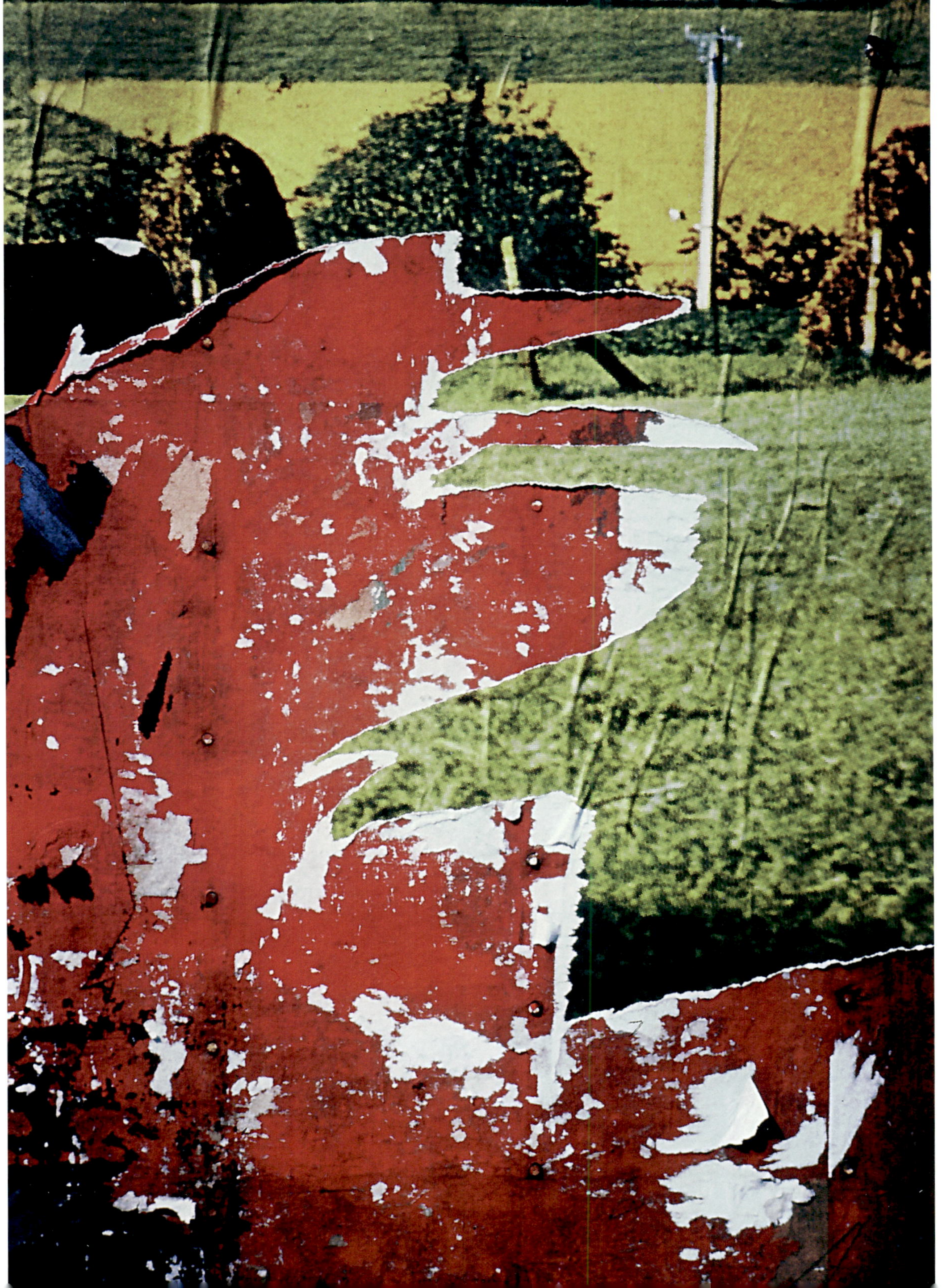

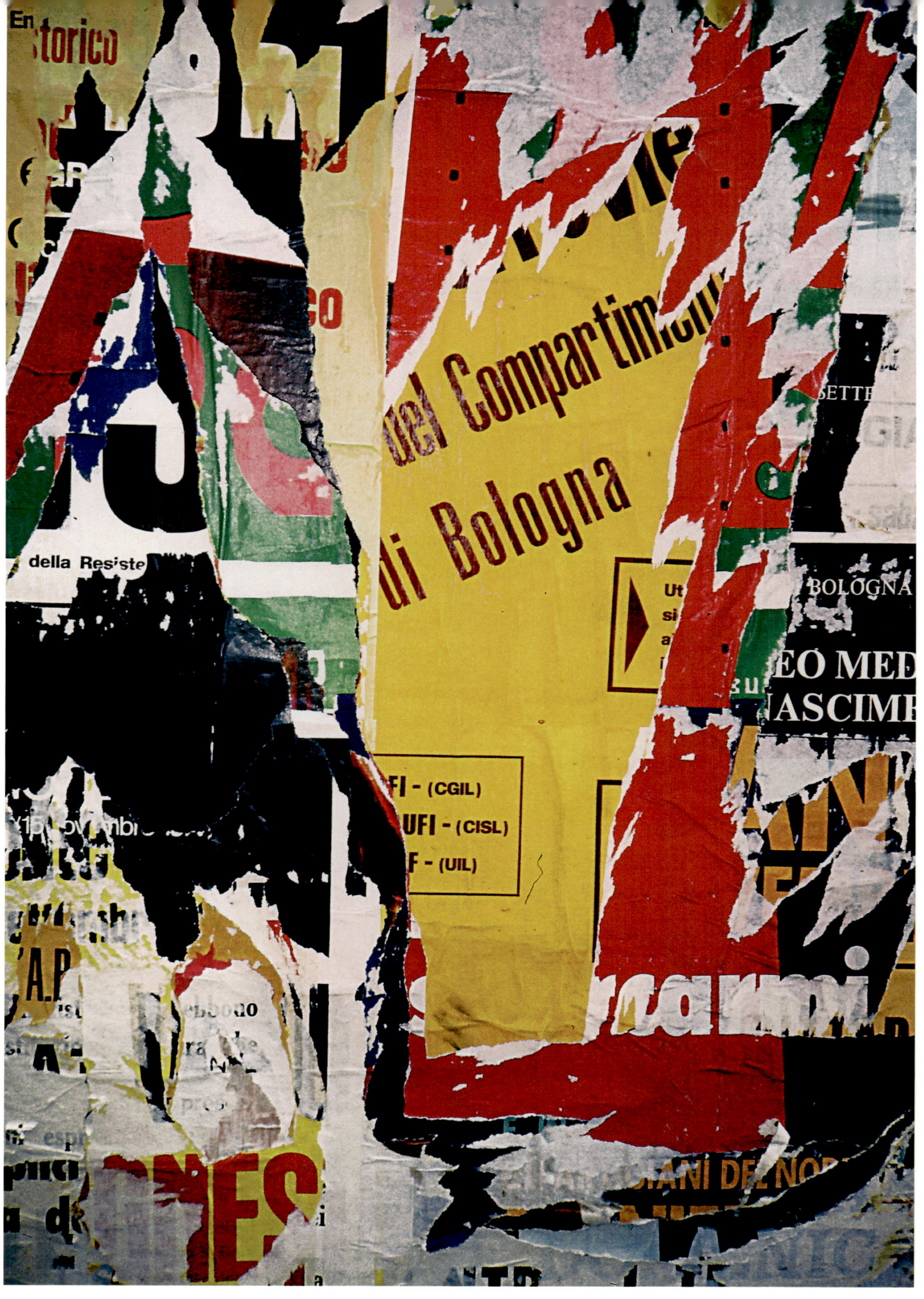
storico
del Compartimento
di Bologna
della Resiste
BOLOGNA
EO MED
ASCIM
FI - (CGIL)
UFI - (CISL)
F - (UIL)
IANI DEL NO

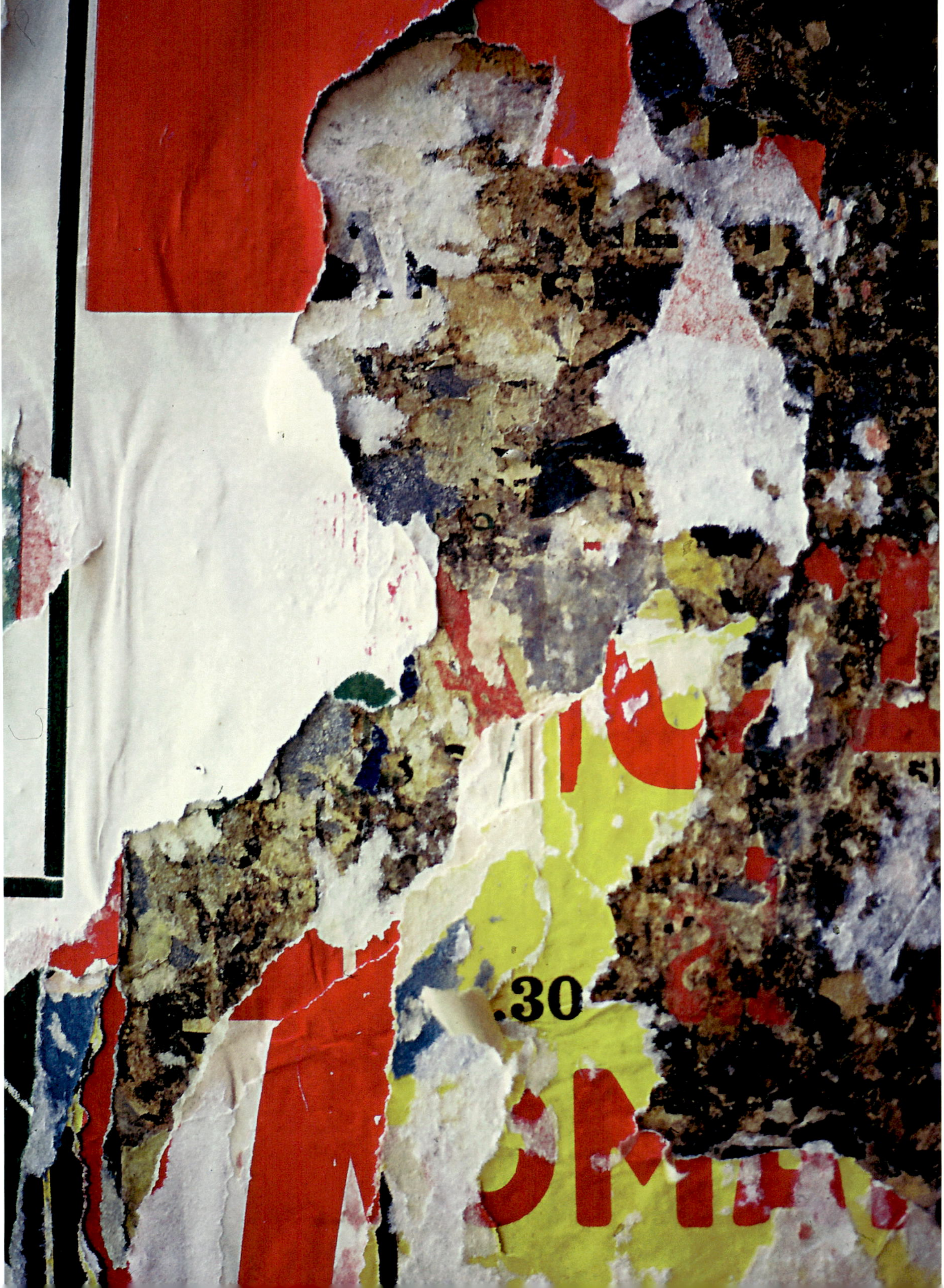

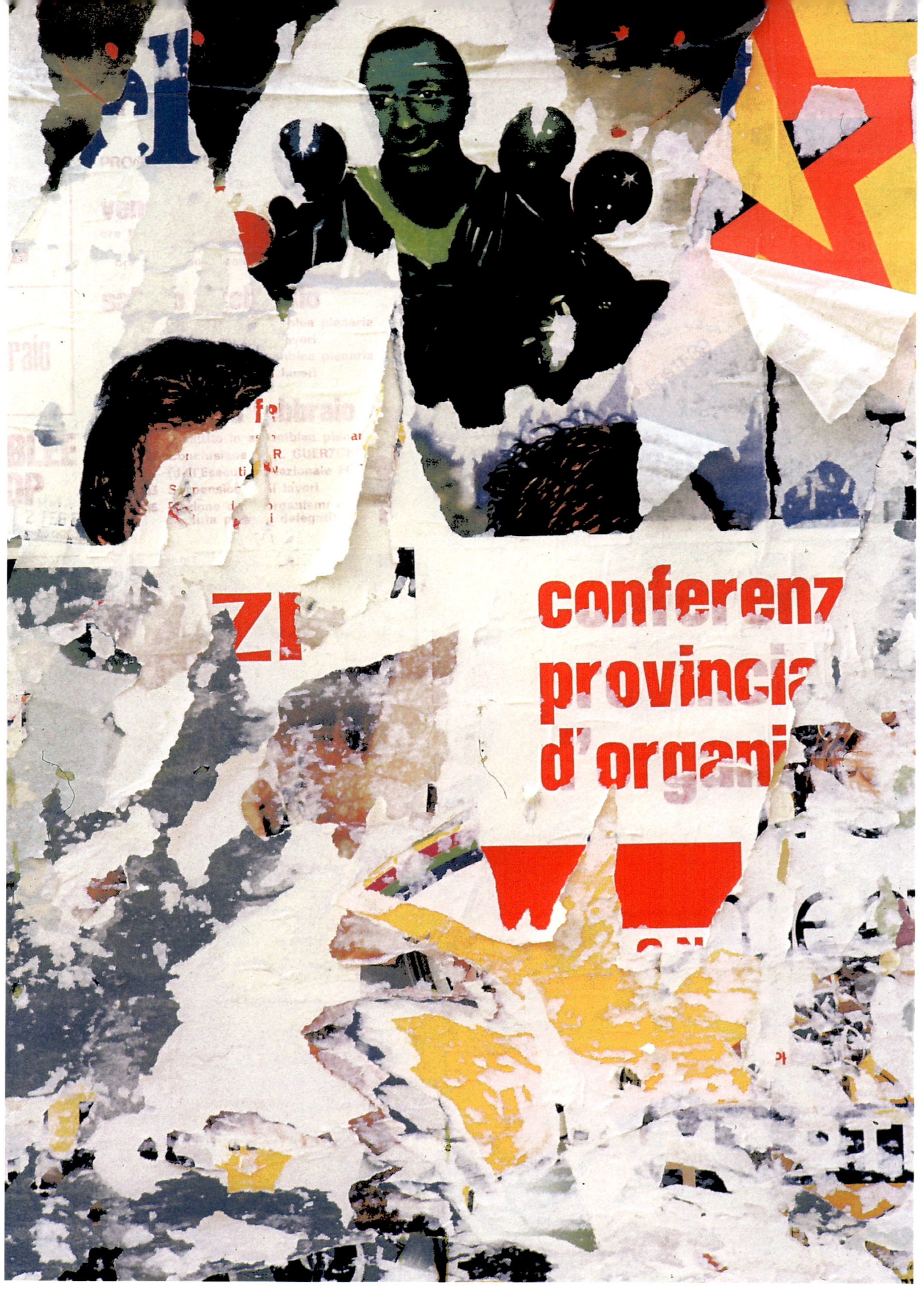
conferenz
provincia
d'organi

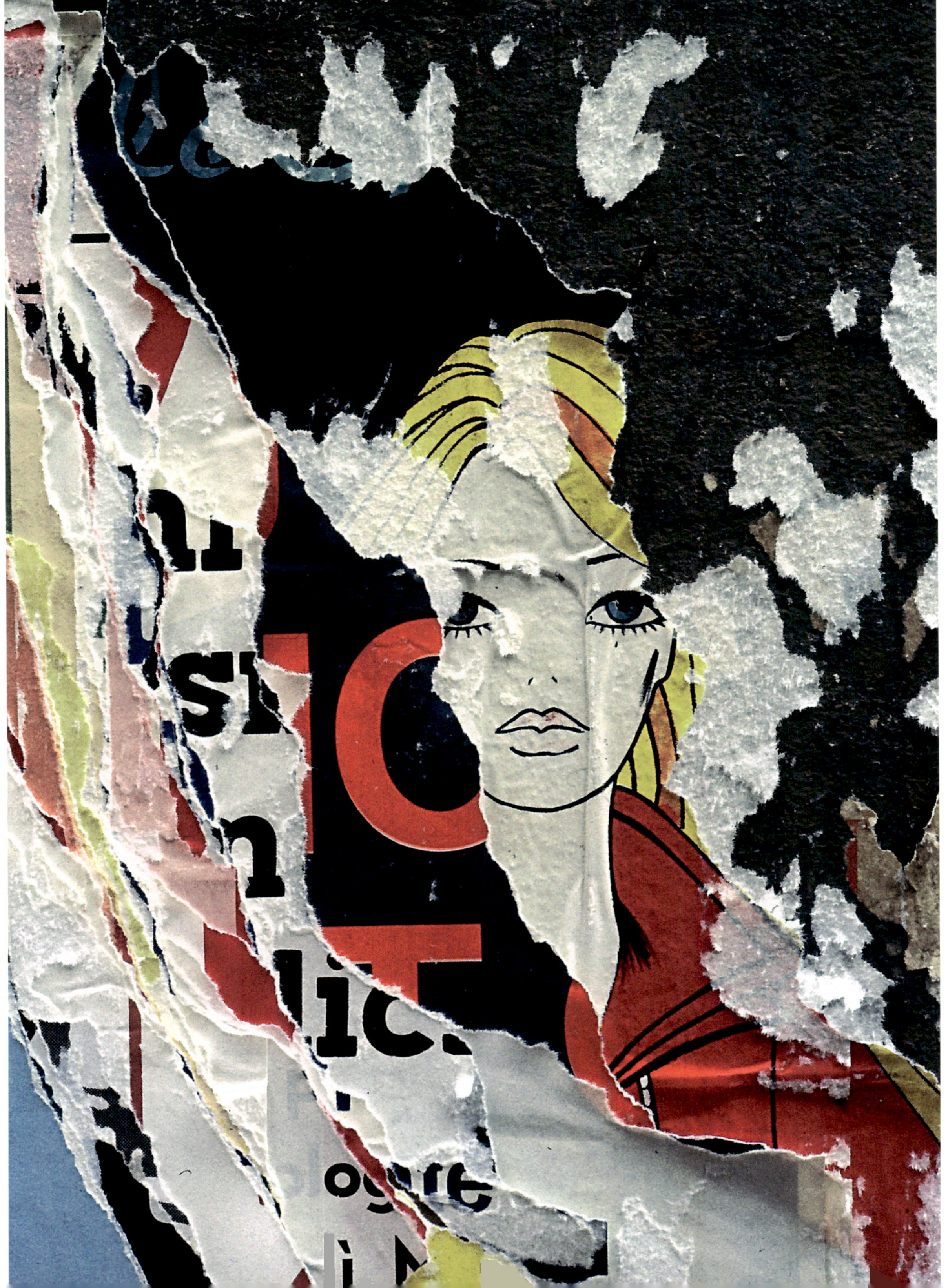

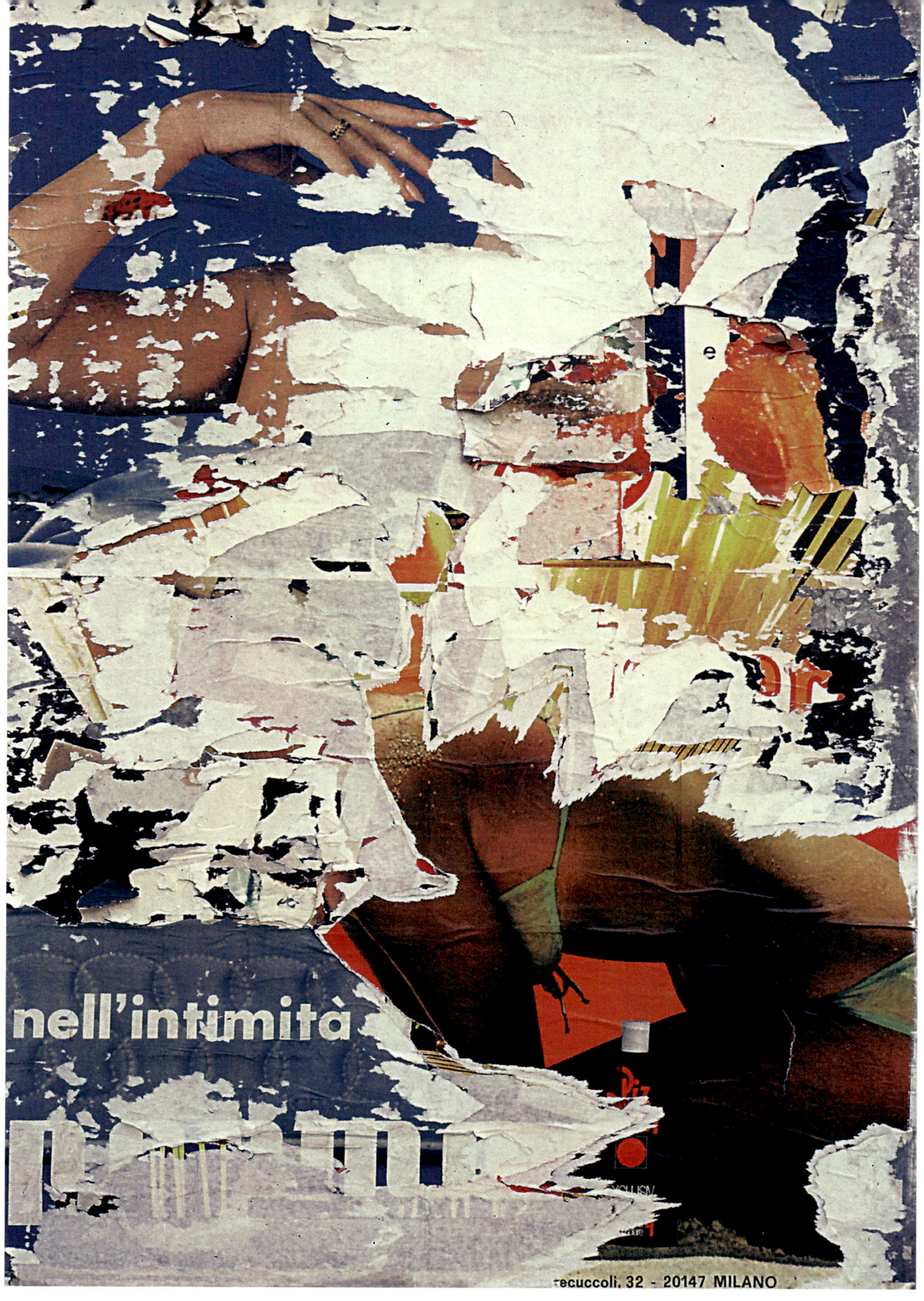

nell'intimità
tecuccoli, 32 - 20147 MILANO

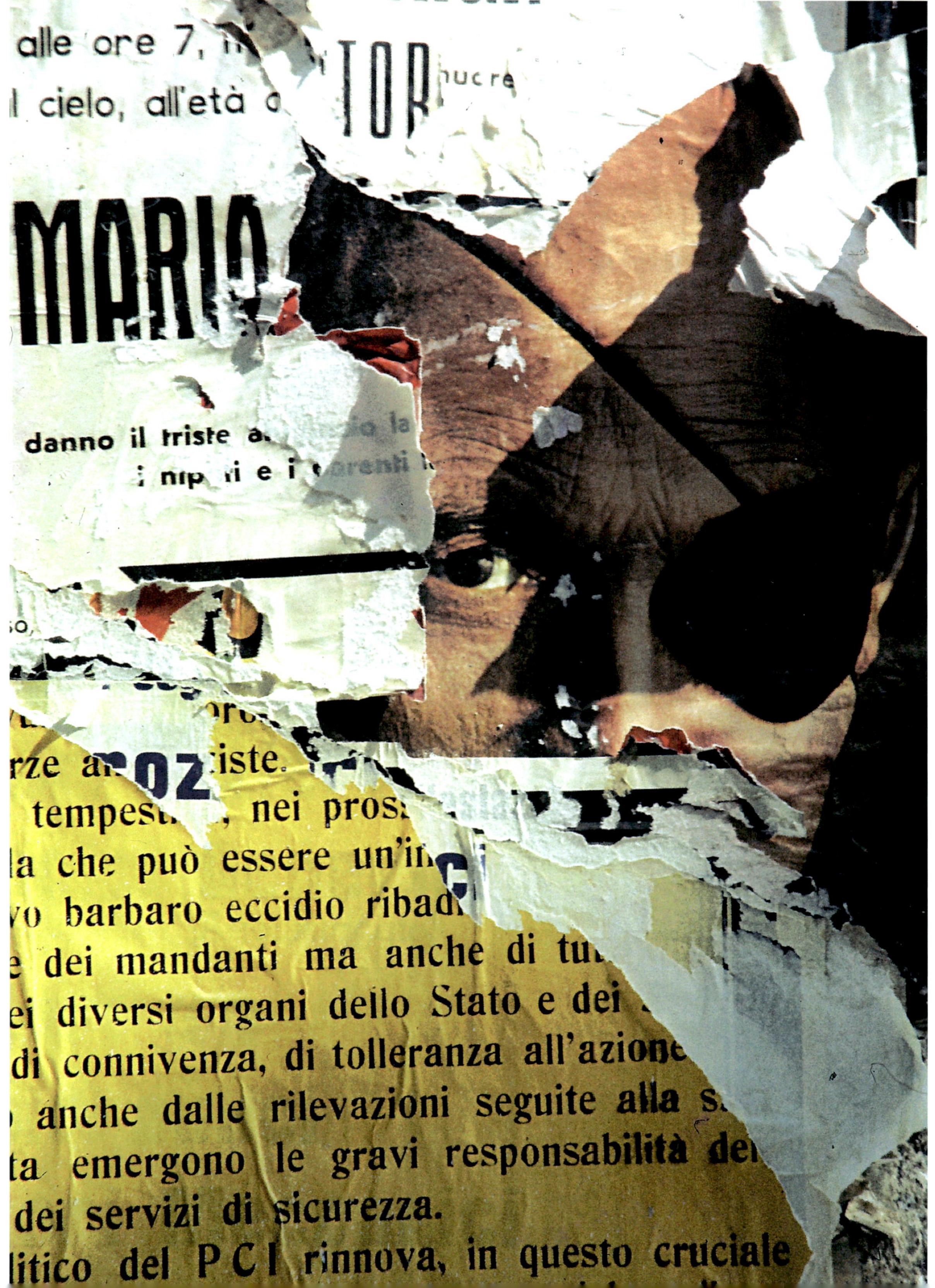
alle ore 7,
I cielo, all'età
TOR
hucre
MARIO
danno il triste a
nip ii e i
rze a oz iste.
tempest , nei pros
la che può essere un'i
vo barbaro eccidio ribad
e dei mandanti ma anche di tu
ei diversi organi dello Stato e dei
di connivenza, di tolleranza all'azione
anche dalle rilevazioni seguite alla s
ta emergono le gravi responsabilità de
dei servizi di sicurezza.
litico del P C I rinnova, in questo cruciale

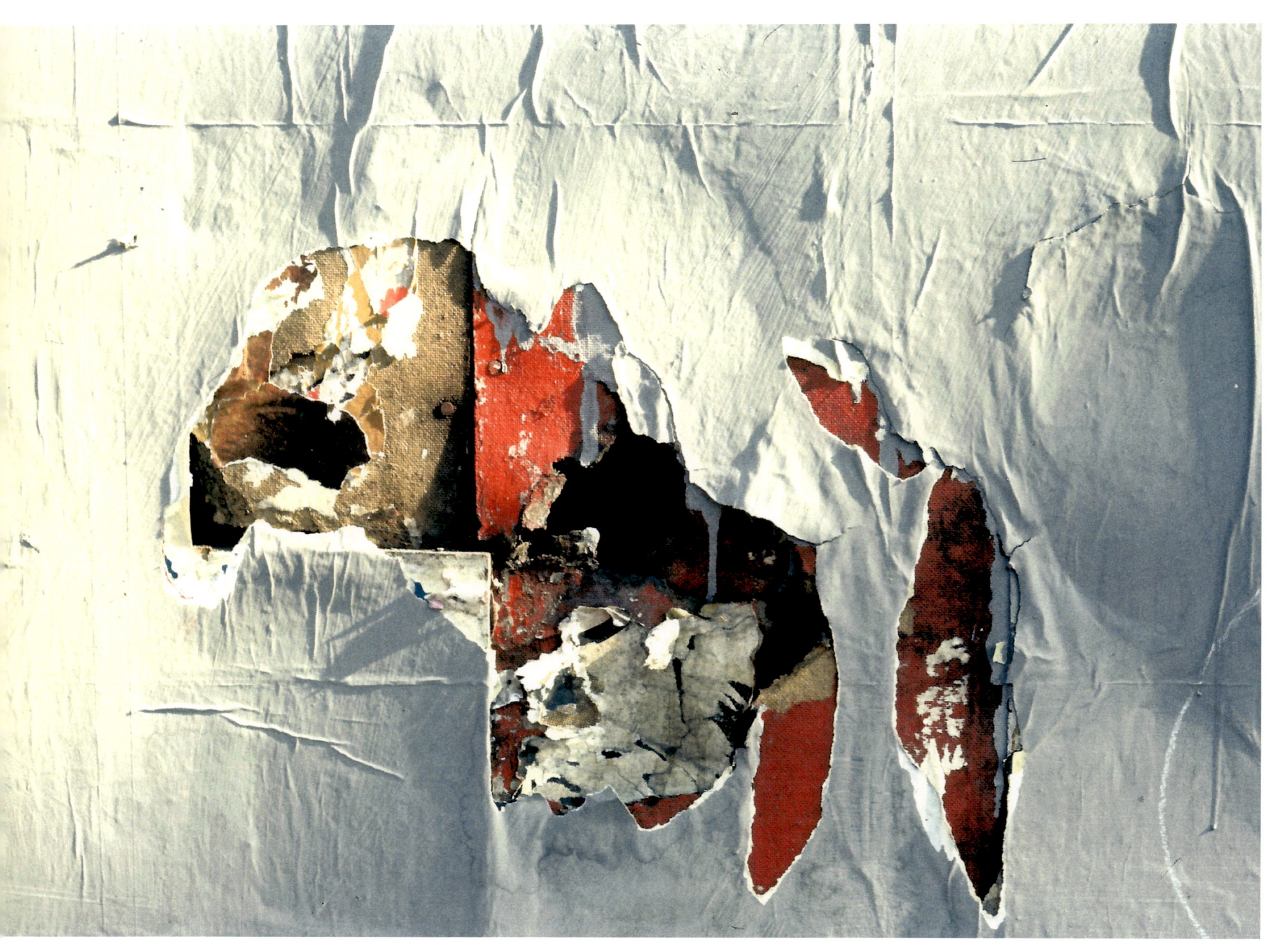

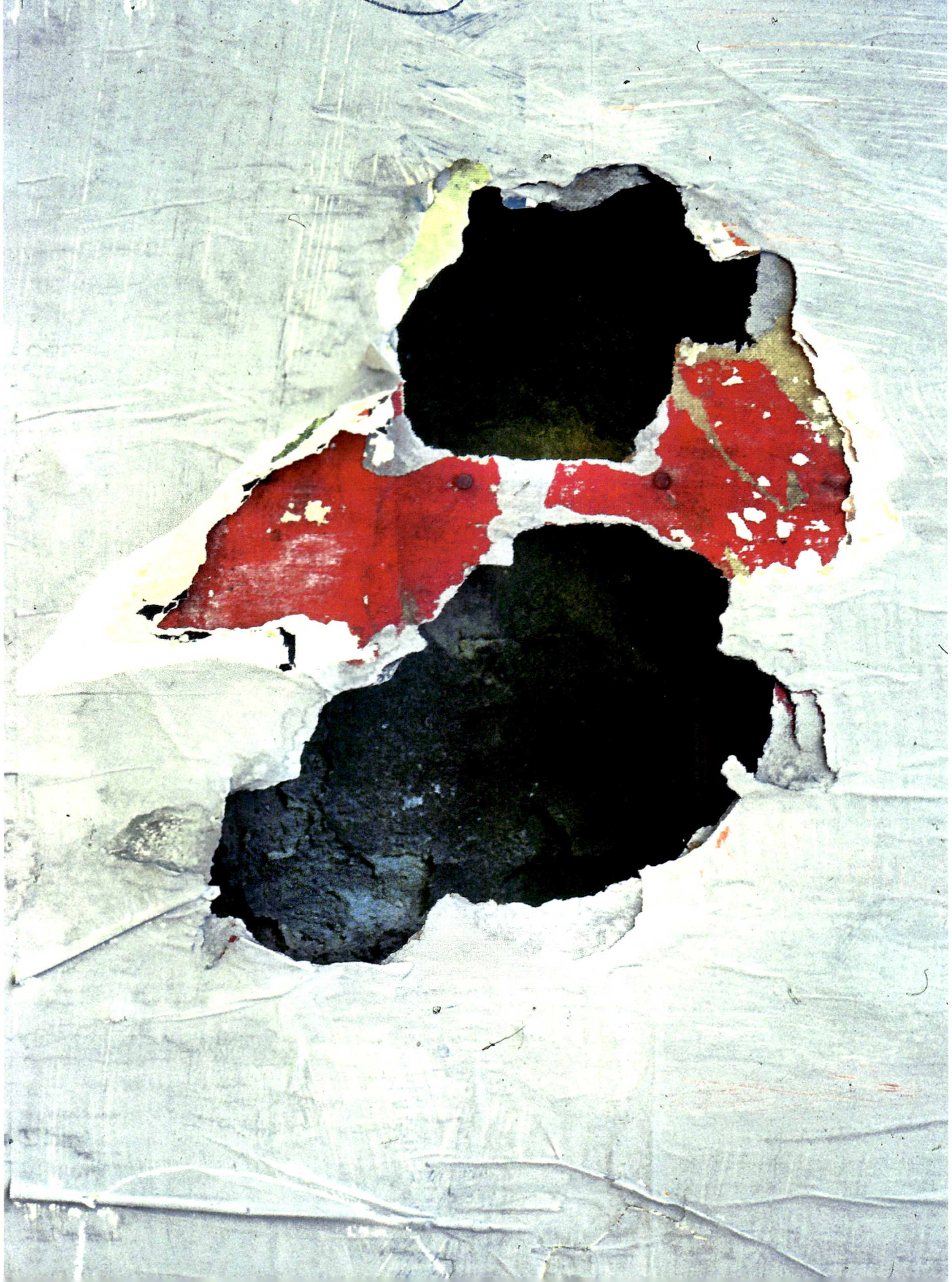

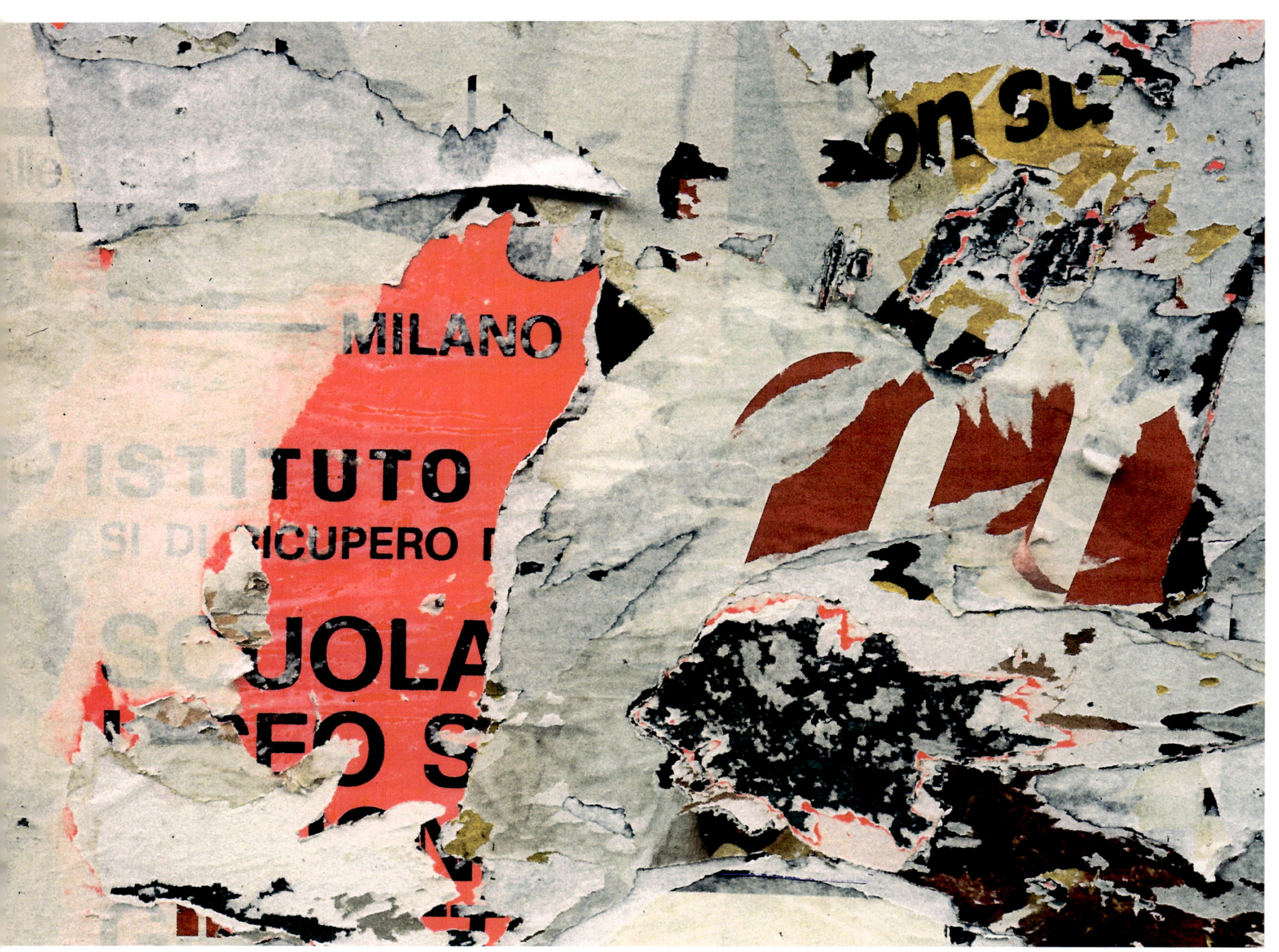
on su
MILANO
ISTITUTO
SI DI RICUPERO
JOLA
CEO S

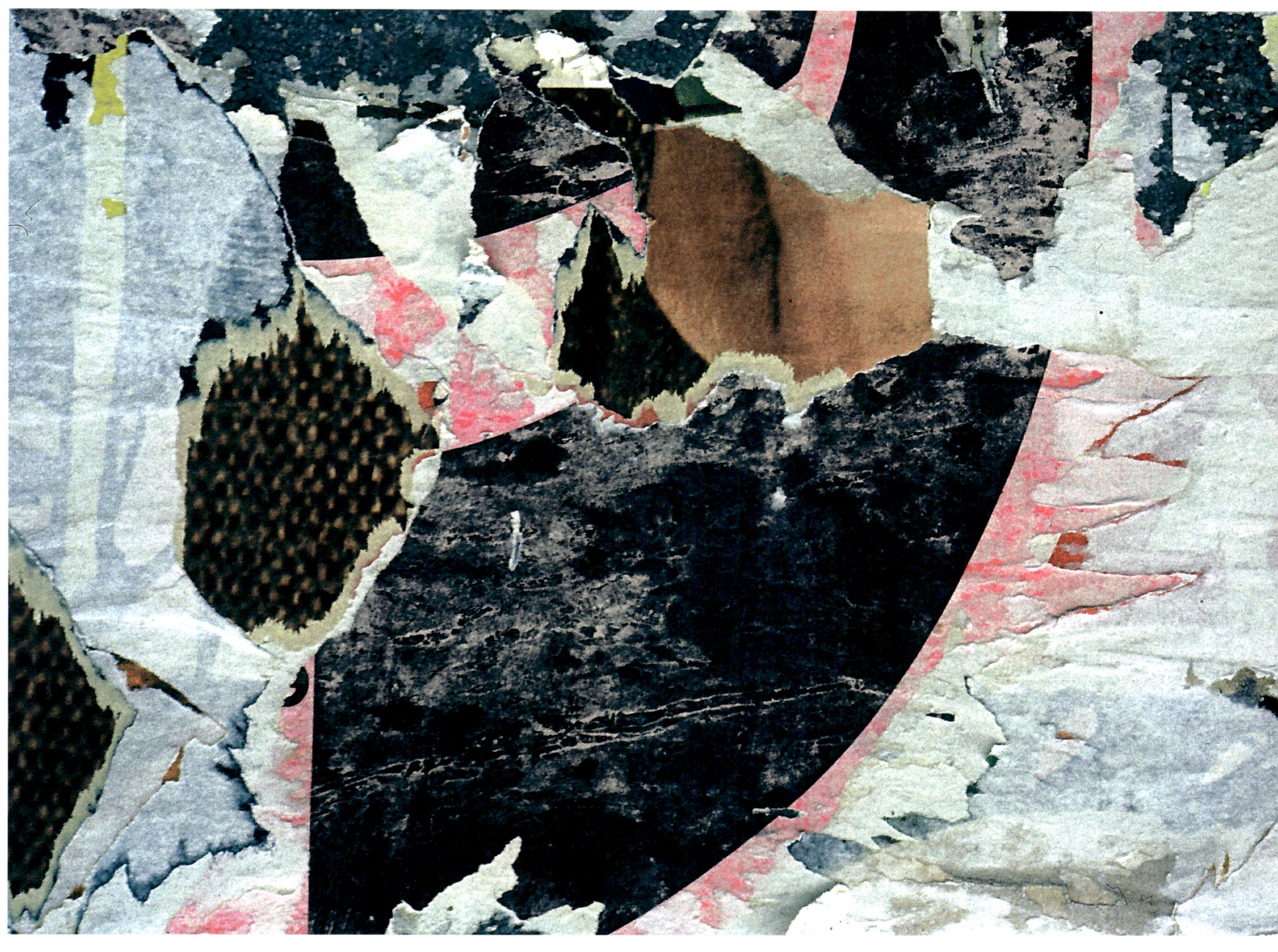

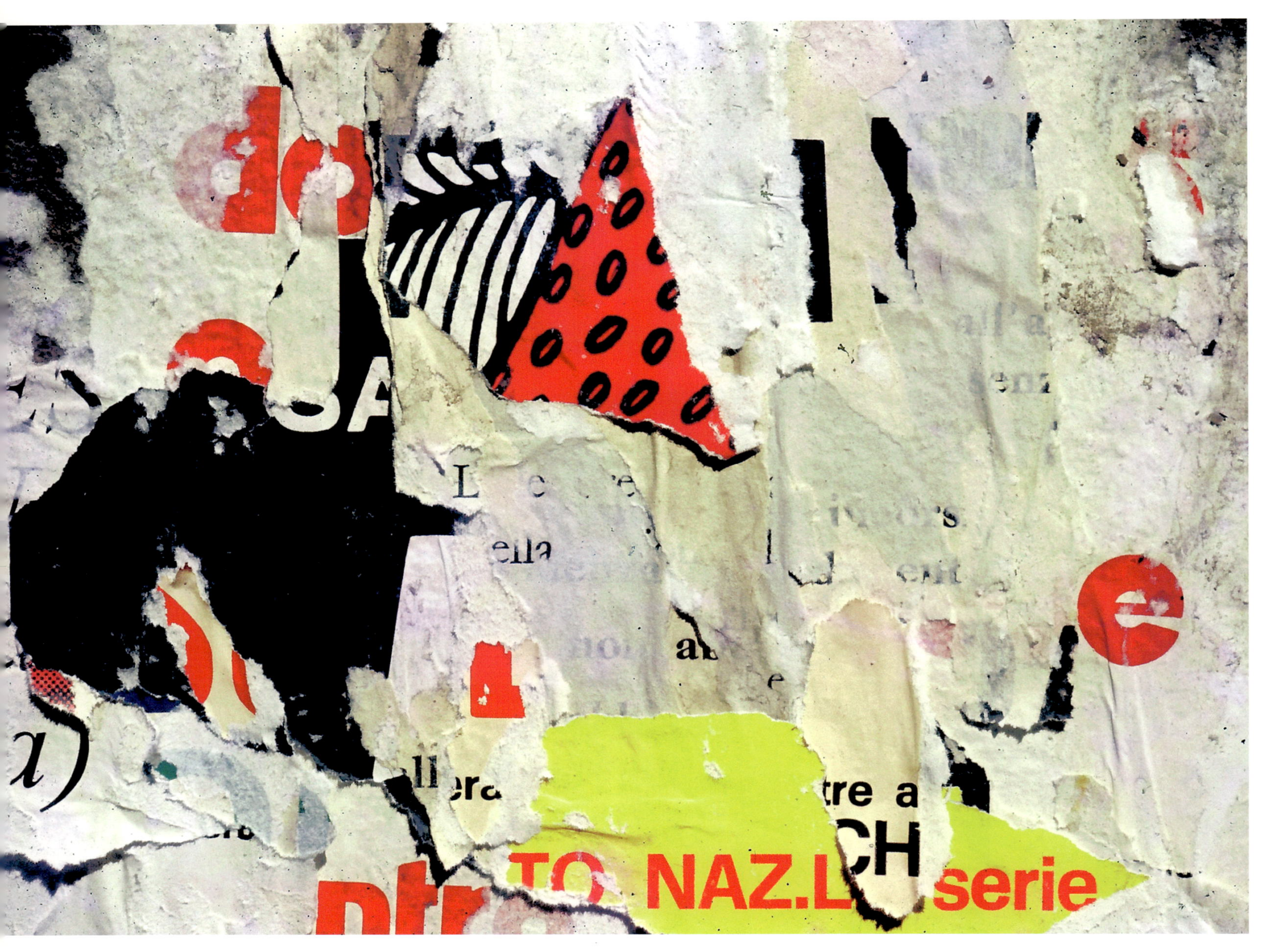
serie
TO. NAZ. CH

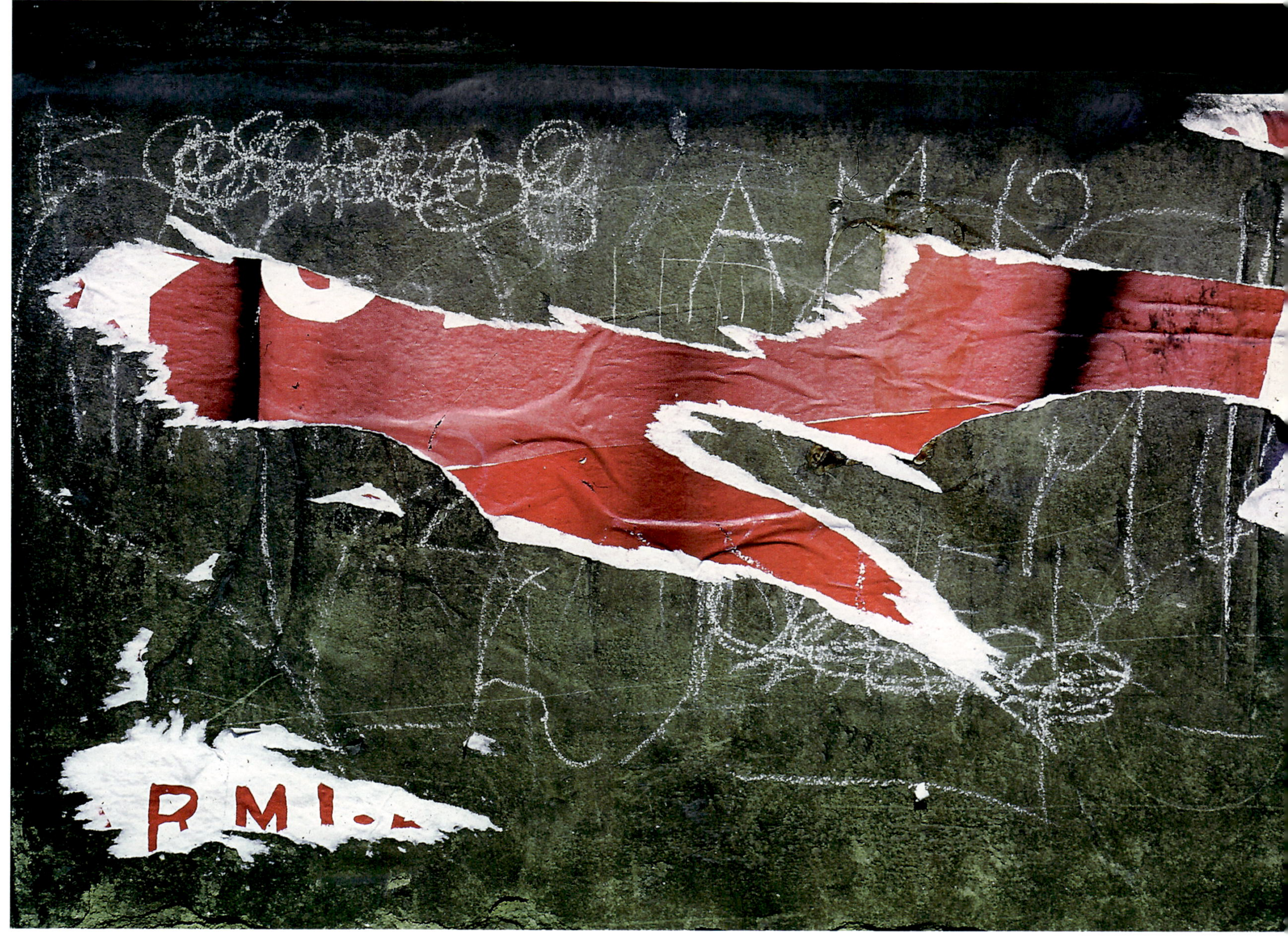
PMI

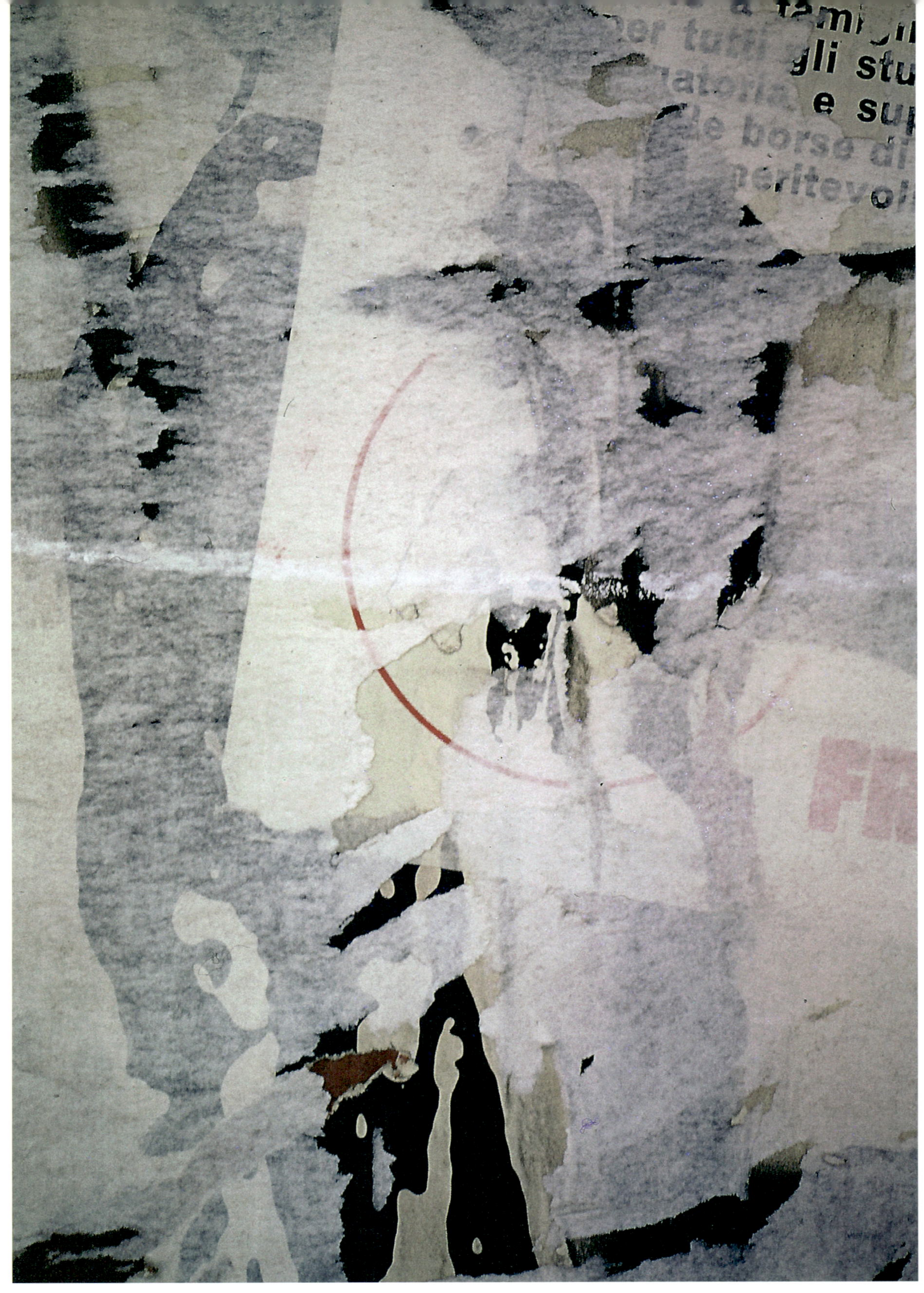
a fami
er tutti gli stu
natoria
e su
le borse di
eritevol
FR

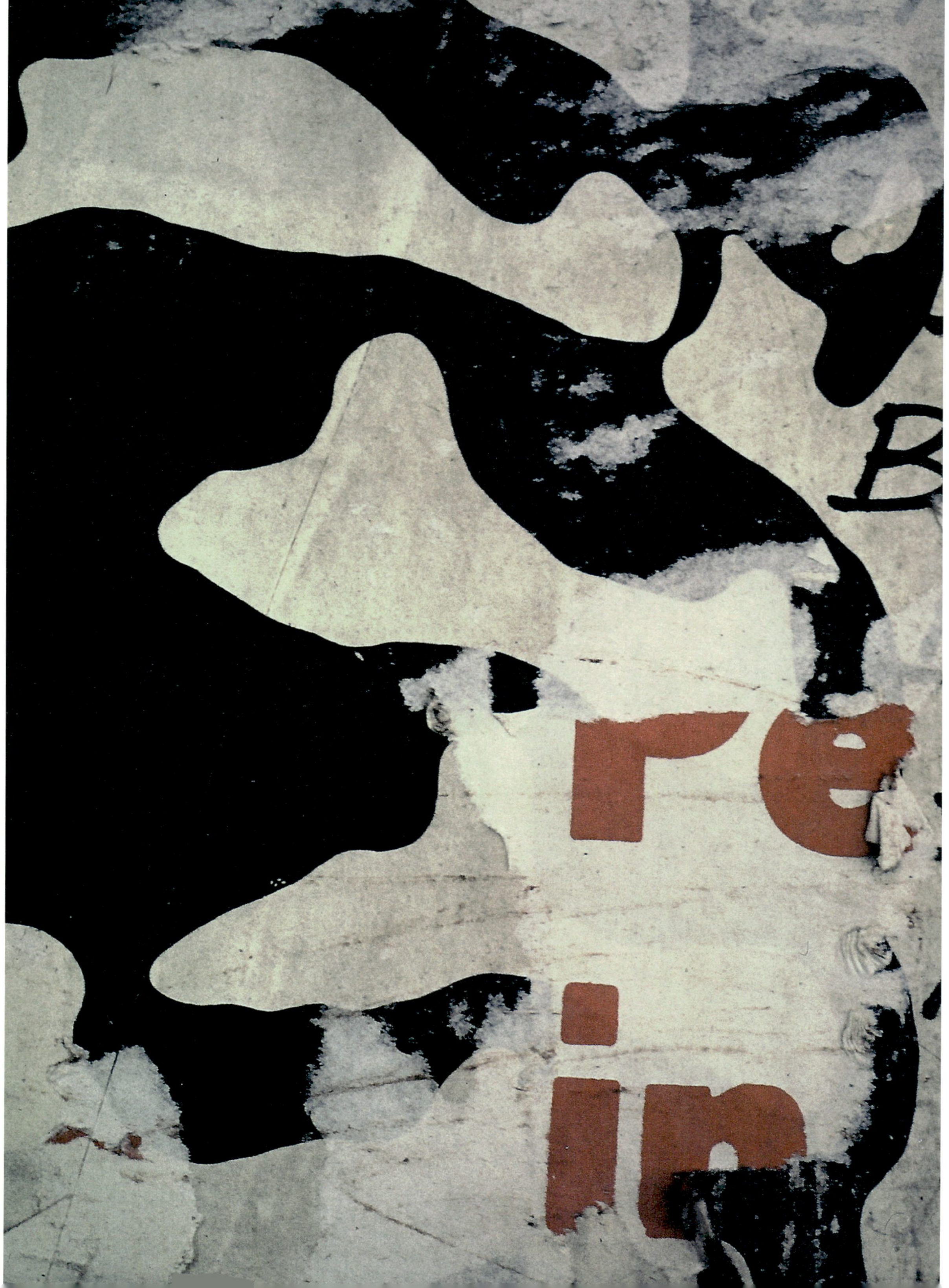

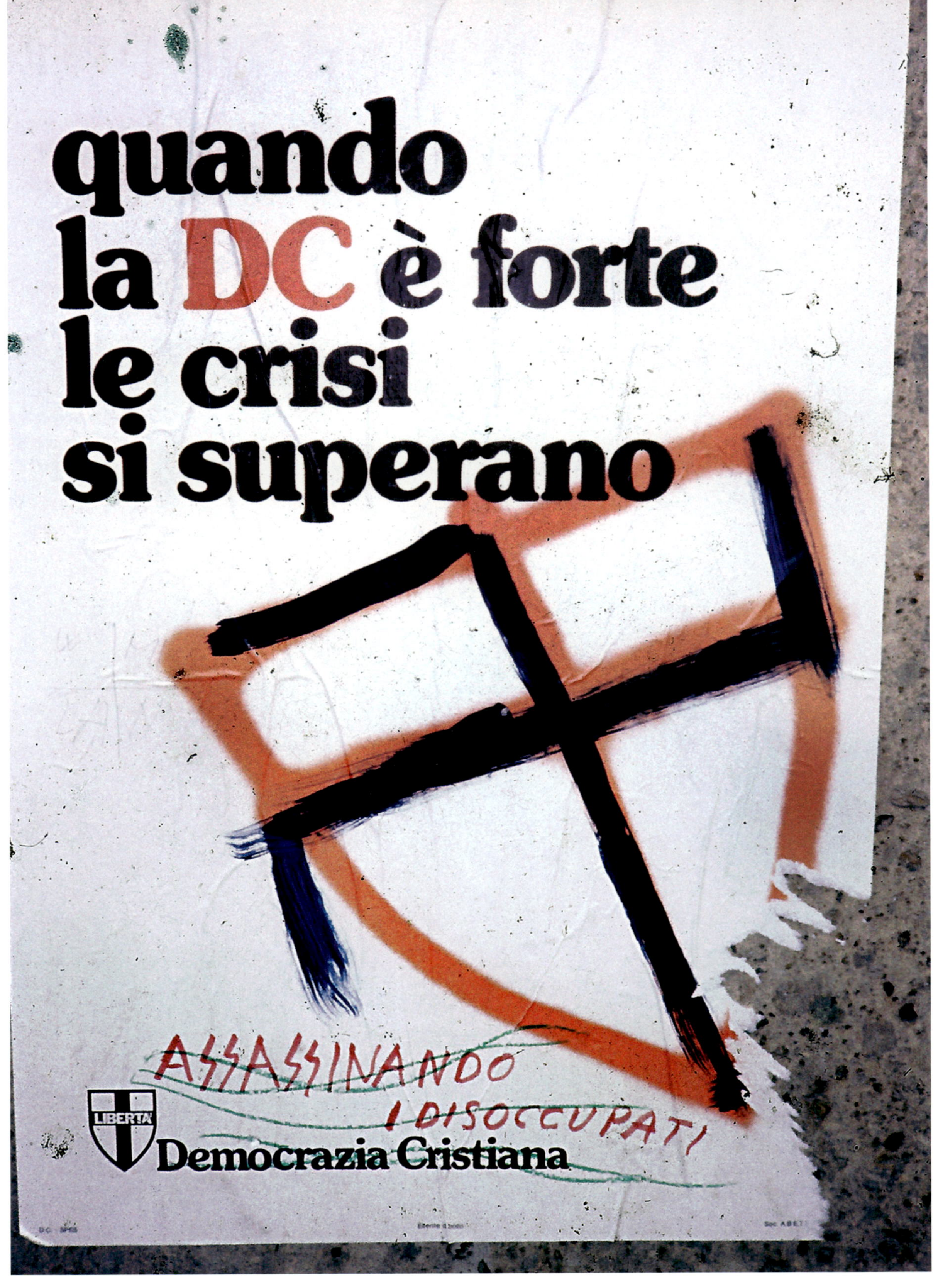

quando
la DC è forte
le crisi
si superano
ASSASSINANDO
I DISOCCUPATI
LIBERTÀ
Democrazia Cristiana

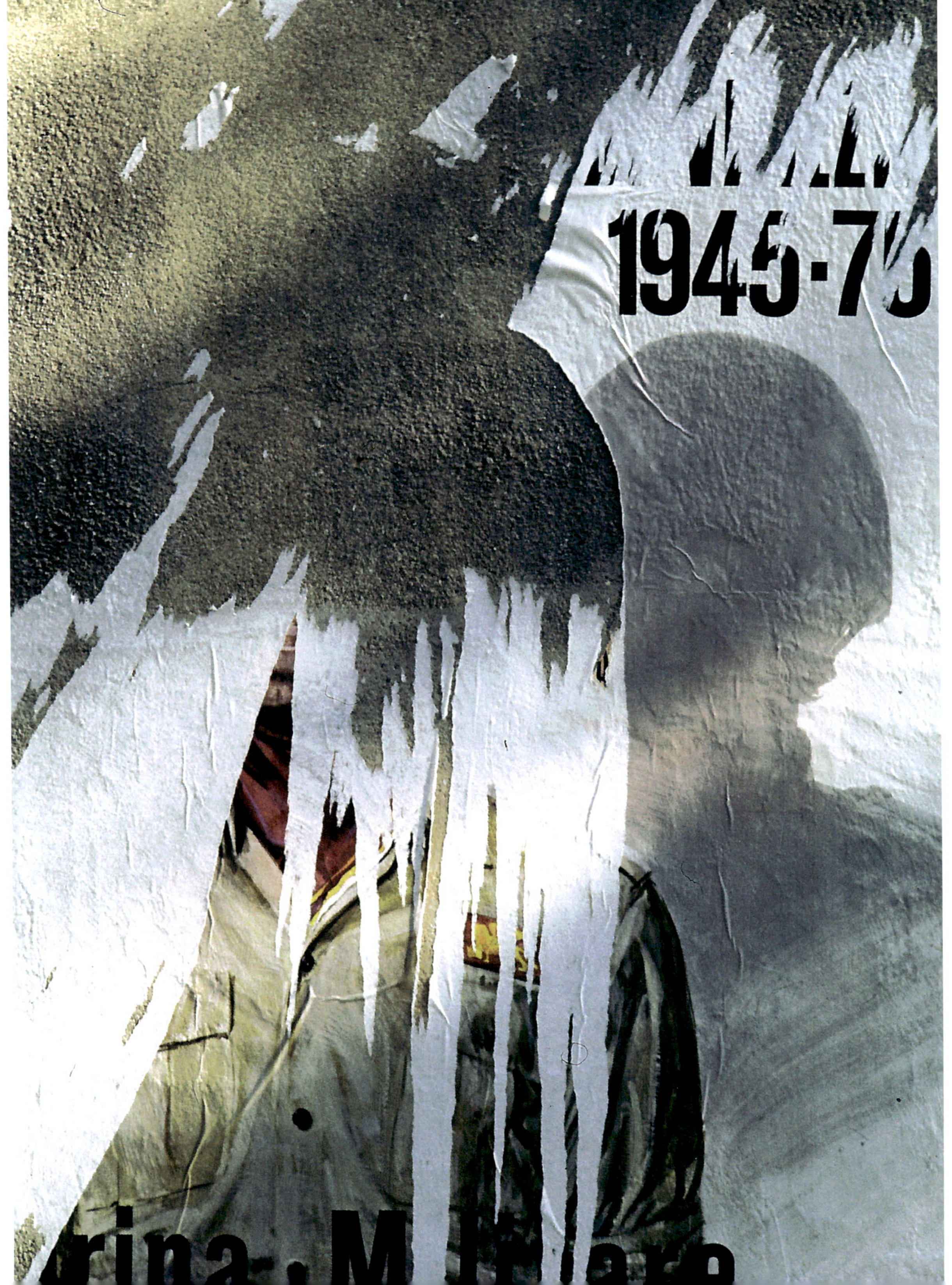
1945-75

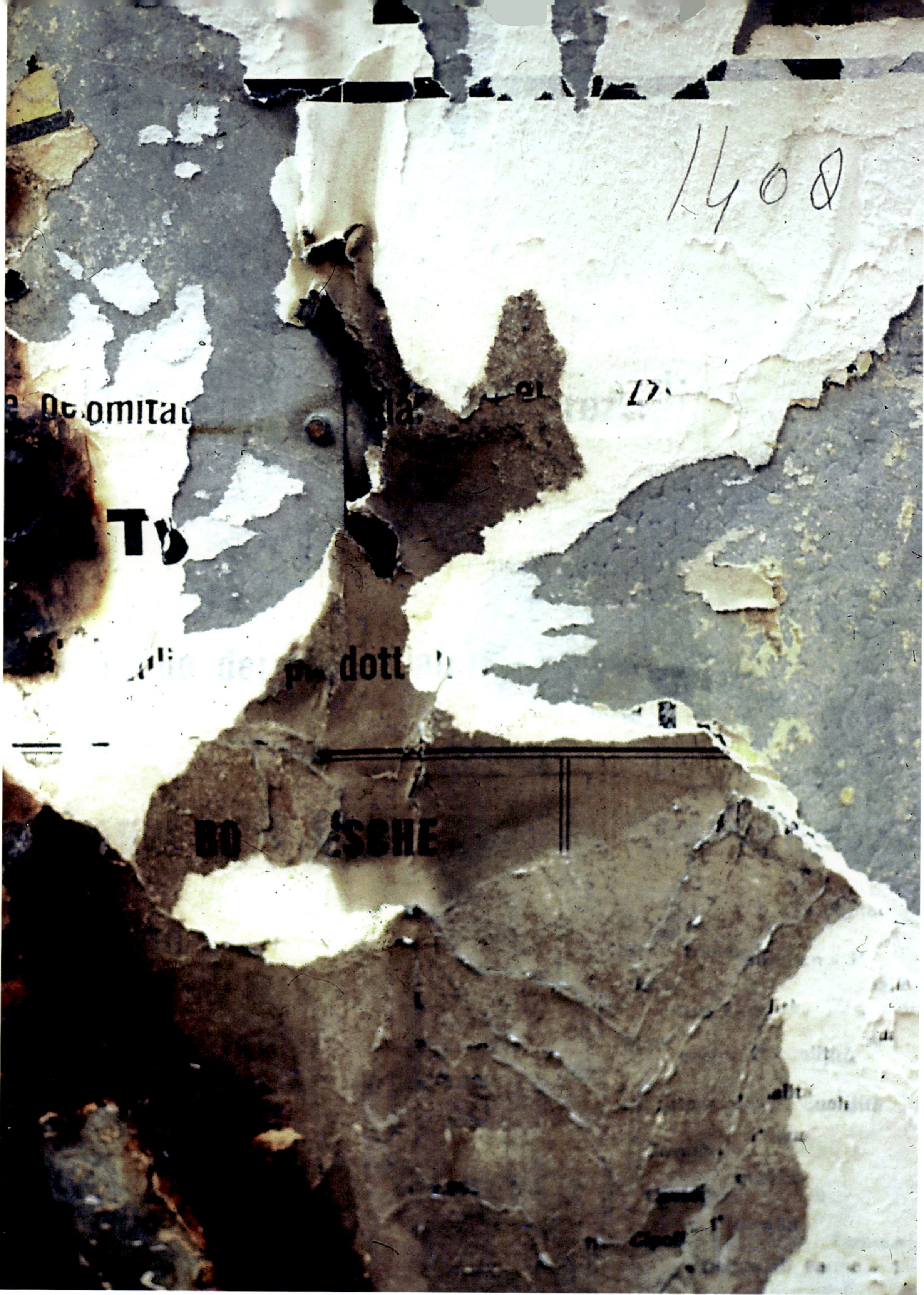
1400
omita
TB
lio dei prodott
BO   ESCHE

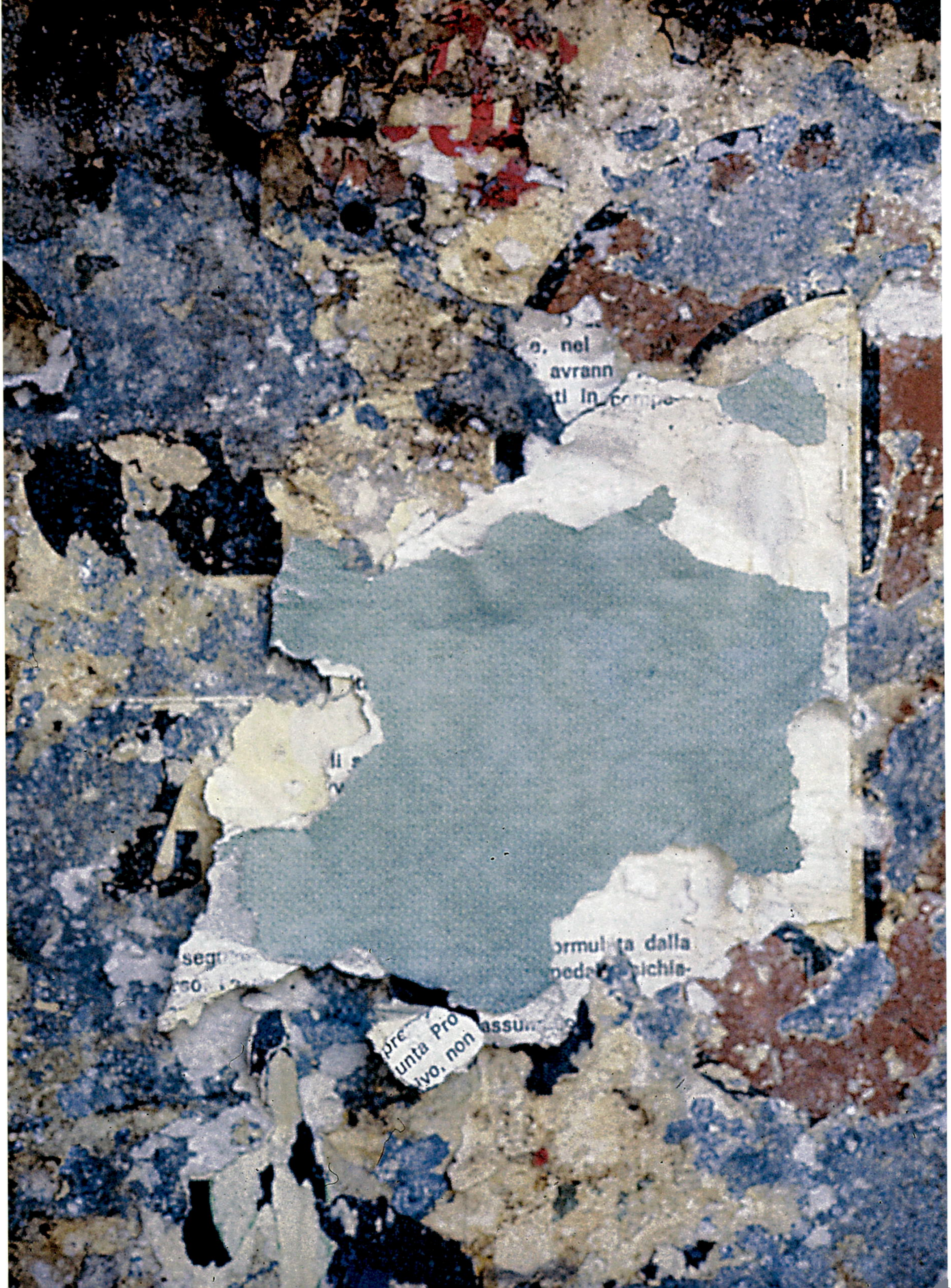

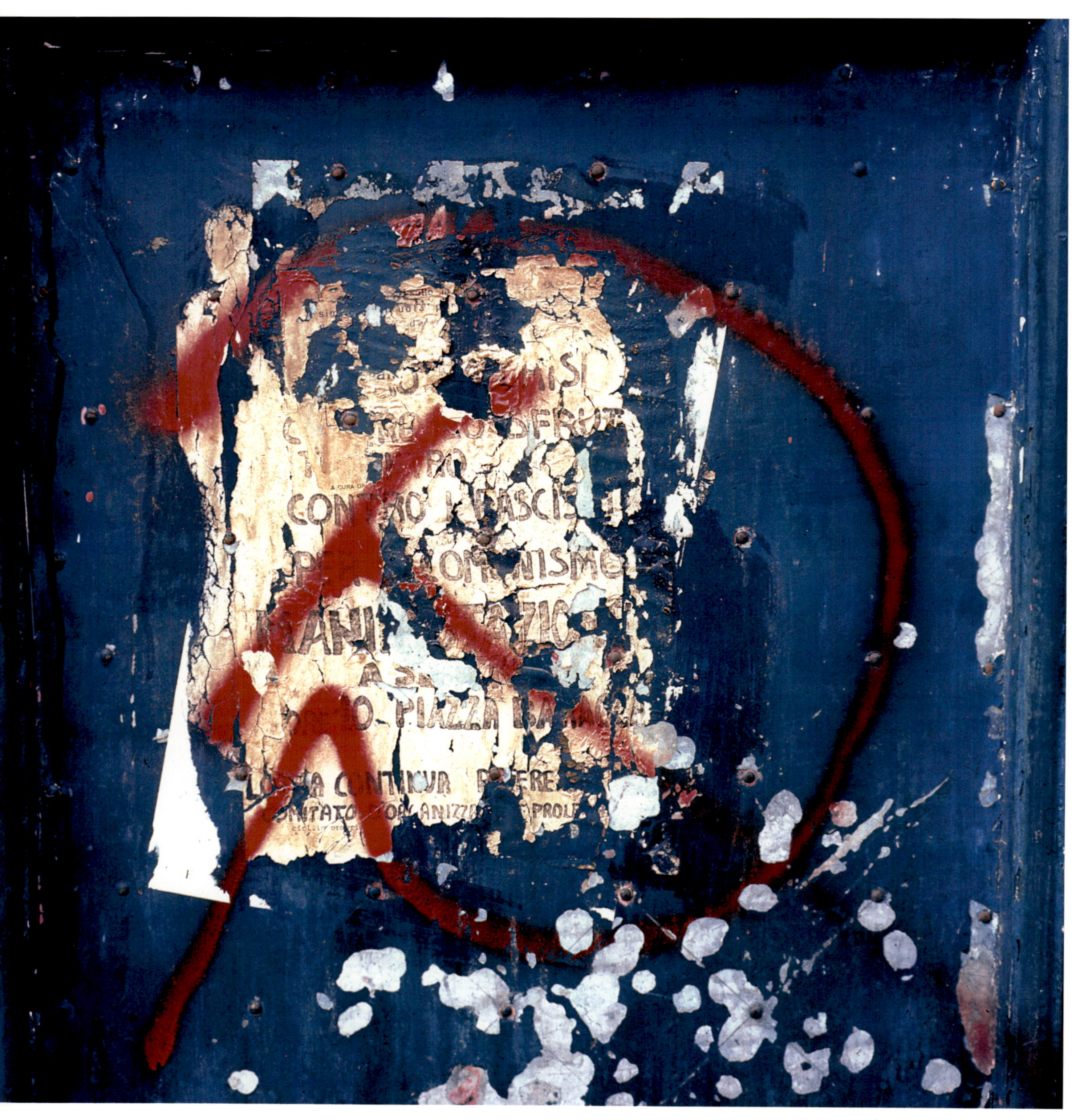
A CURA D
CONTRO I FASCI
OMUNISMO
ANI AZIO
O PIAZZA D
LOTTA CONTINUA P FRE
OMITATO ORGANIZZ PROL

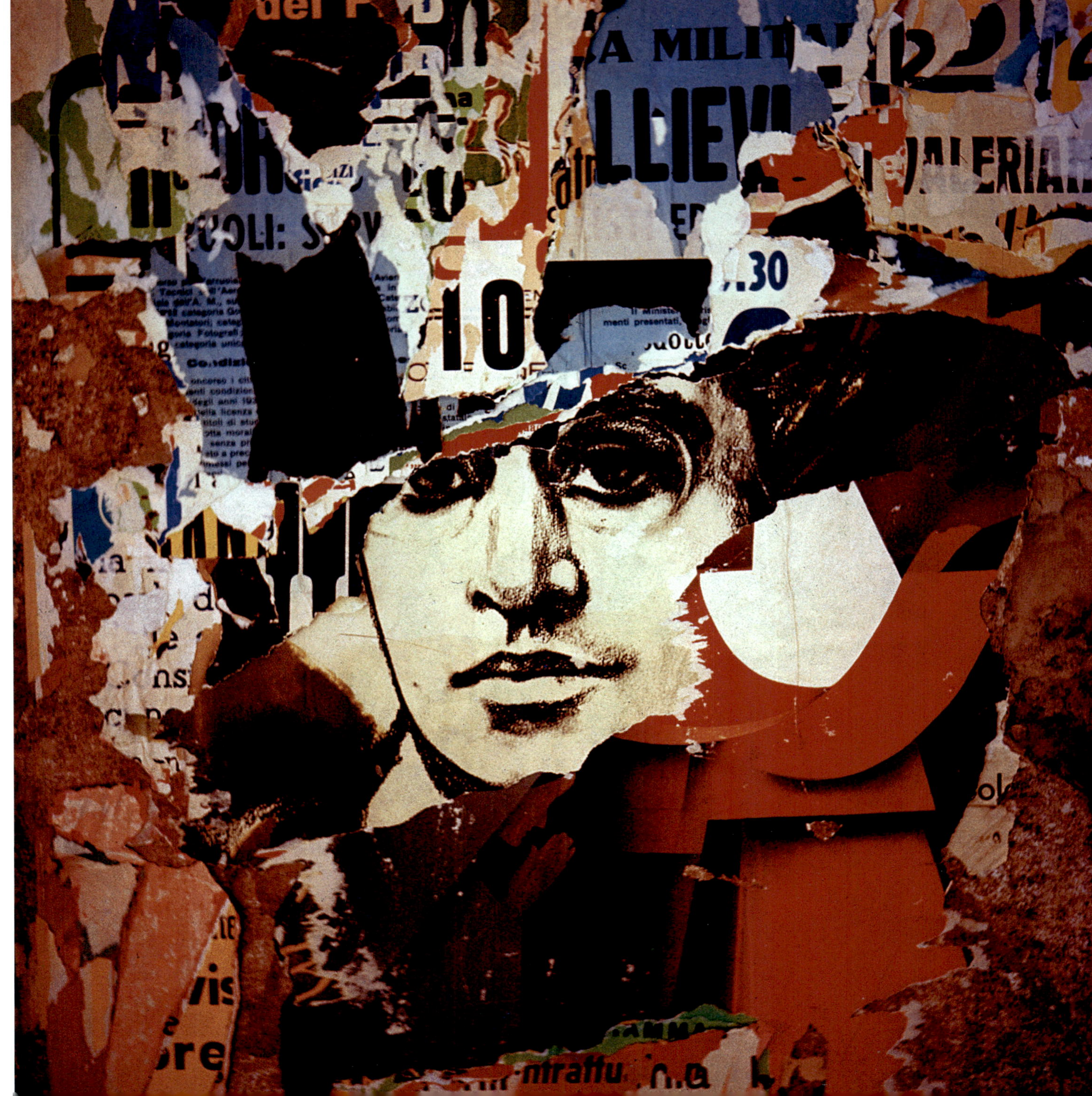

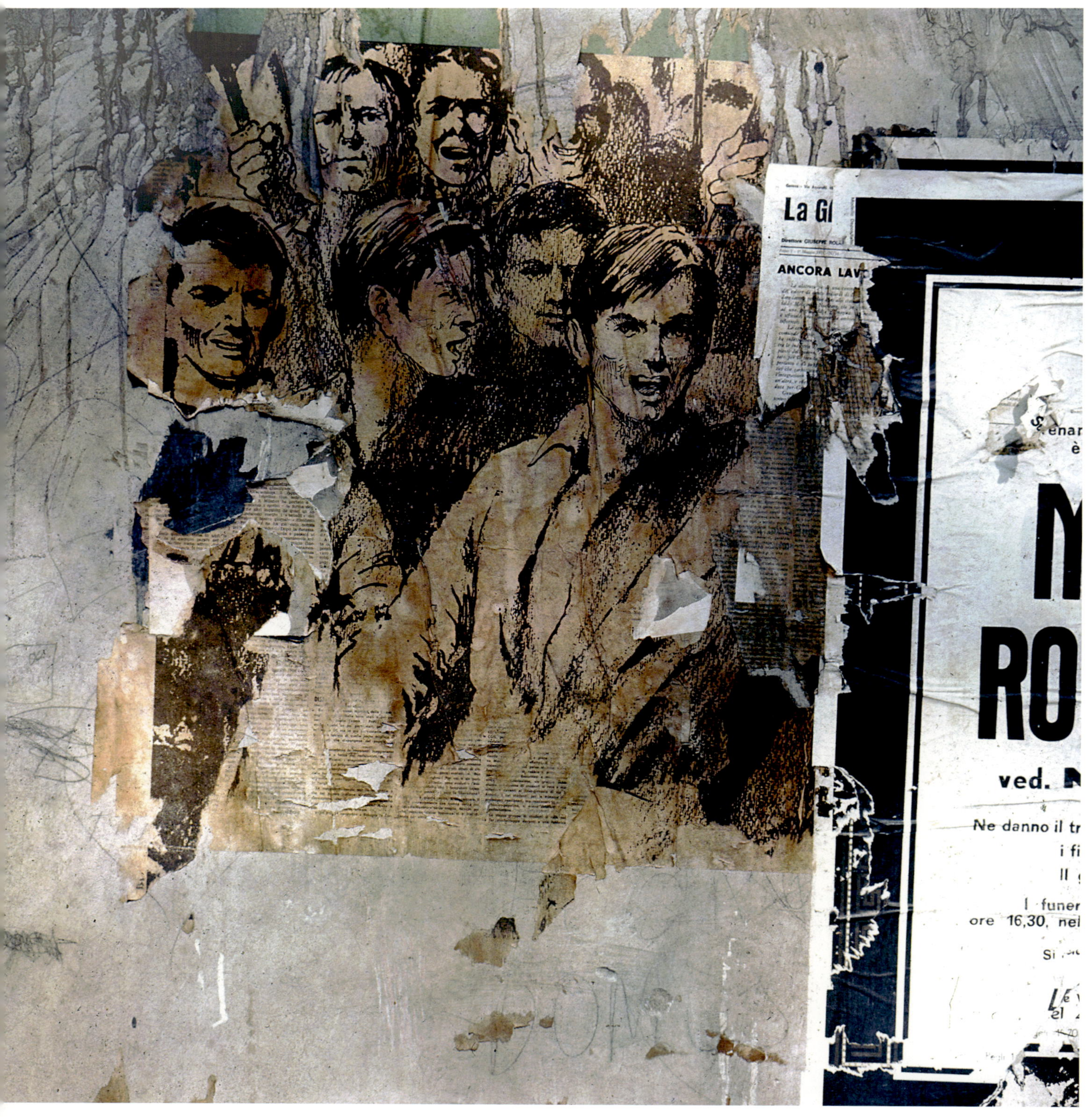

Genova - Via Assarotti
La Gi
Direttore GIUSEPPE ROLL
ANCORA LAV
ved. N
Ne danno il tr
i fi
Il g
I funer
ore 16,30, nel
Si
M
RO

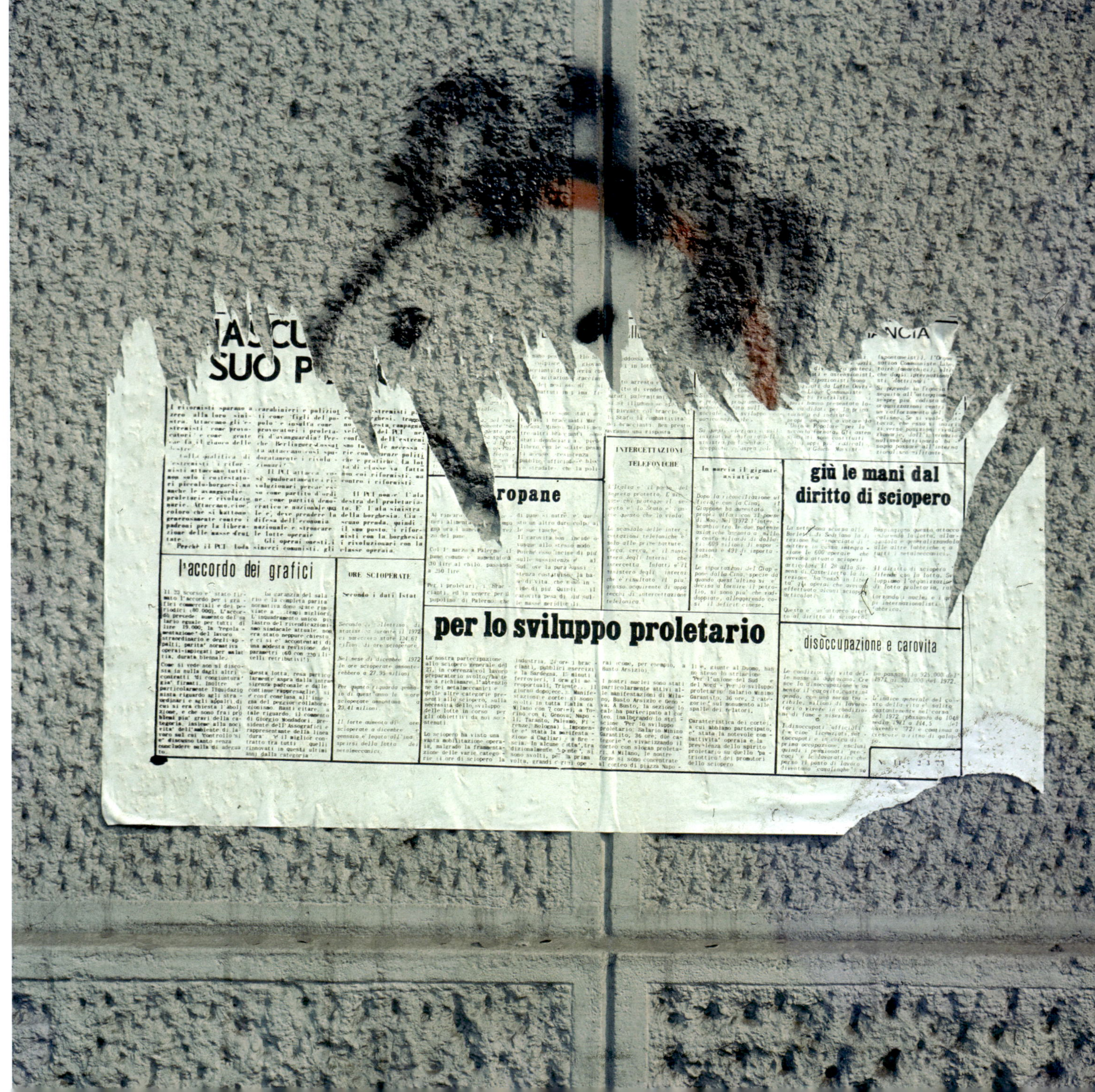
SUO P
giù le mani dal
diritto di sciopero
l'accordo dei grafici
ORE SCIOPERATE
INTERCETTAZIONI
TELEFONICHE
per lo sviluppo proletario
disoccupazione e carovita

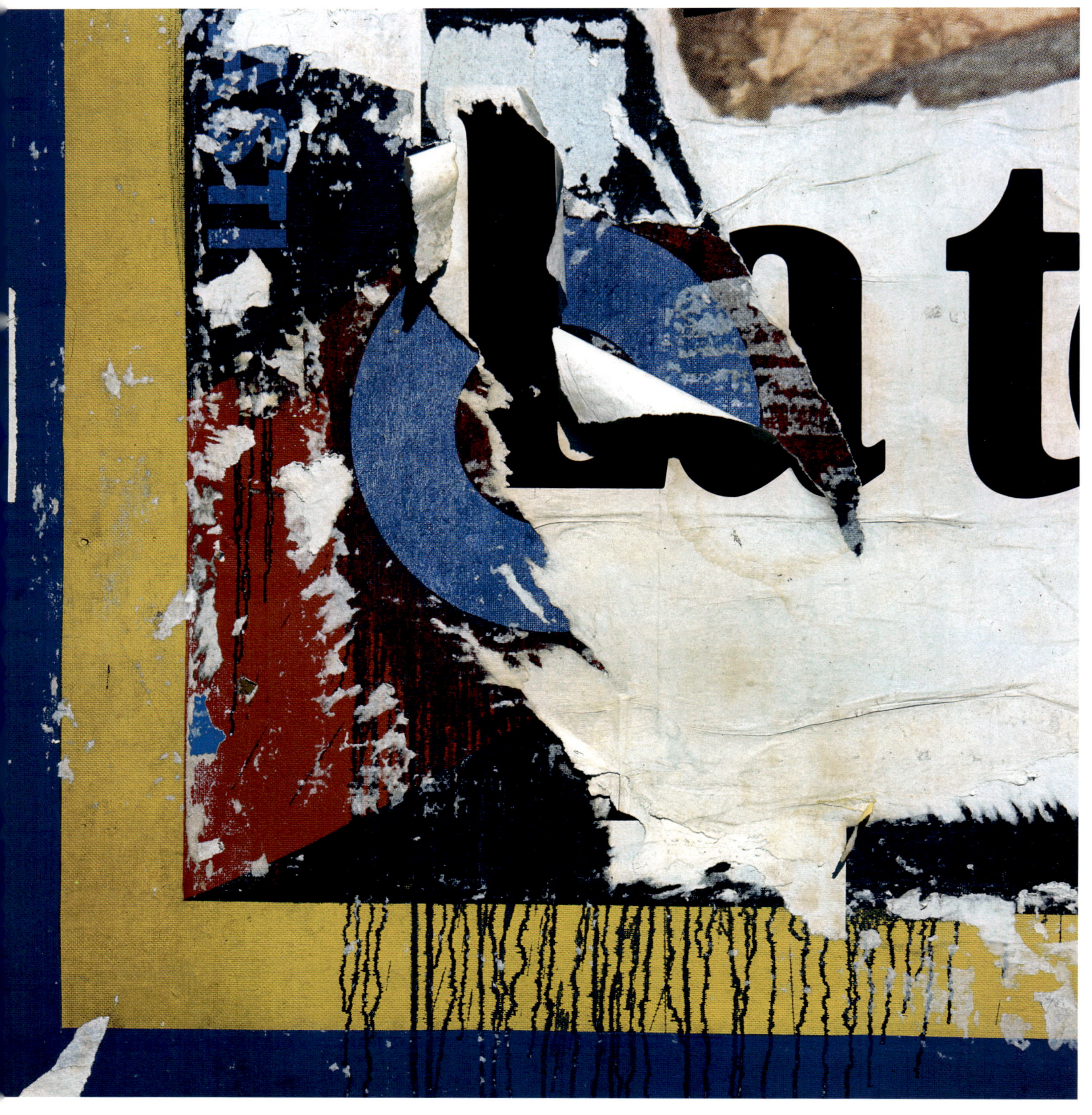

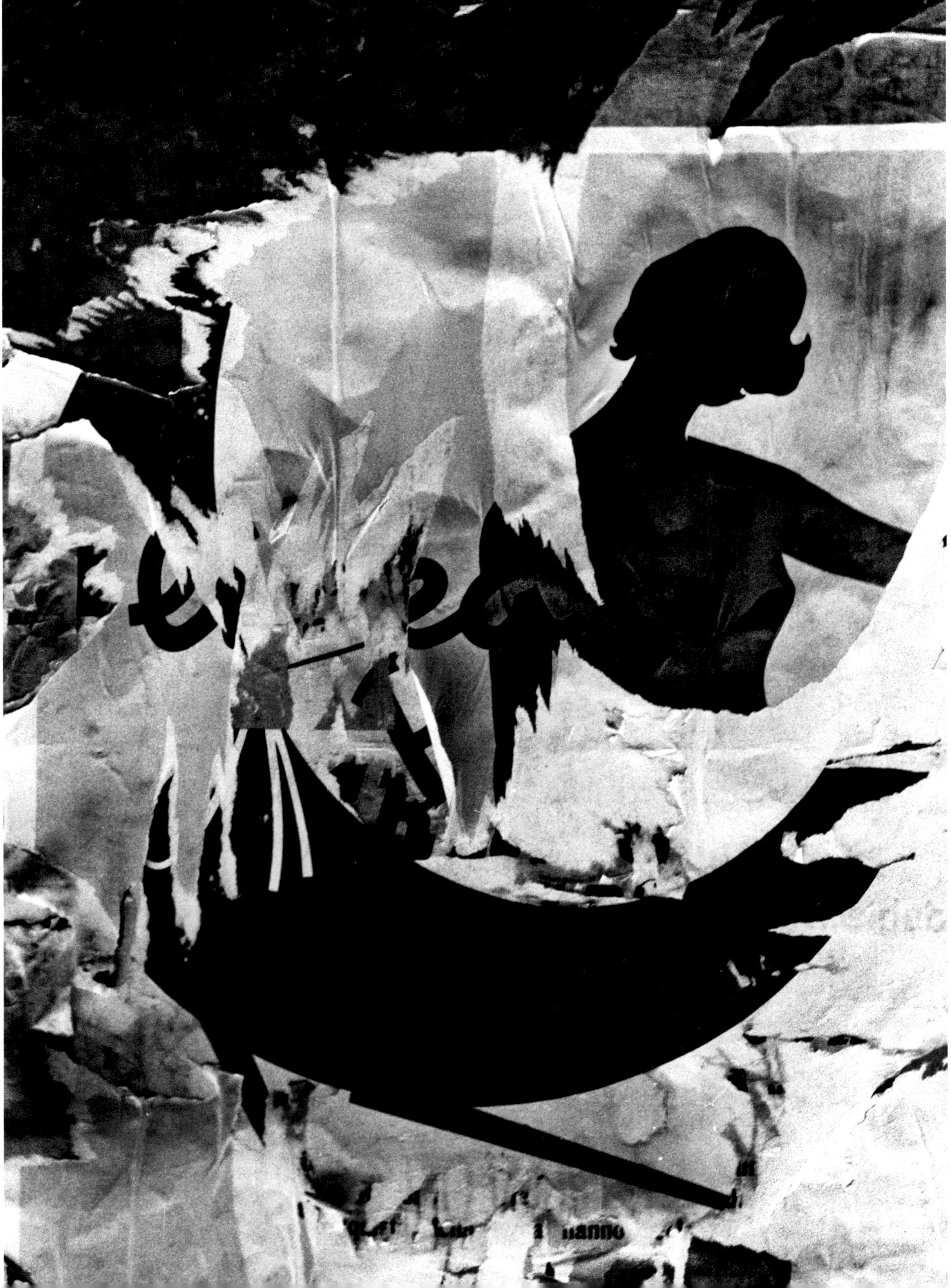

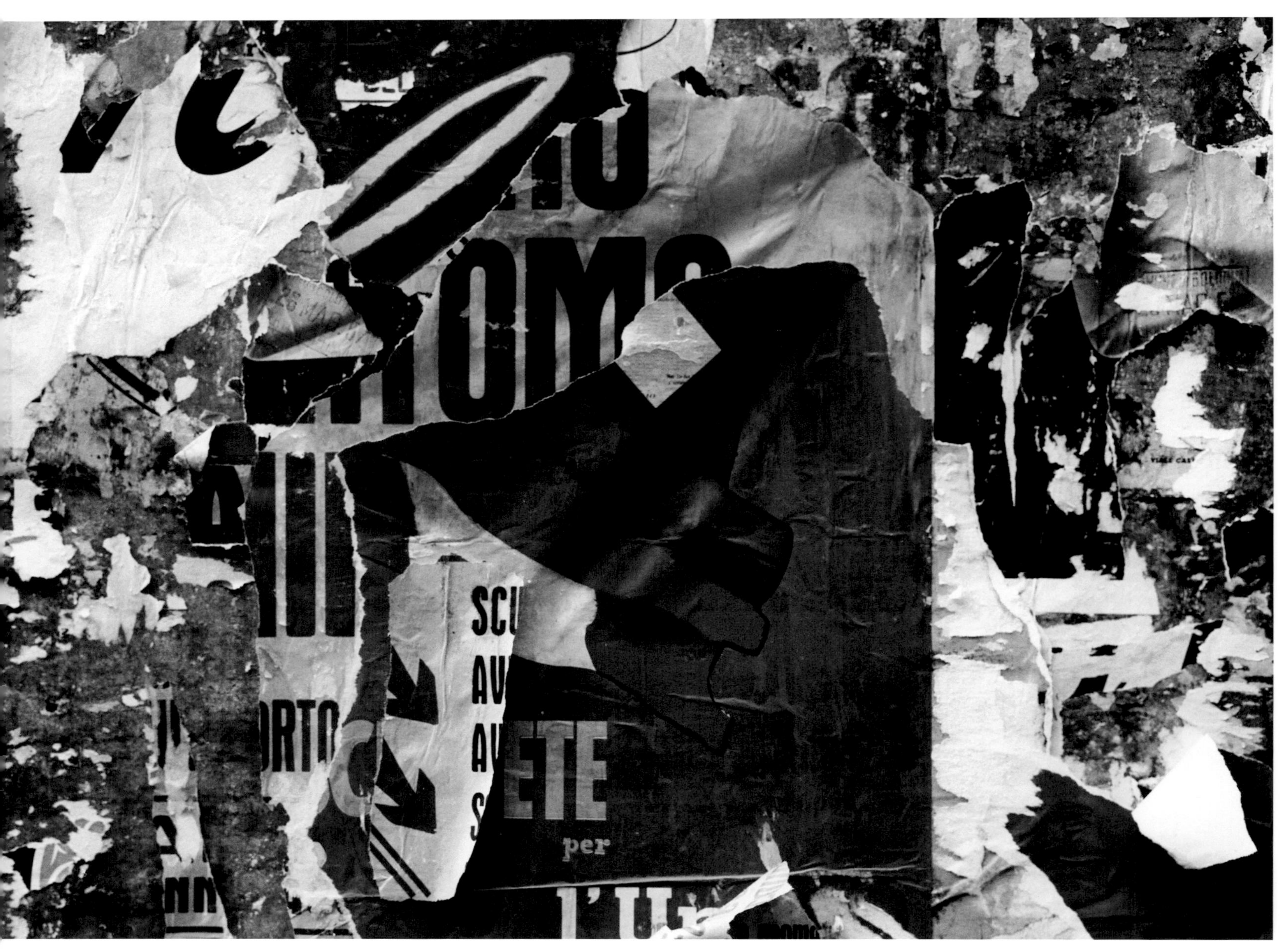
UOMS
SCU
AV
AVETE
S
per
l'U

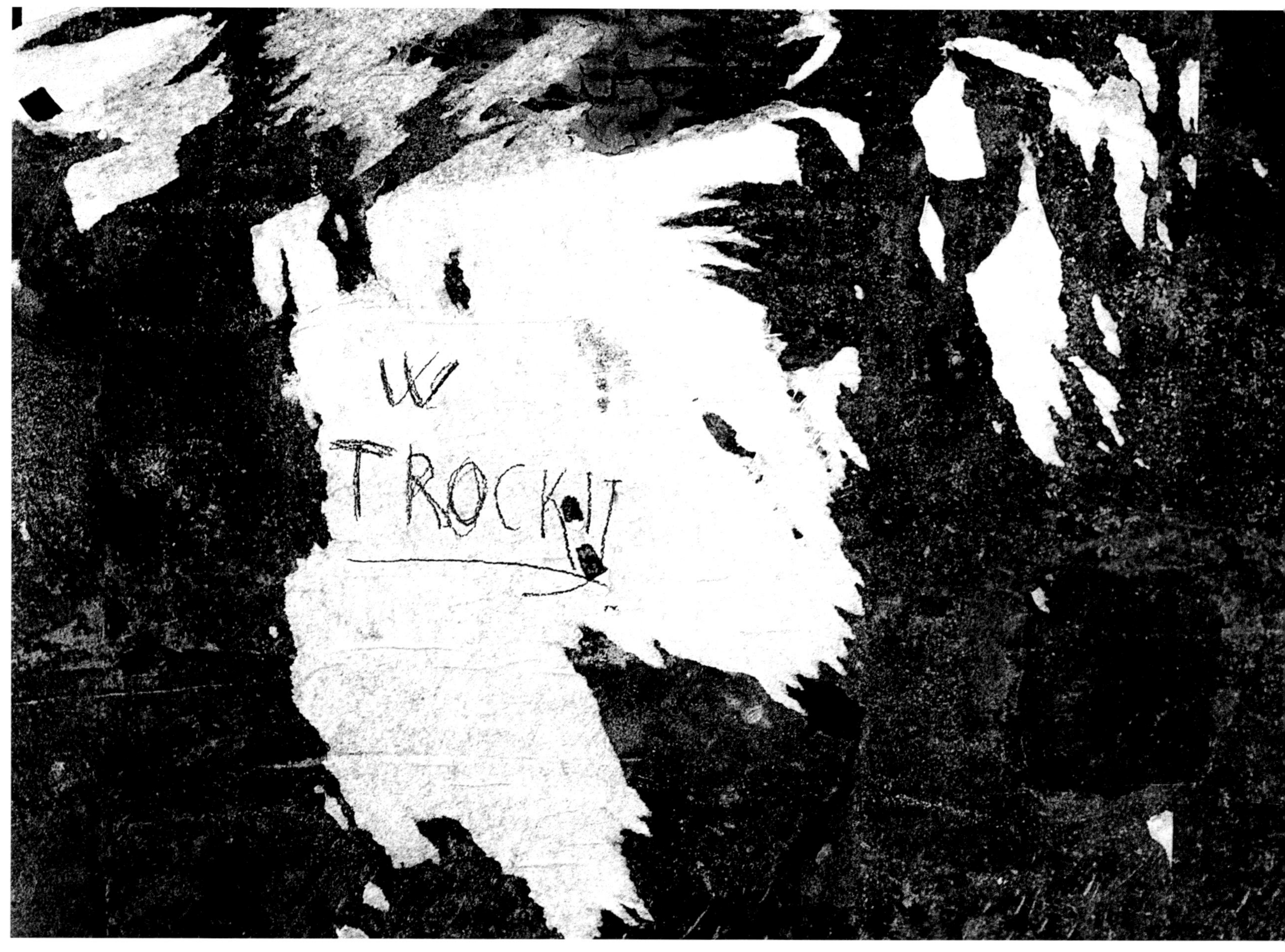

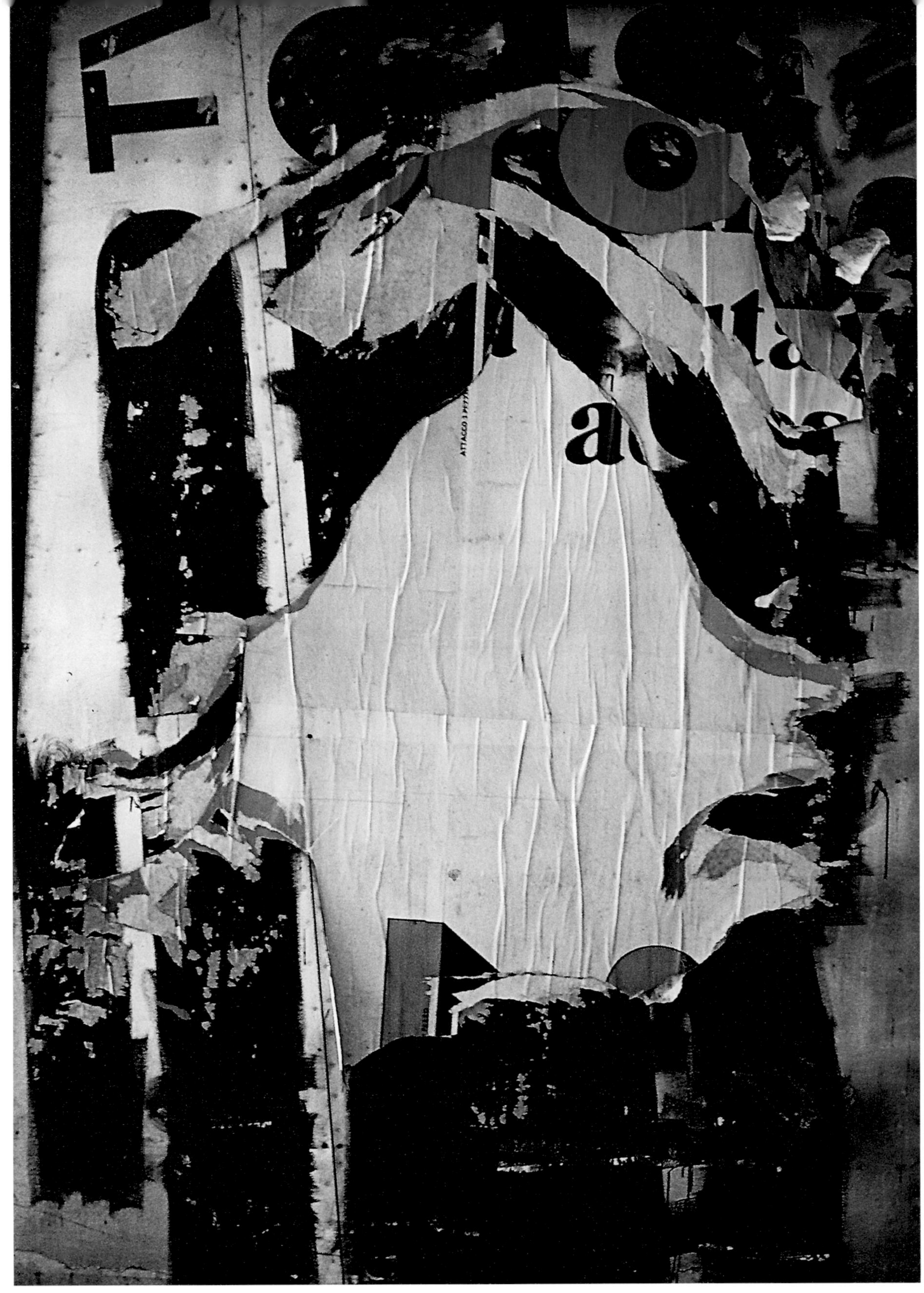

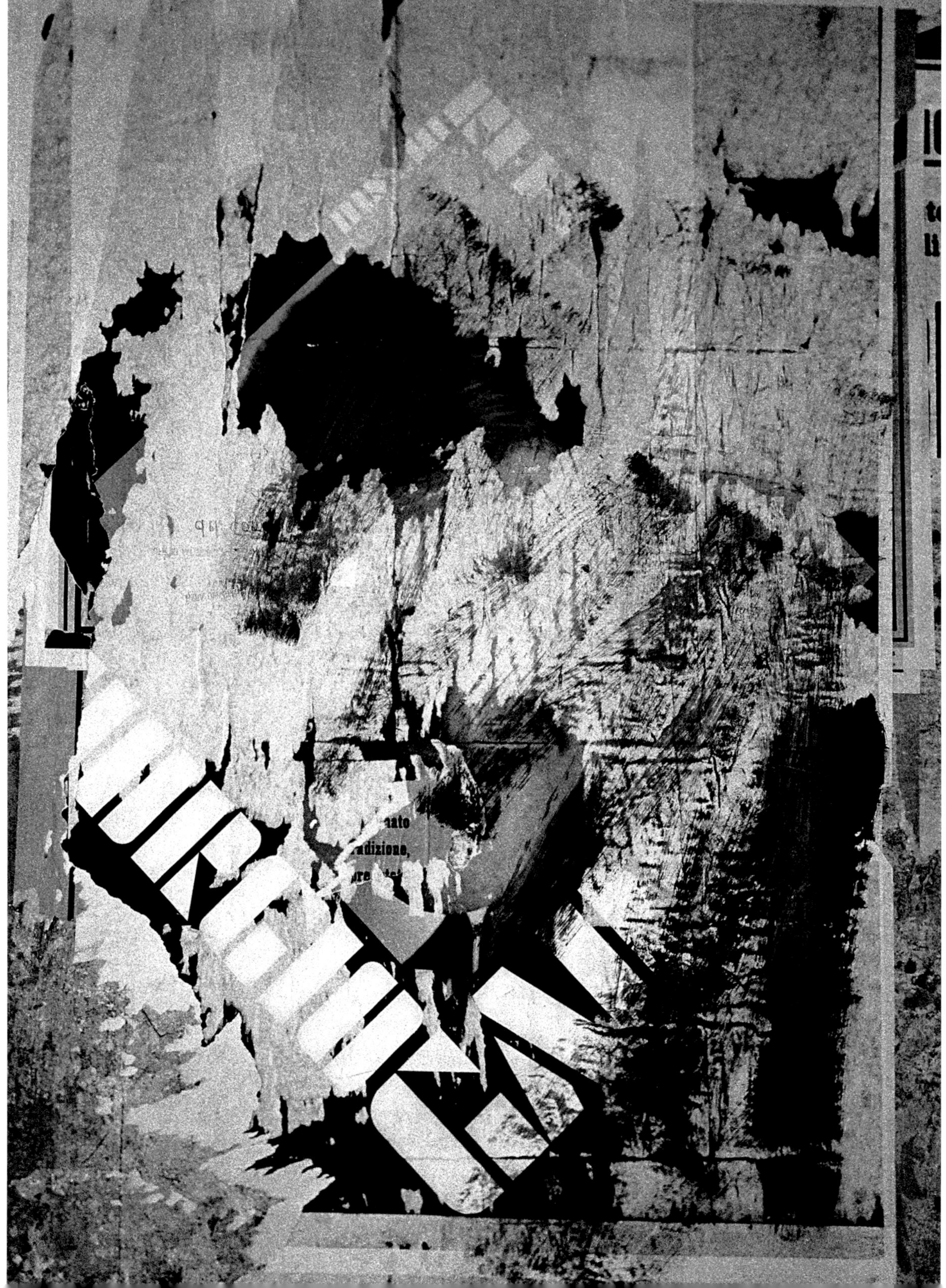

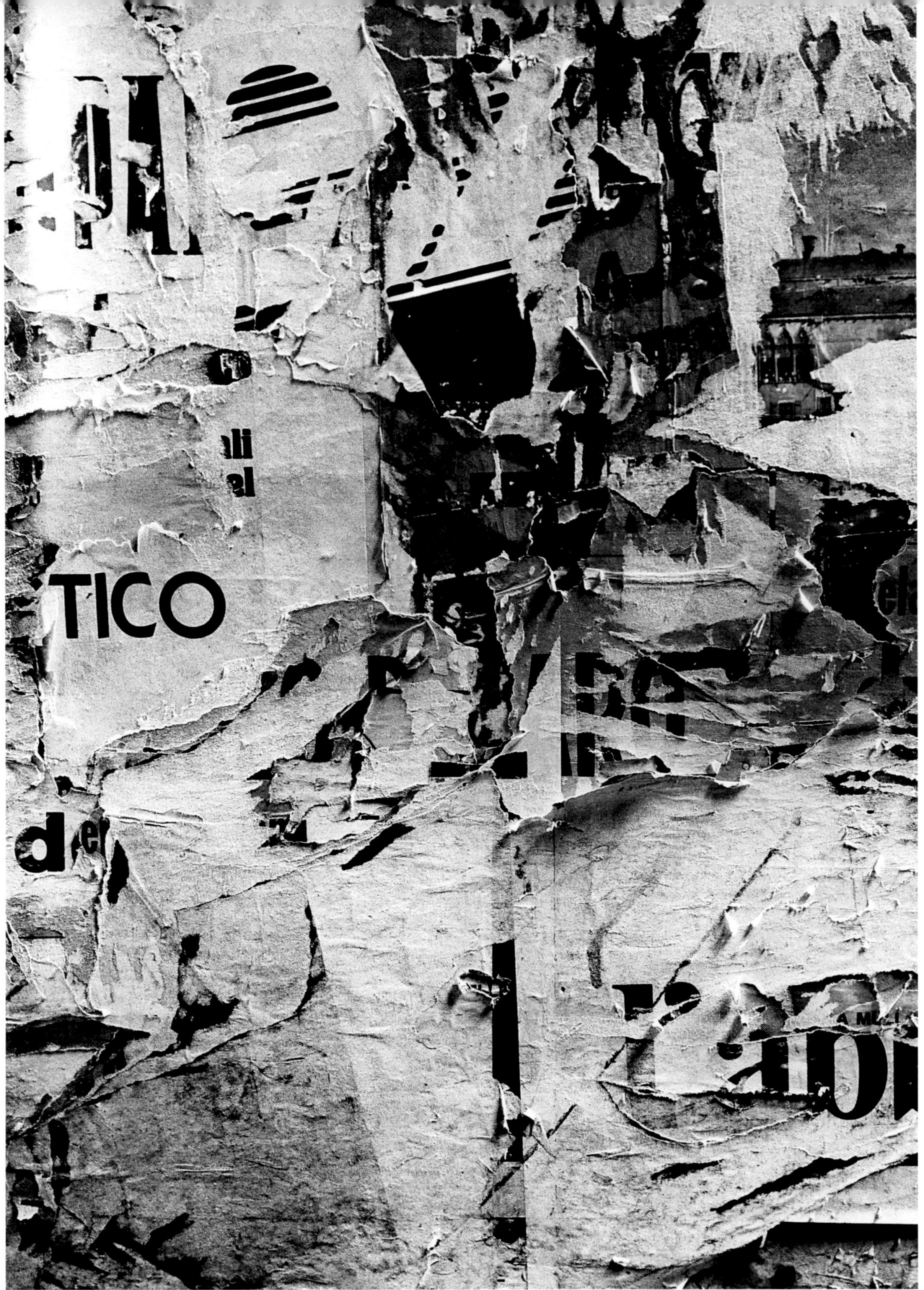

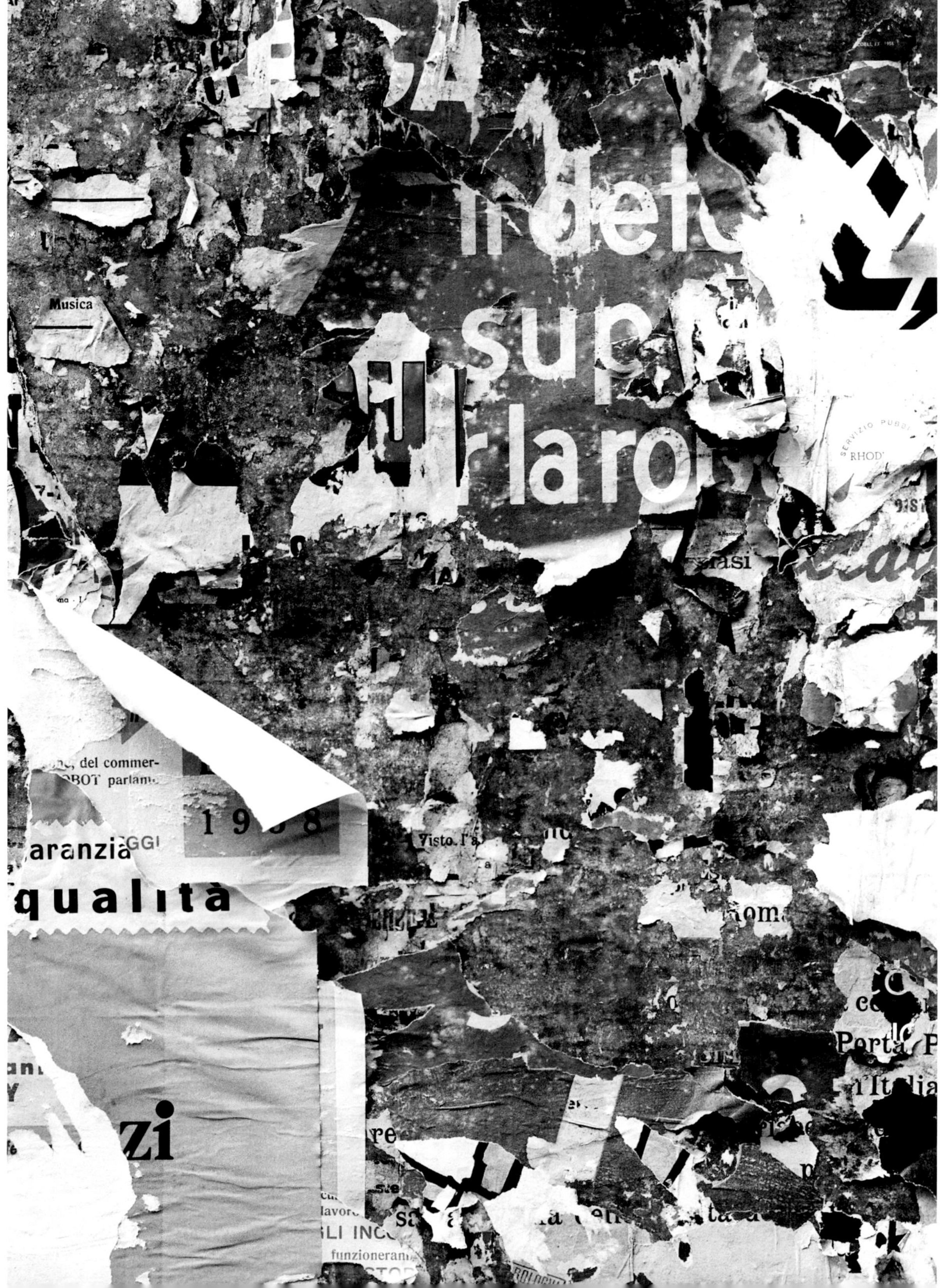
Musica
rdel
sup
rla ro
RHOD'
, del commer-
BOT parlan
1958
aranzia
qualità
zi

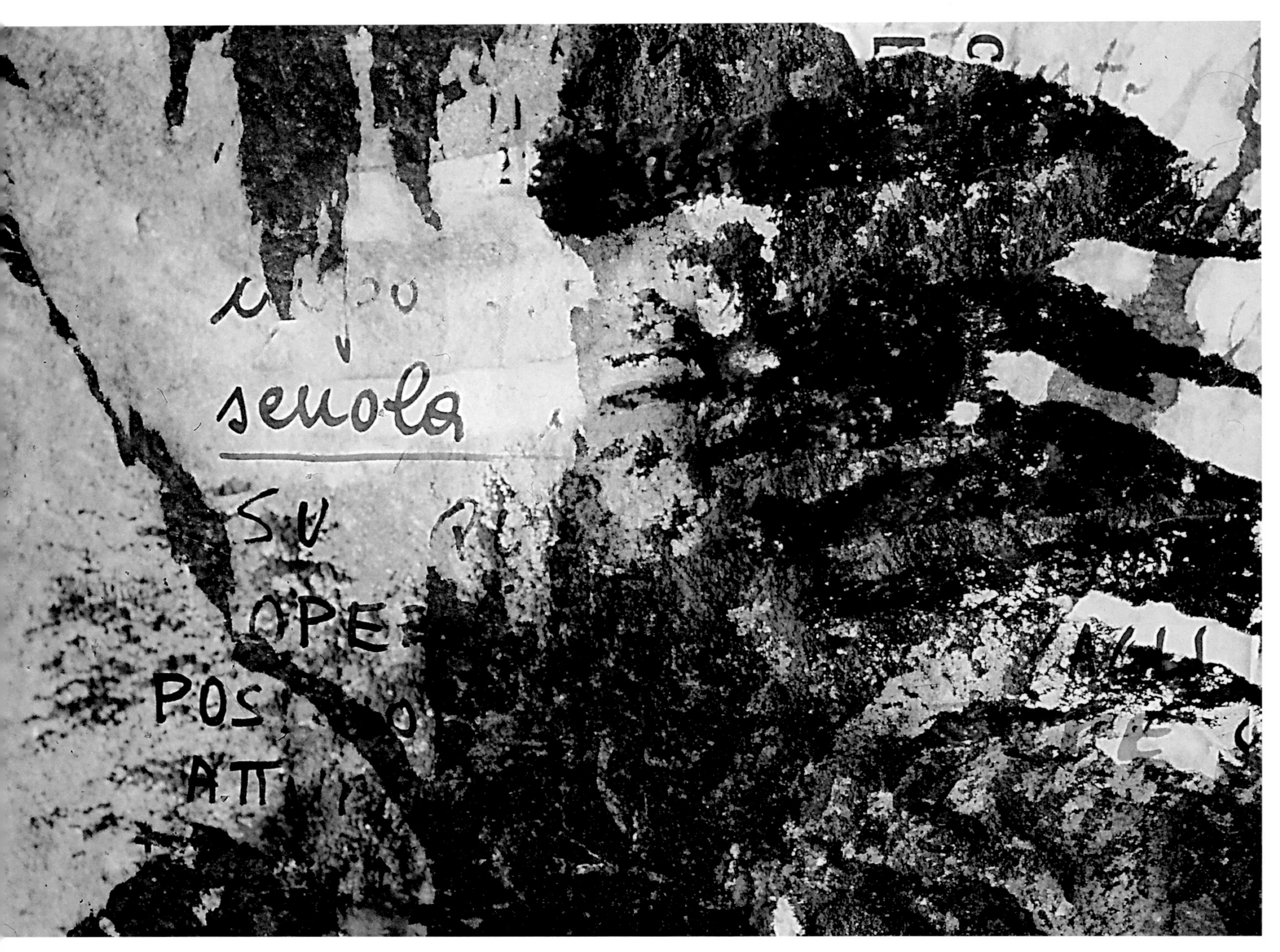
nuovo
scuola
SU
OPE
POS
AT

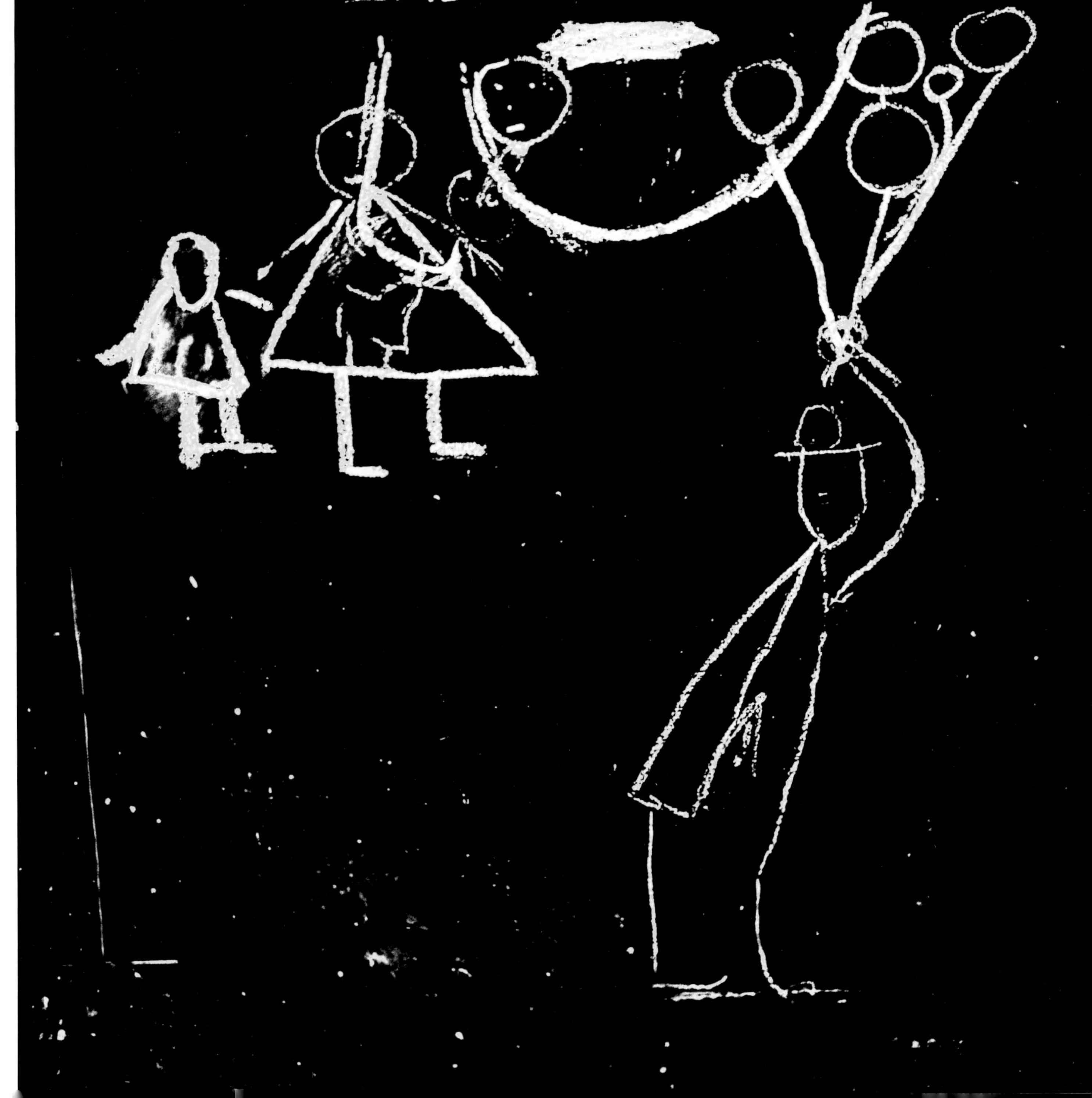

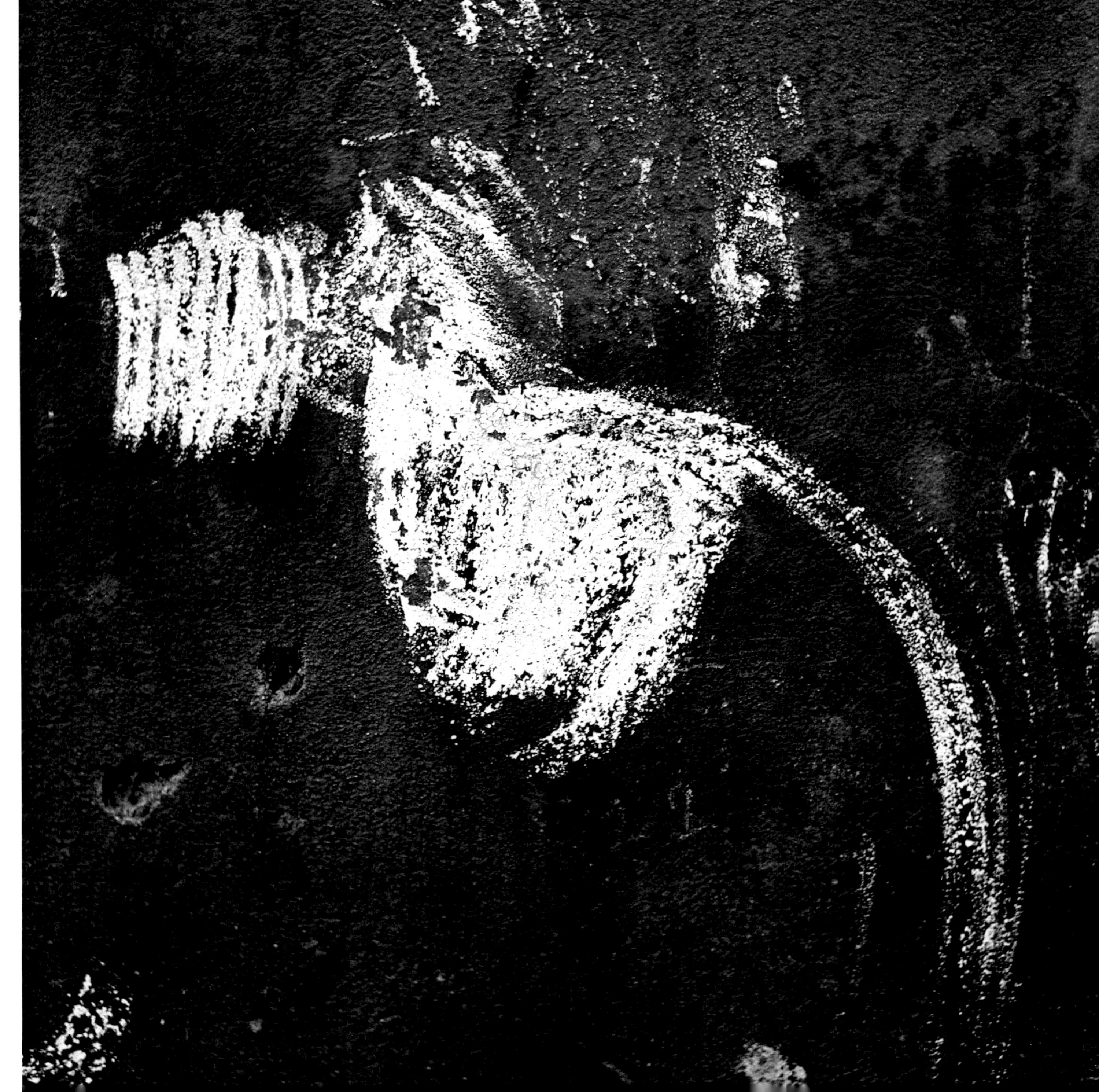

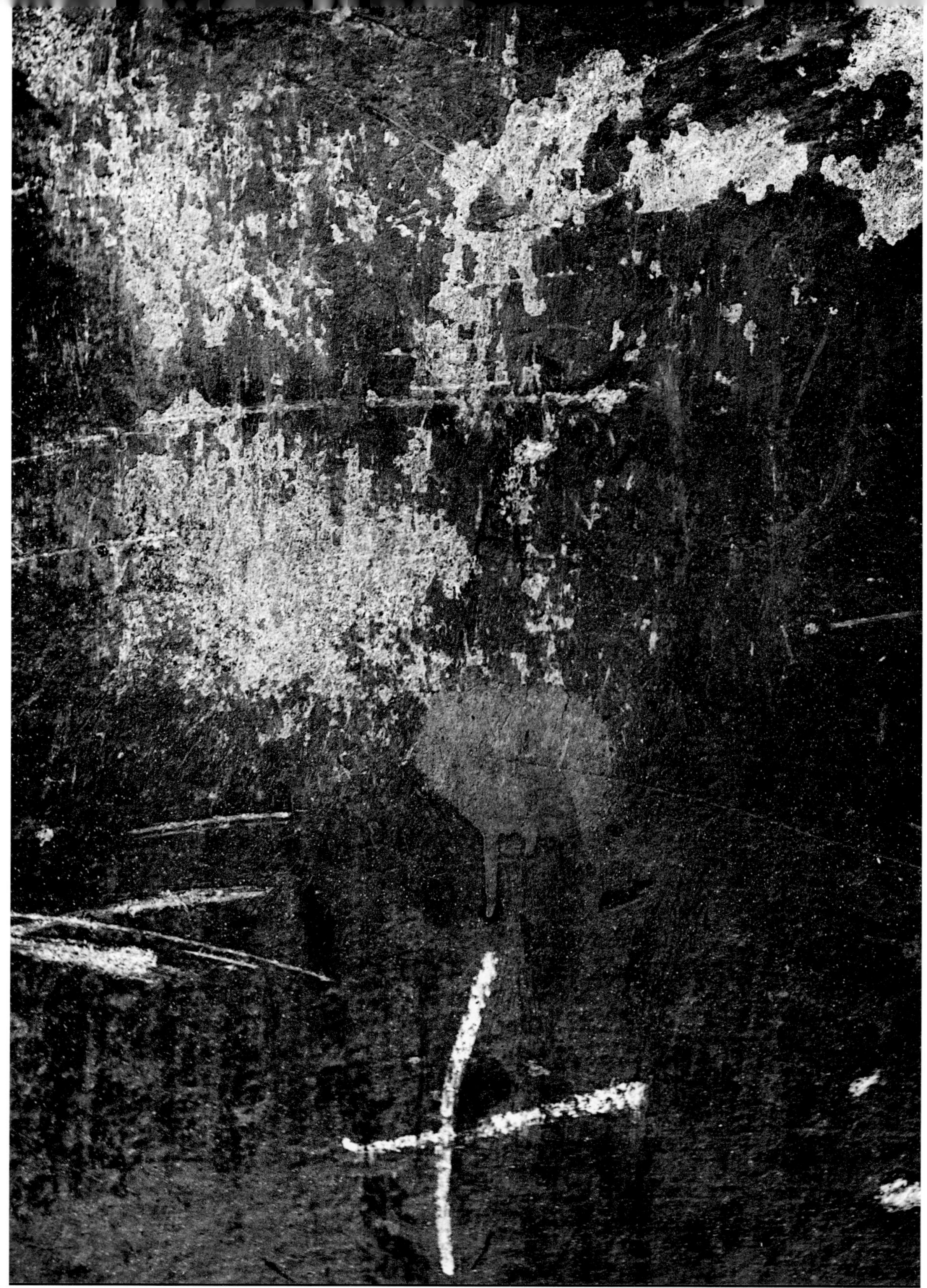

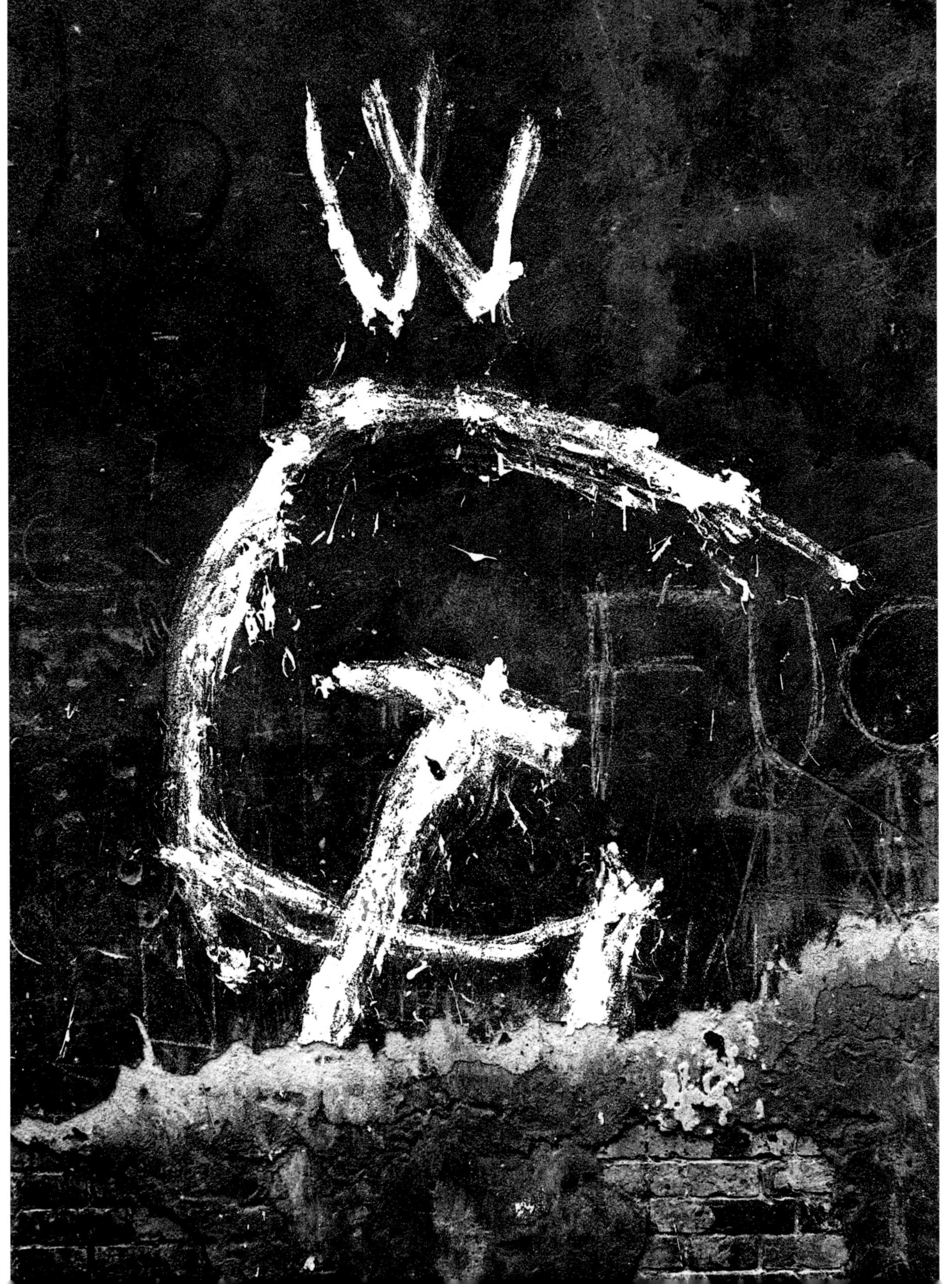

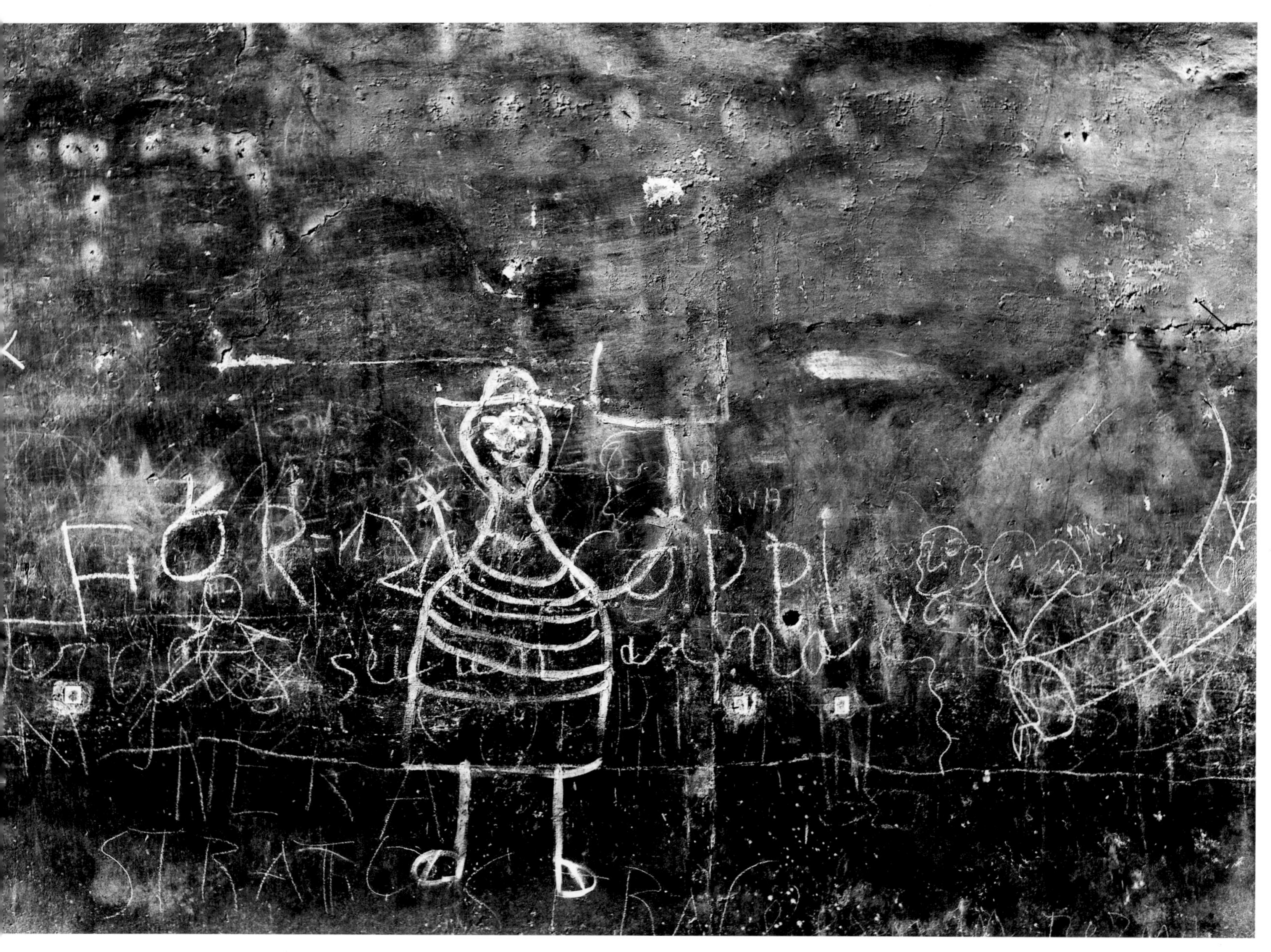

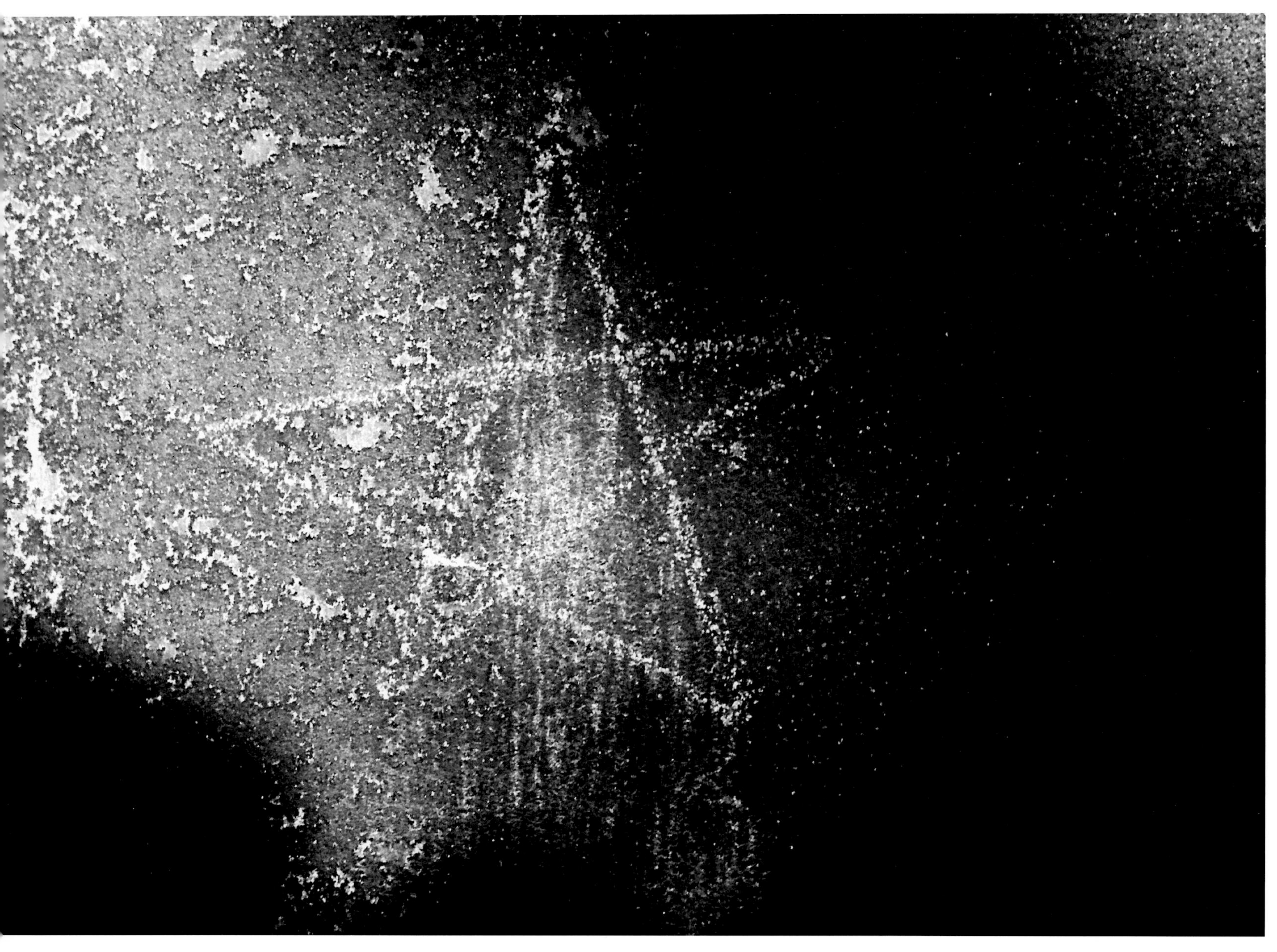

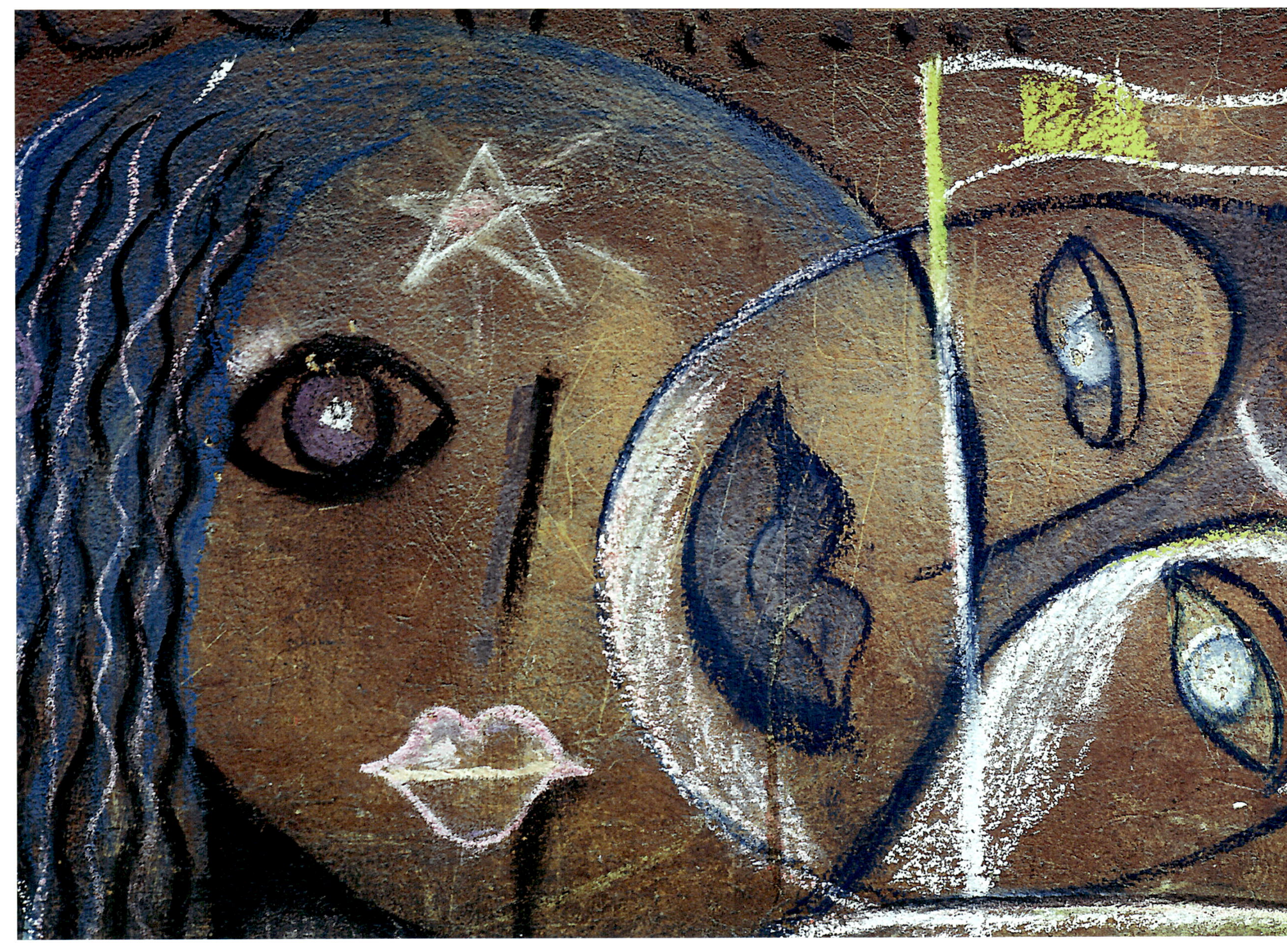

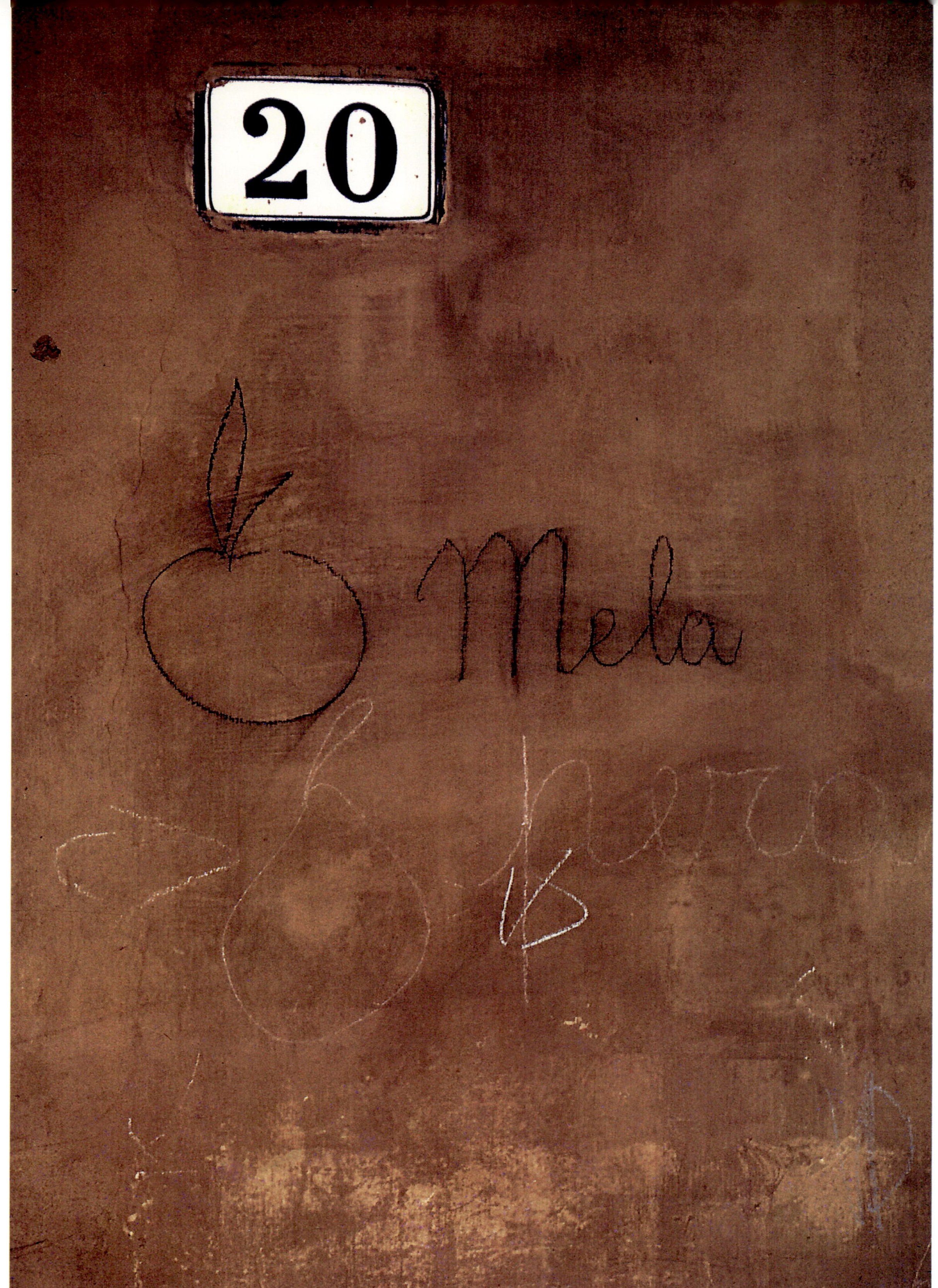
20
Mela
Pera

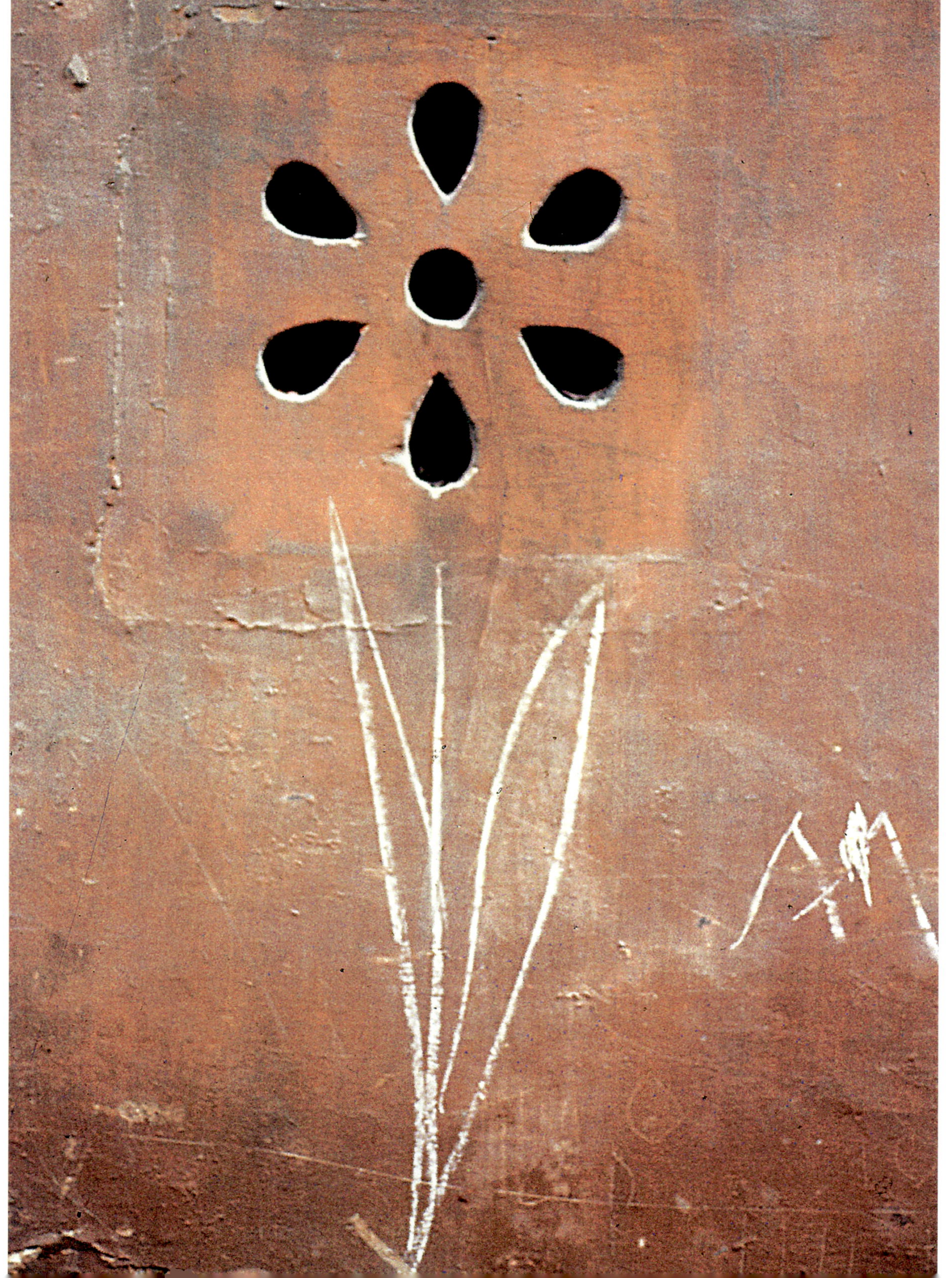

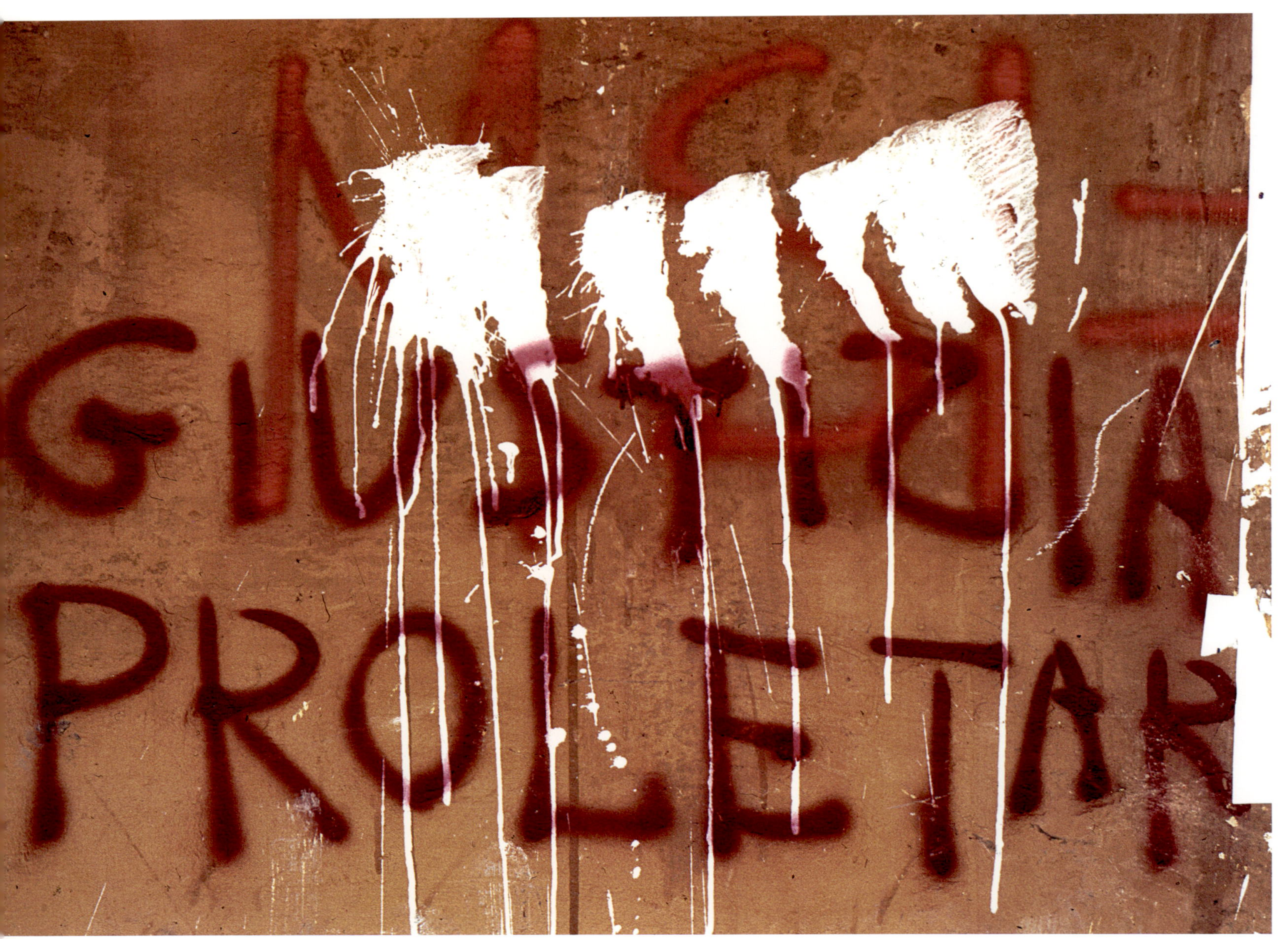
GIUSTIZIA
PROLETAR

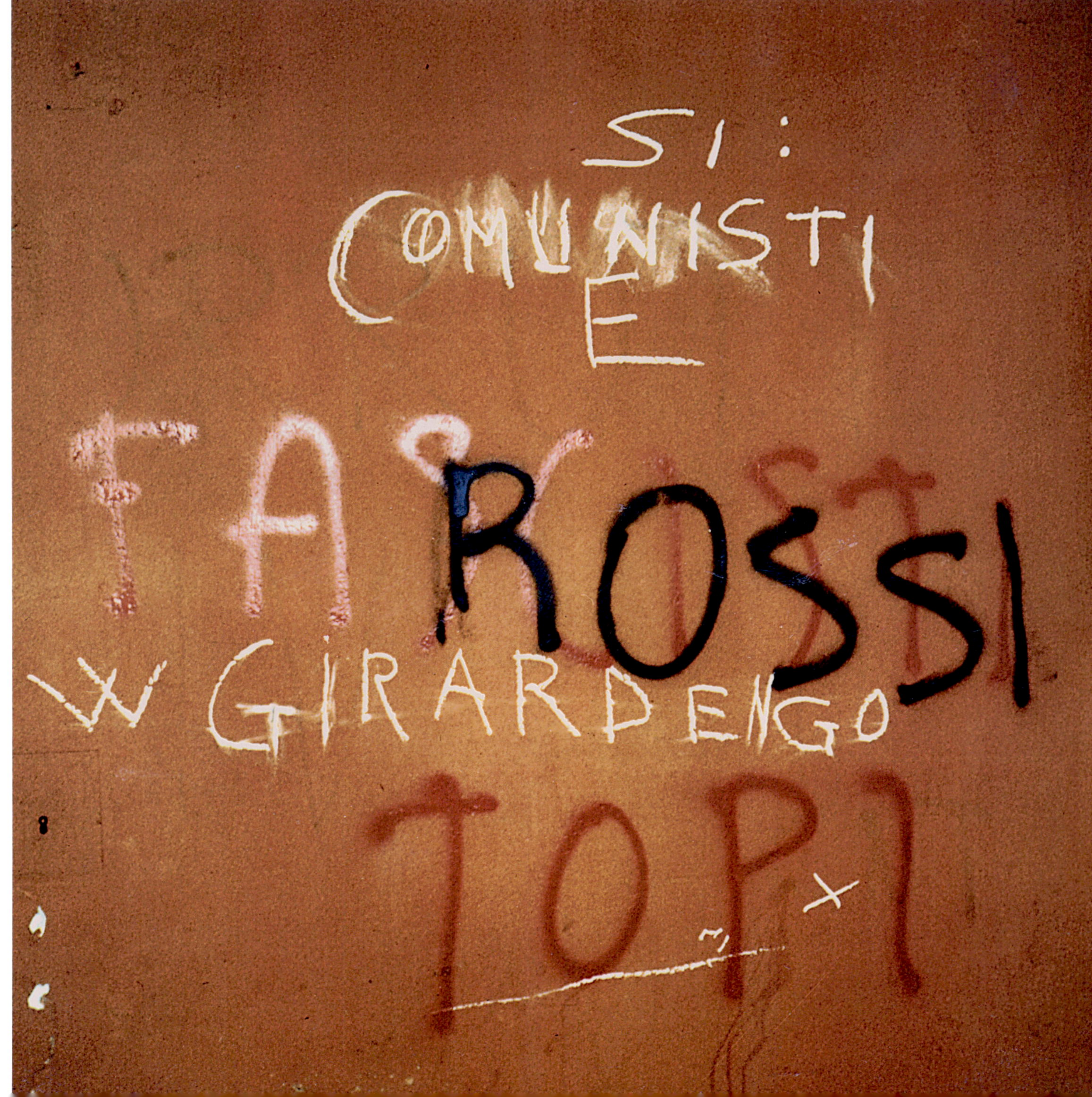
Si:
COMUNISTI
E
FASCISTI
ROSSI
W GIRARDENGO
TOPI

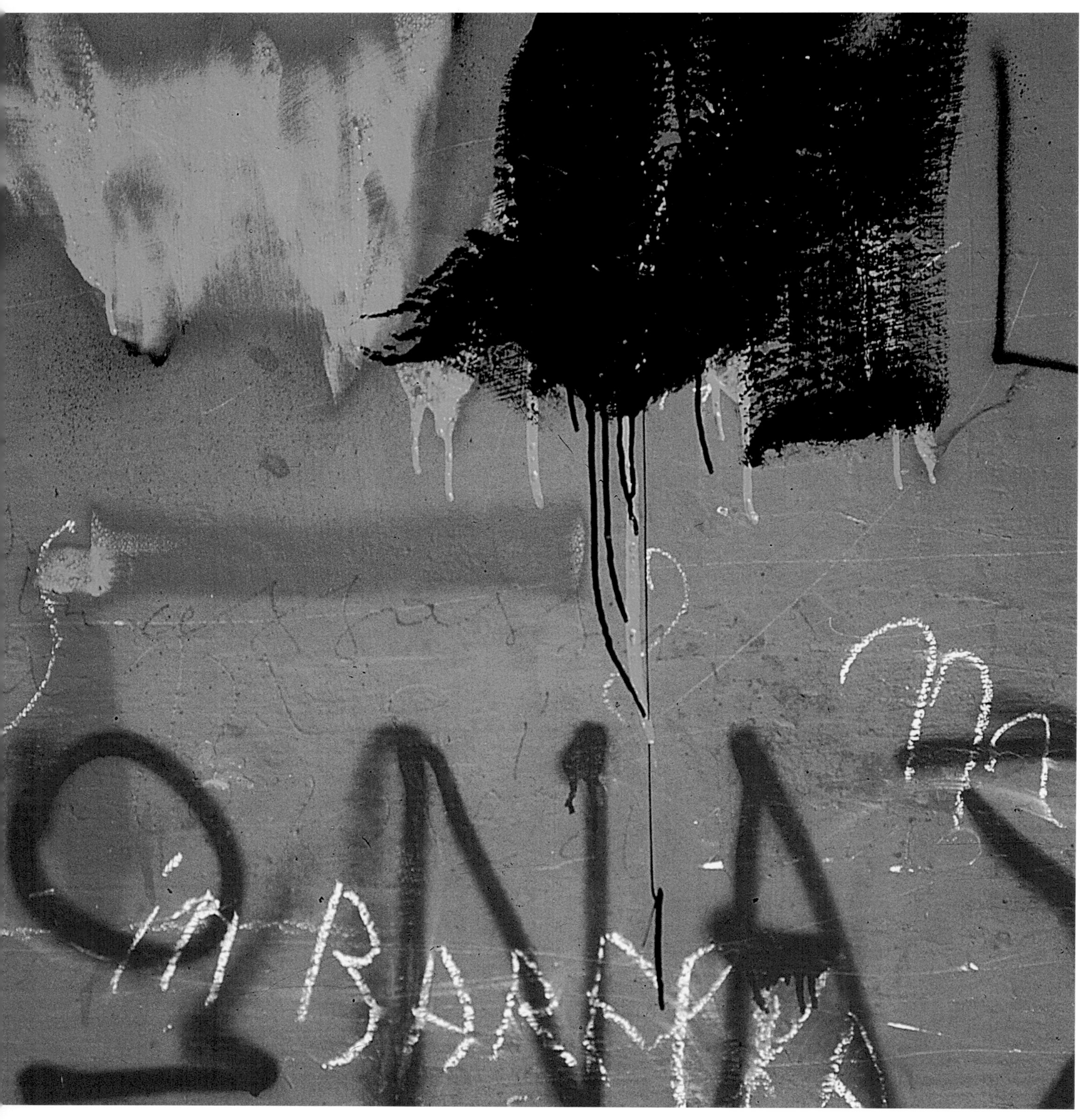

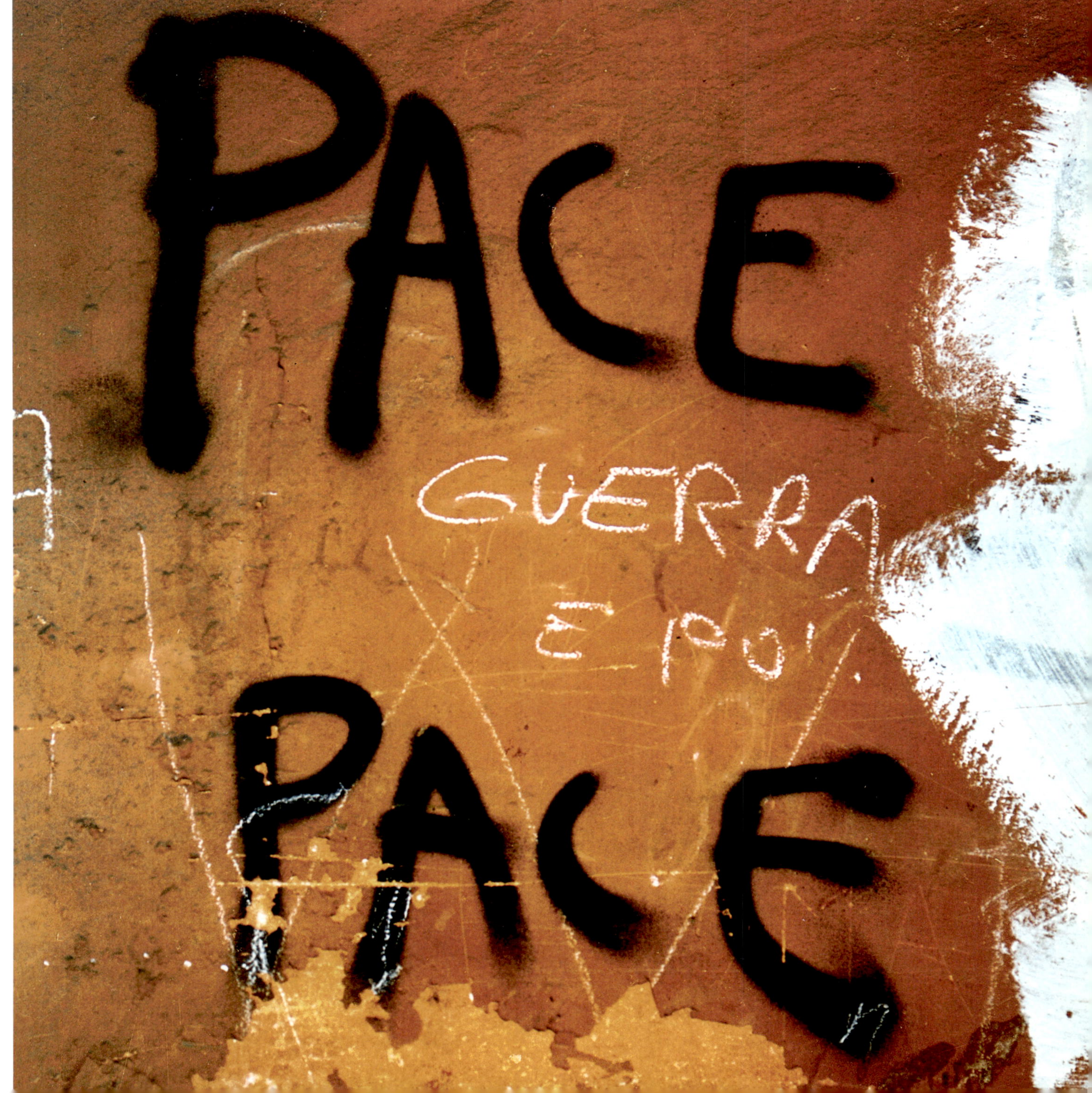
PACE
GUERRA
E POI
PACE

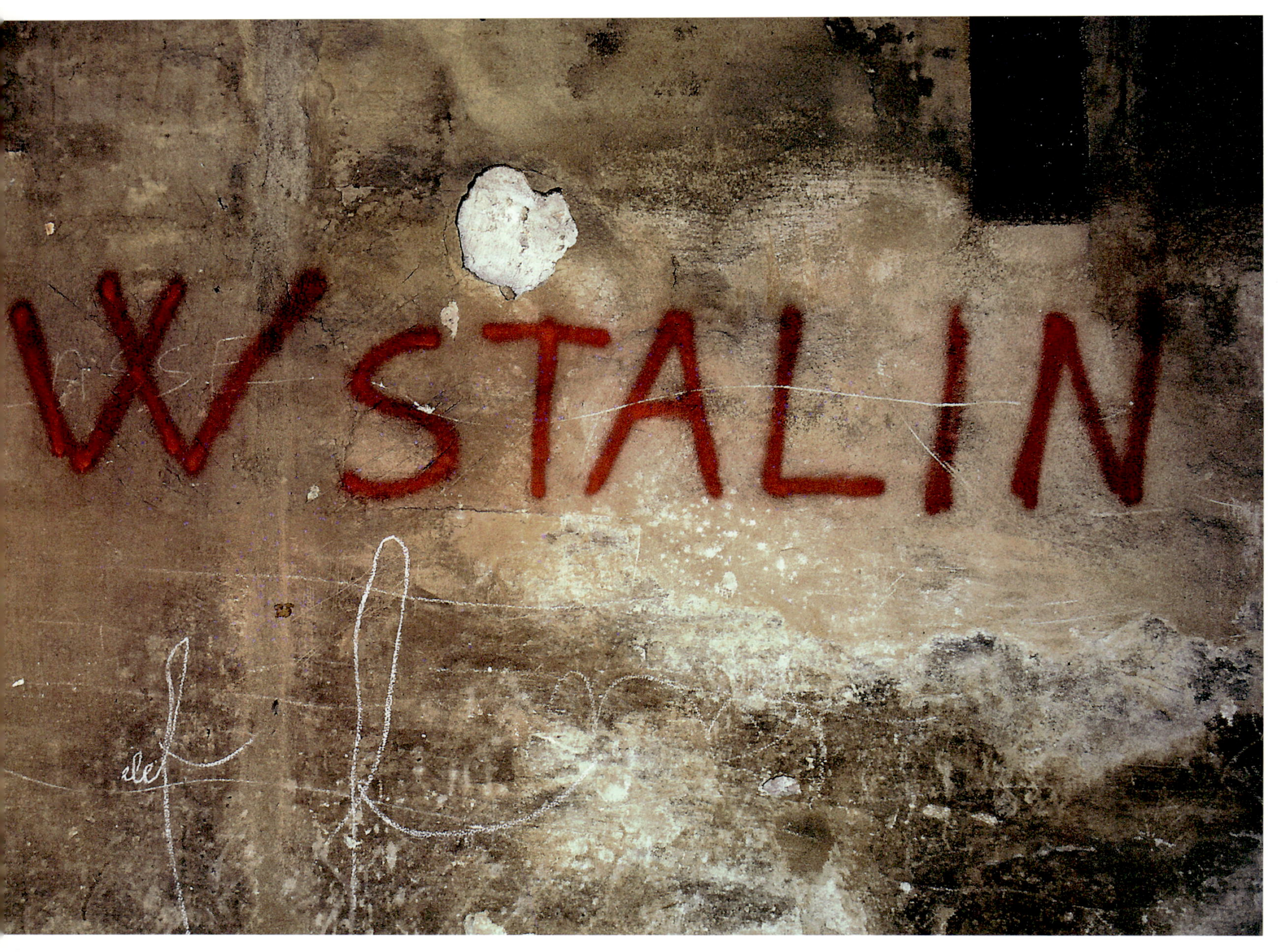
W STALIN

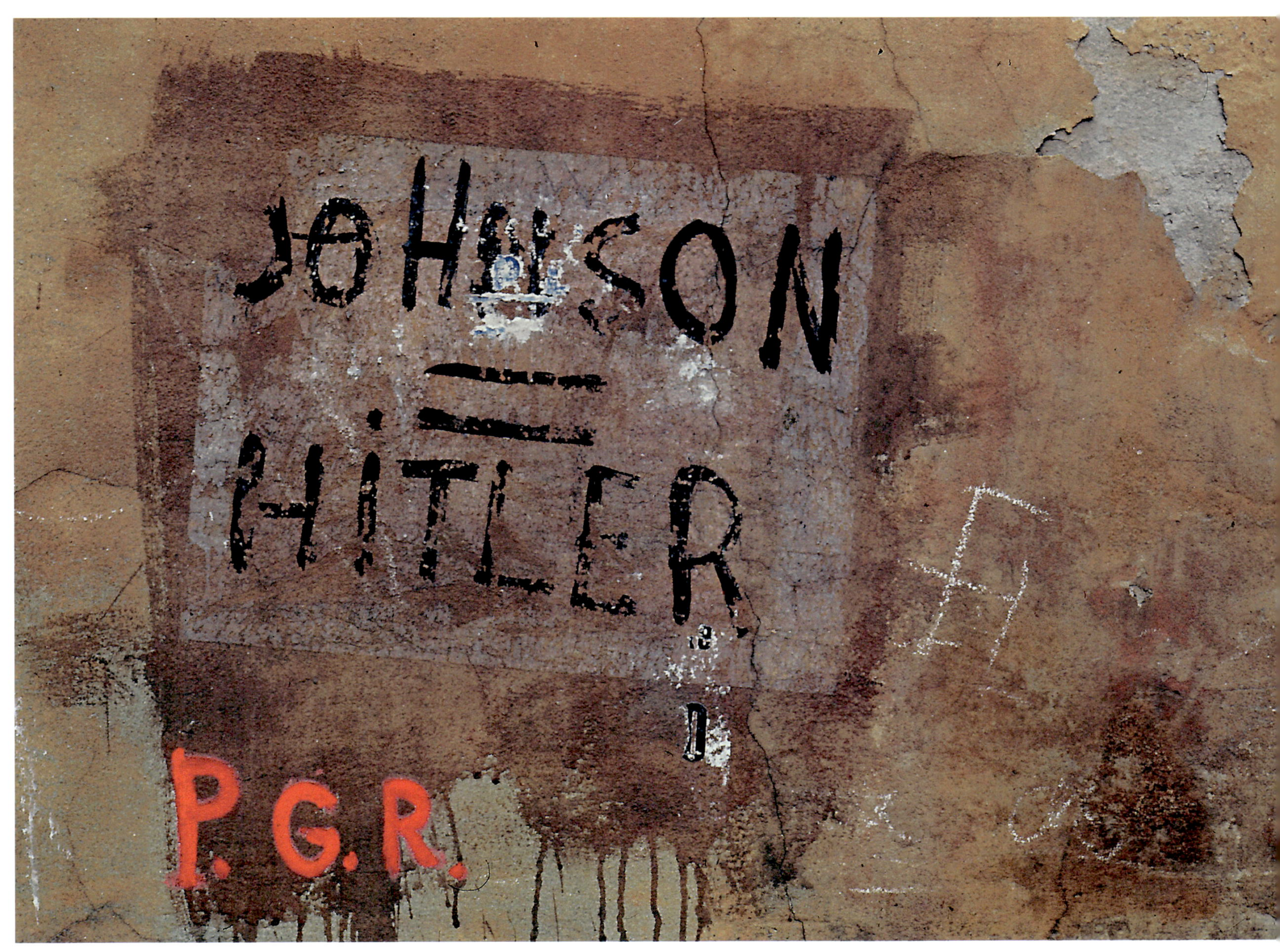
JOHNSON
HITLER
P.G.R.

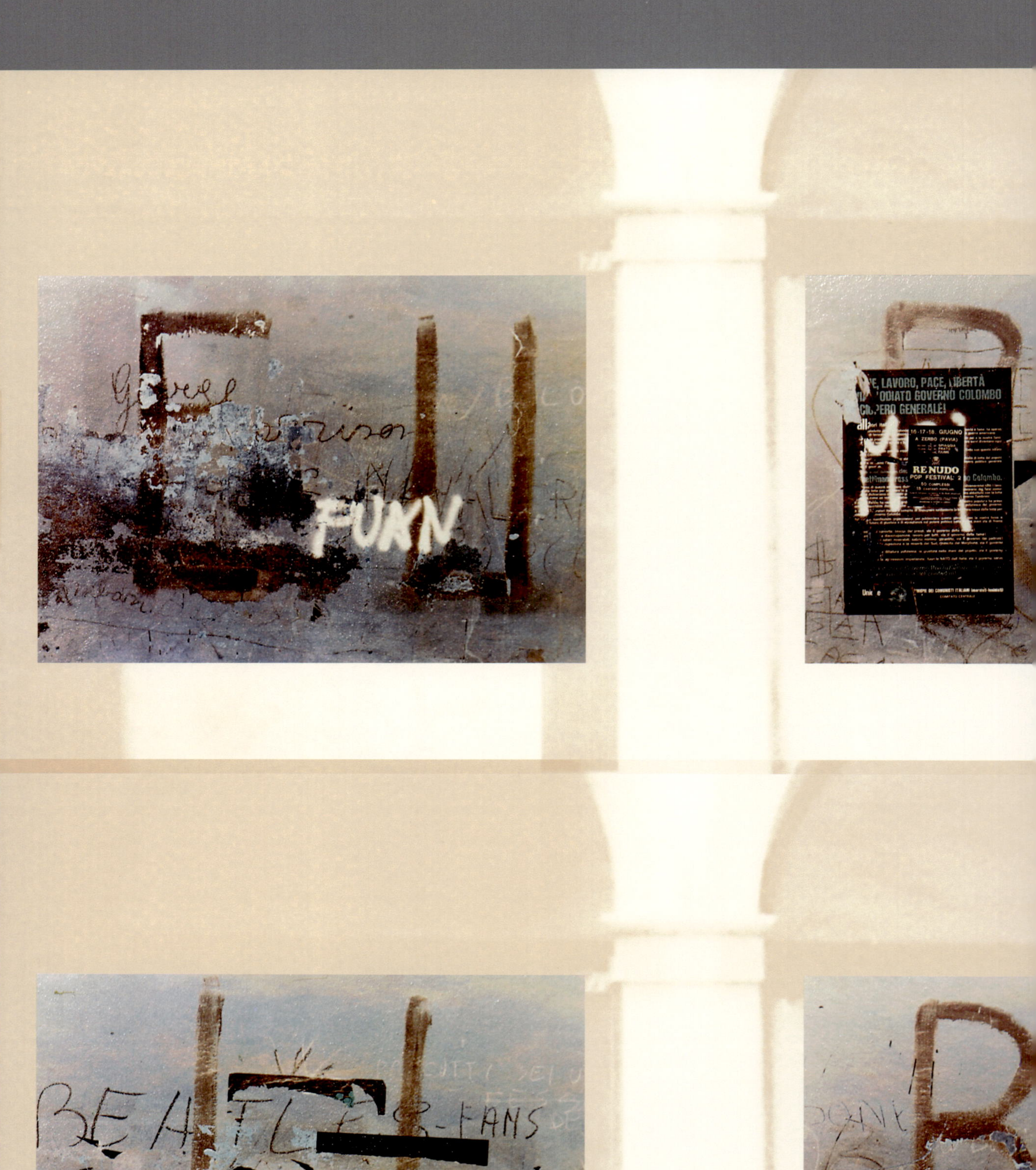
FUKN
BEATLES FANS
E, LAVORO, PACE, LIBERTÀ
ODIATO GOVERNO COLOMBO
SCIOPERO GENERALE!
16-17-18 GIUGNO
A ZERBO (PAVIA)
RE NUDO
POP FESTIVAL: 2 Colombo.

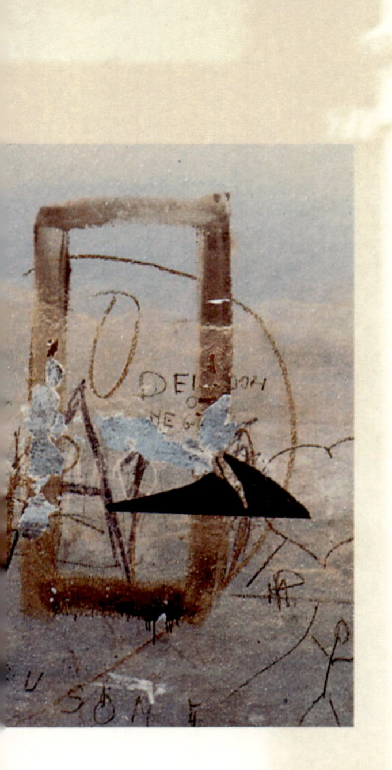
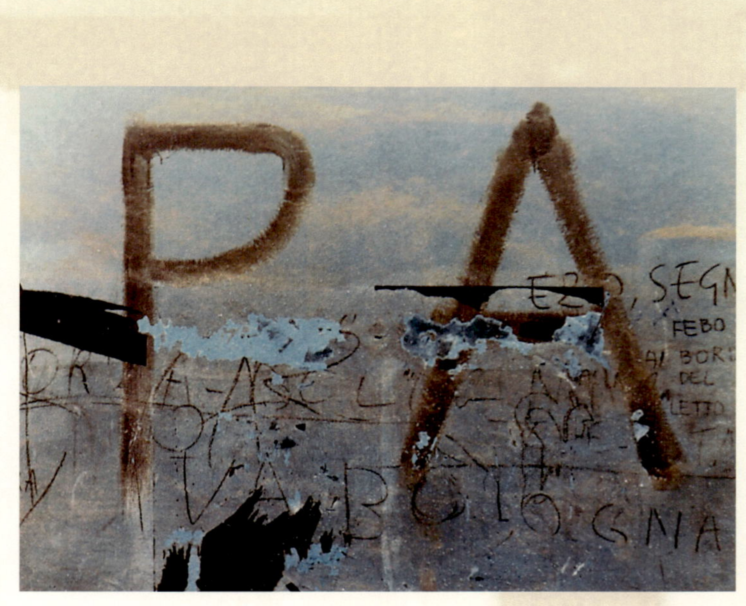
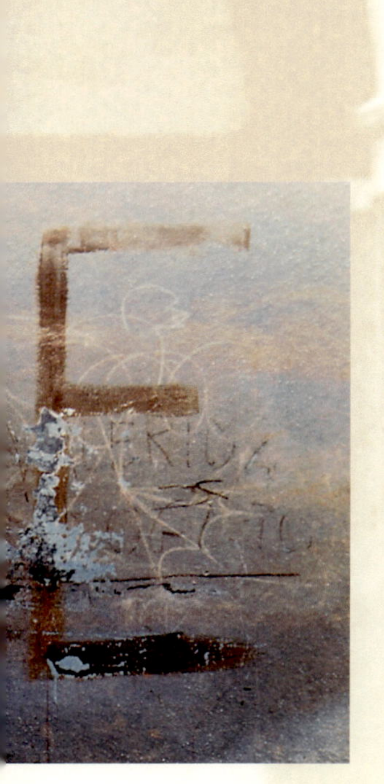
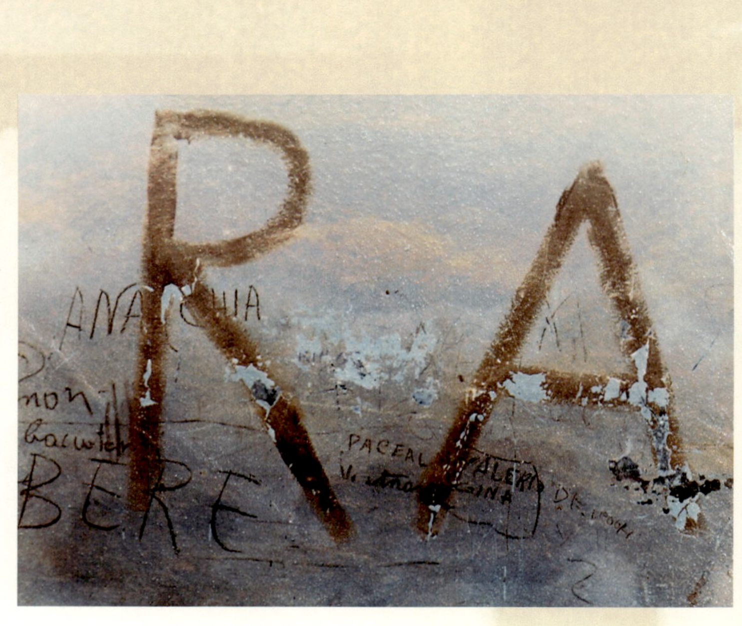

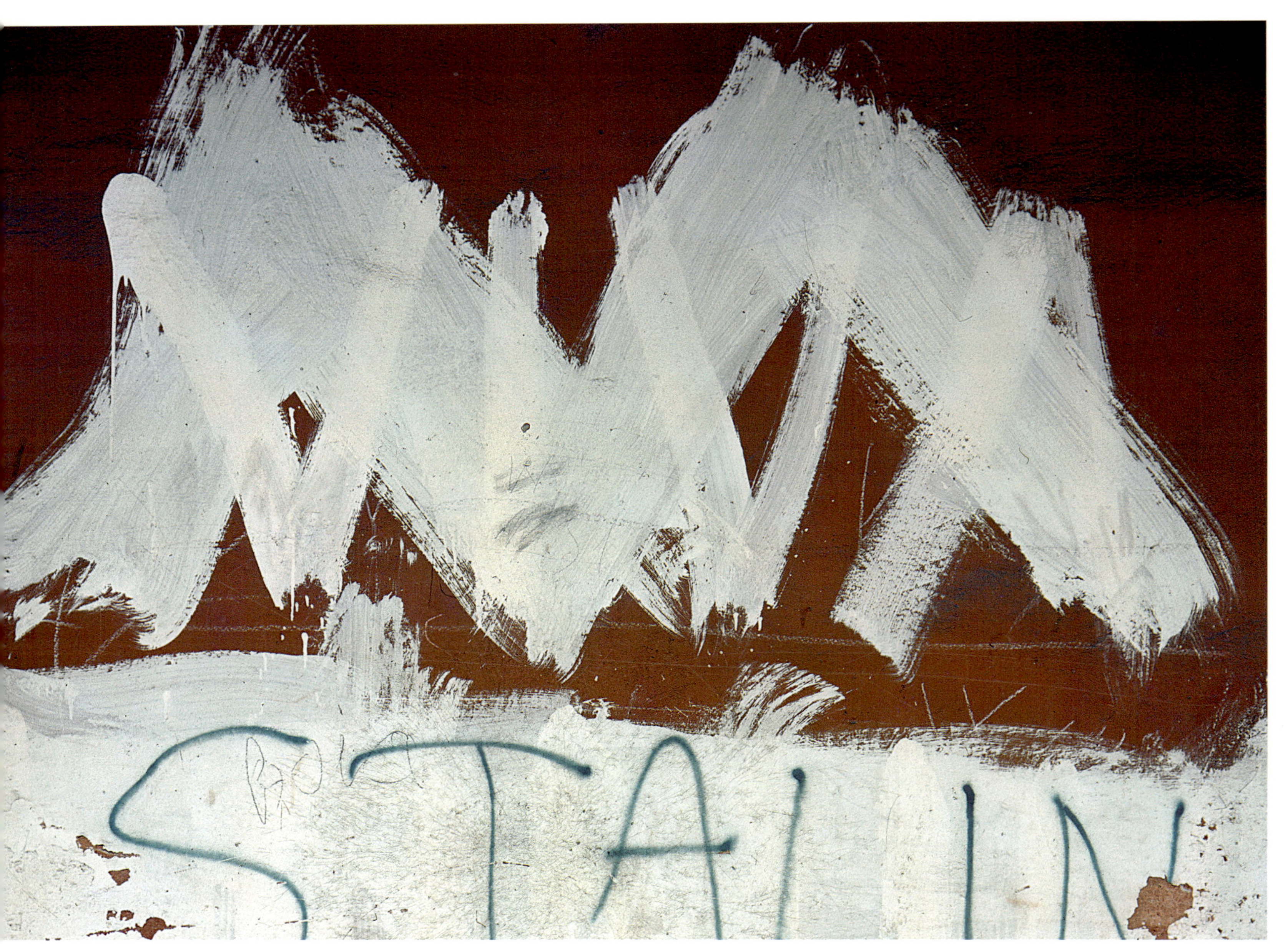

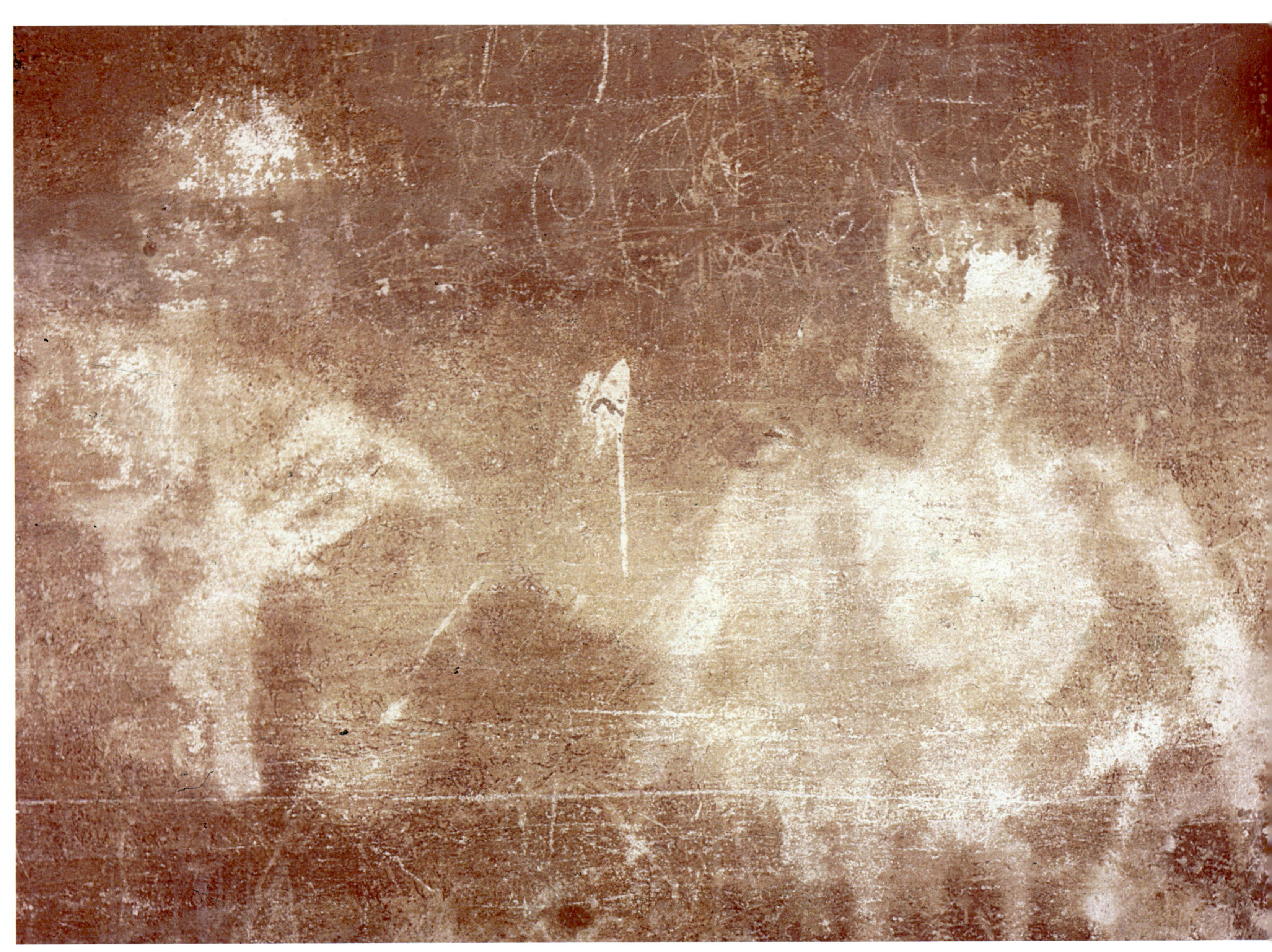

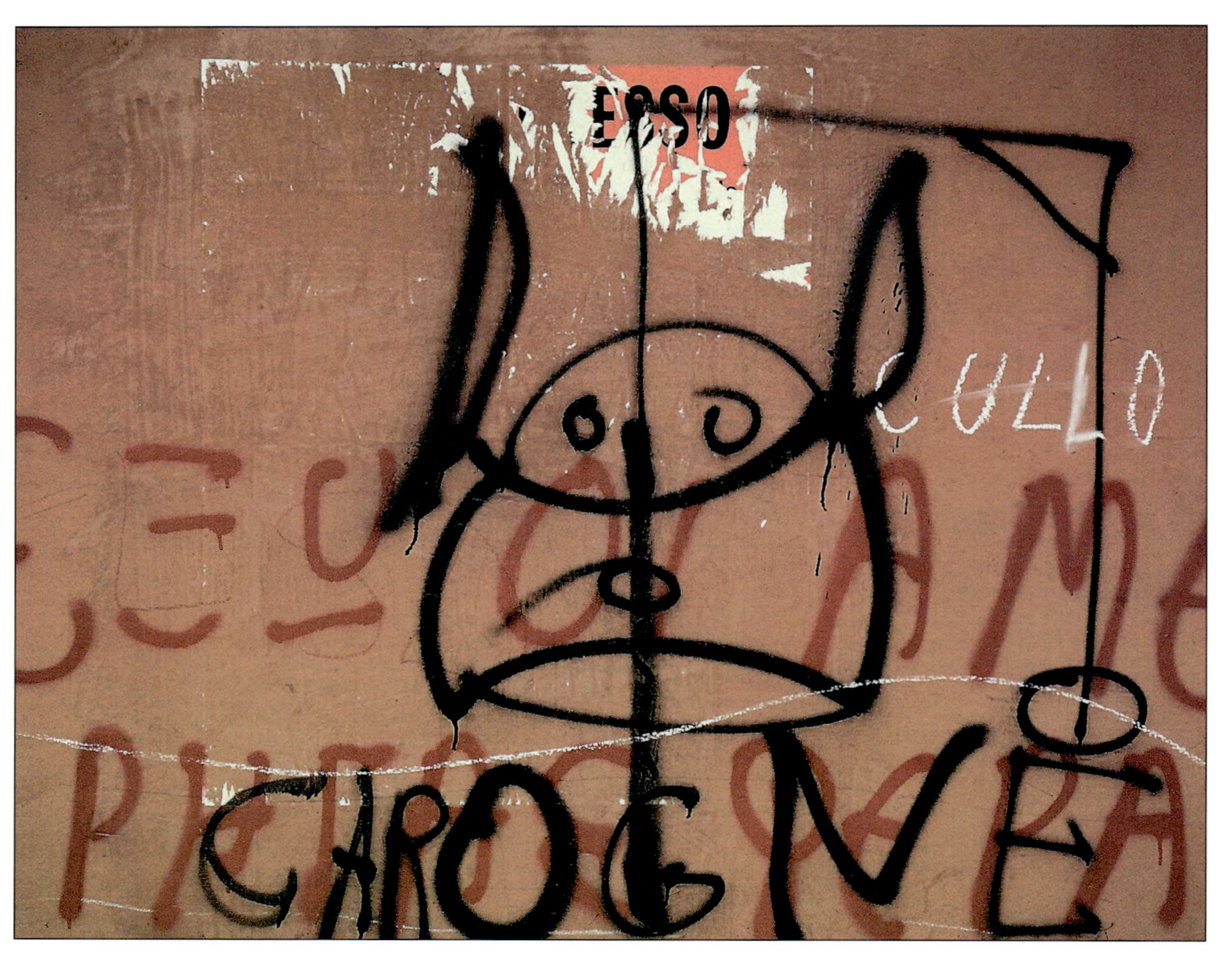

ESSO
CAROGNE

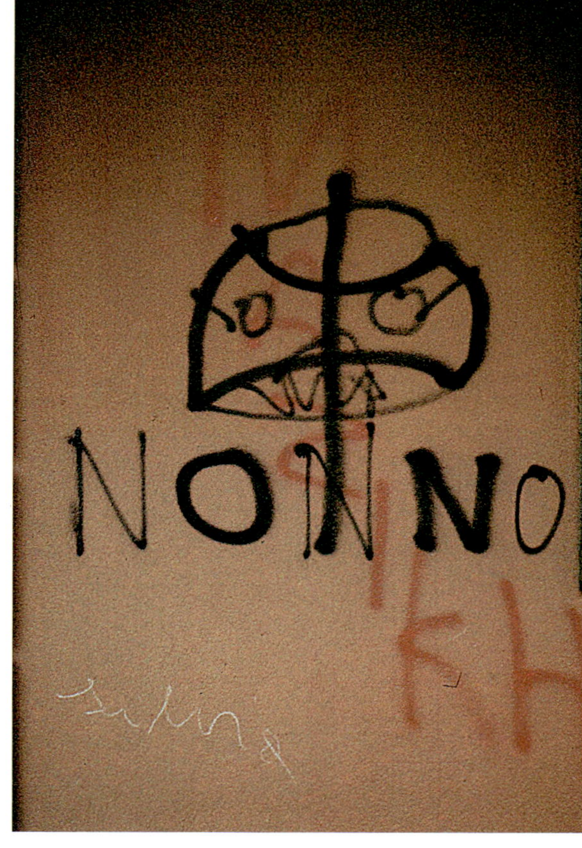

NONNO

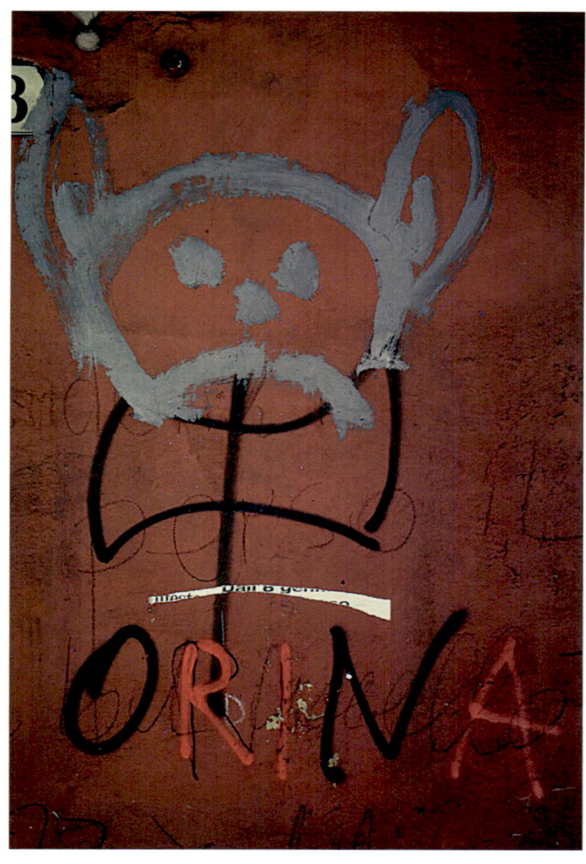

ORINA

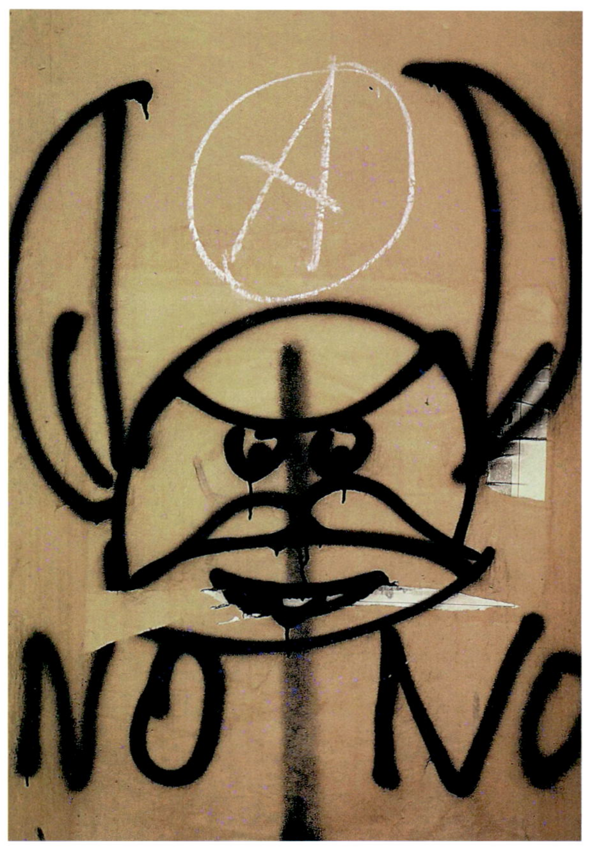
NO NO

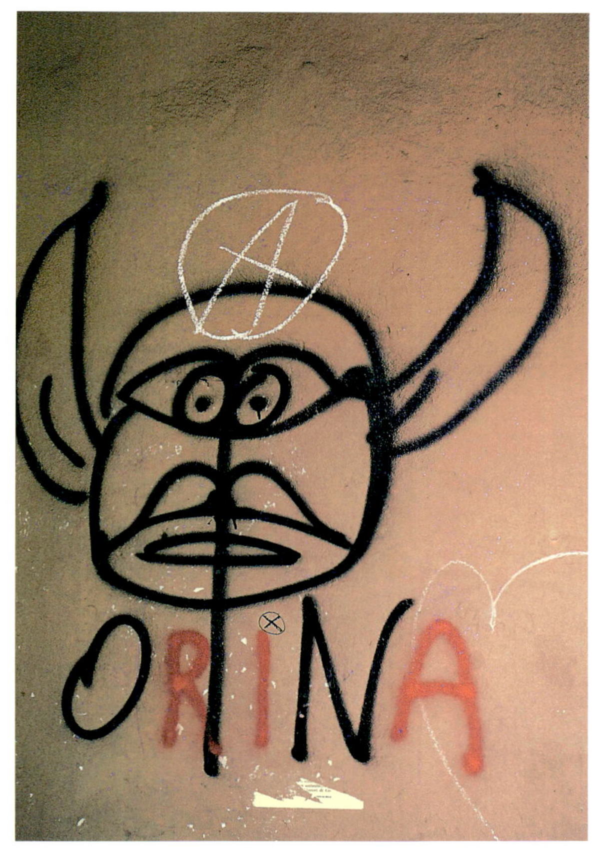
ORINA

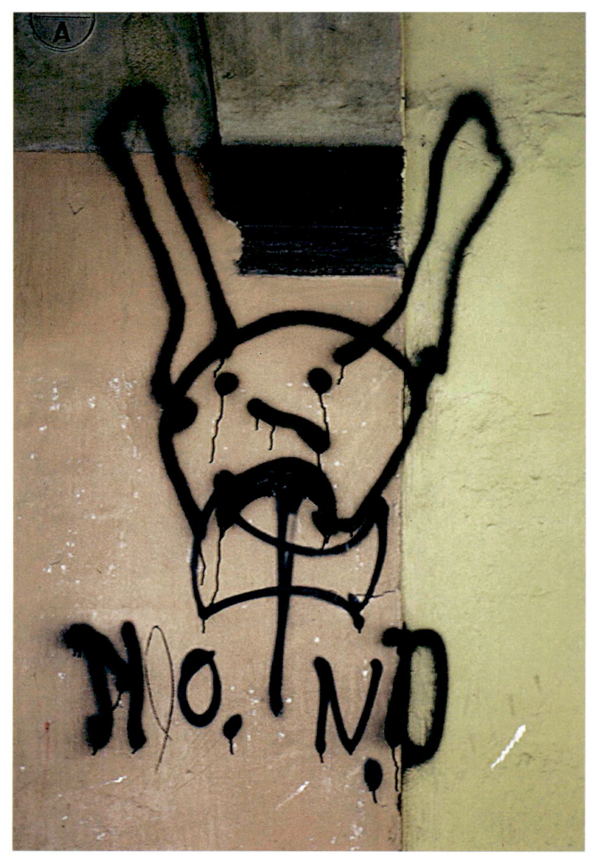
NO. NO

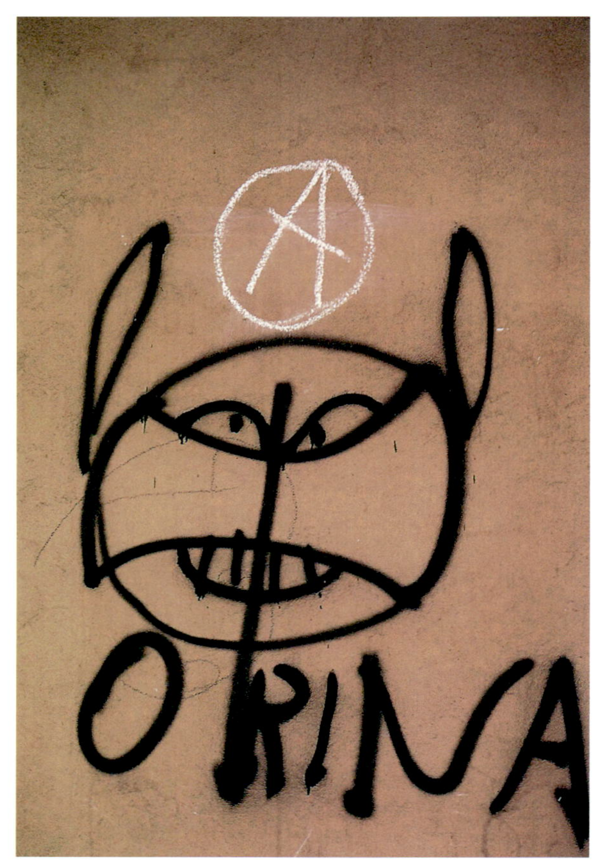
ORINA

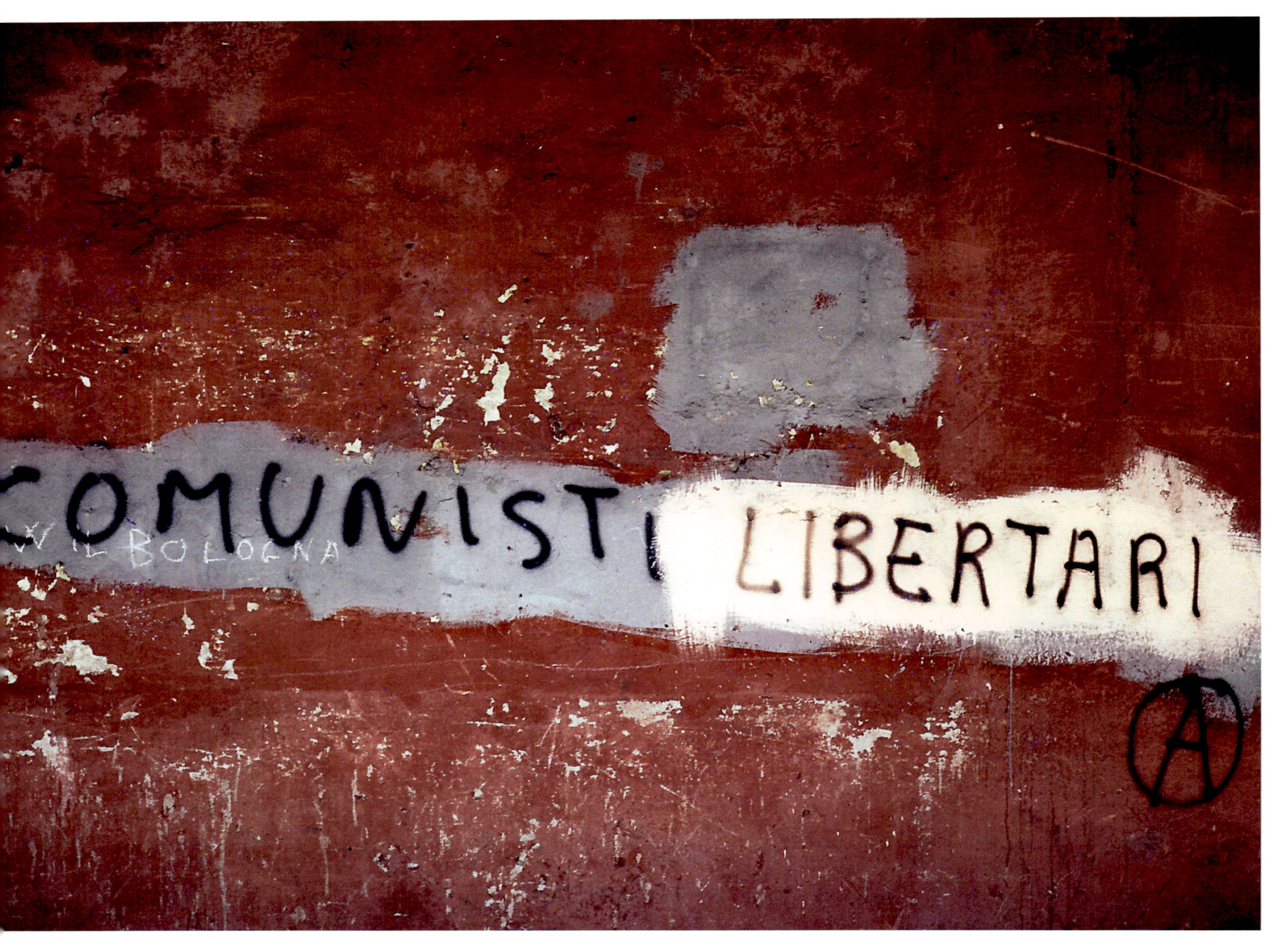

W IL BOLOGNA
COMUNISTI LIBERTARI

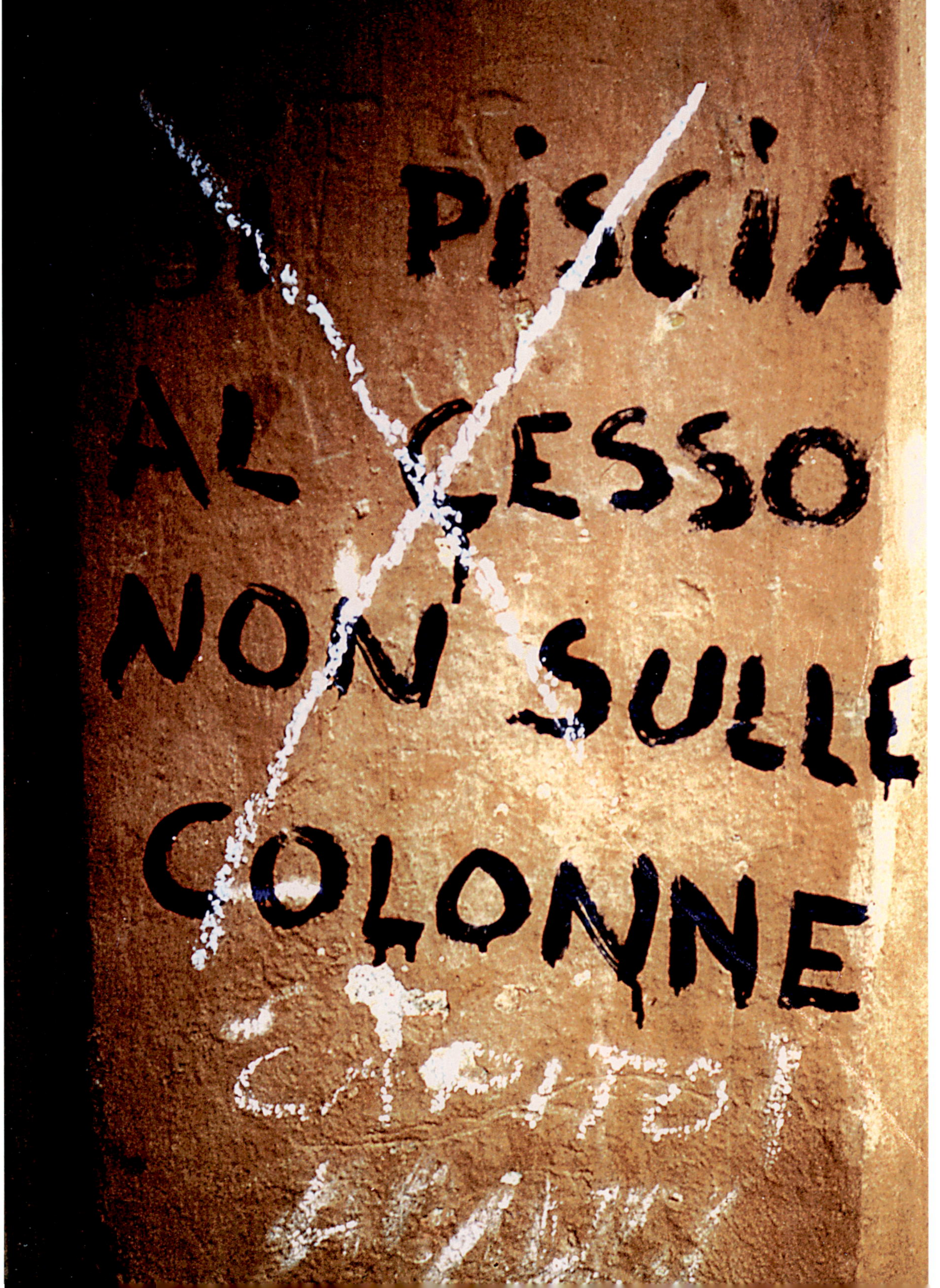
PISCIA
AL CESSO
NON SULLE
COLONNE

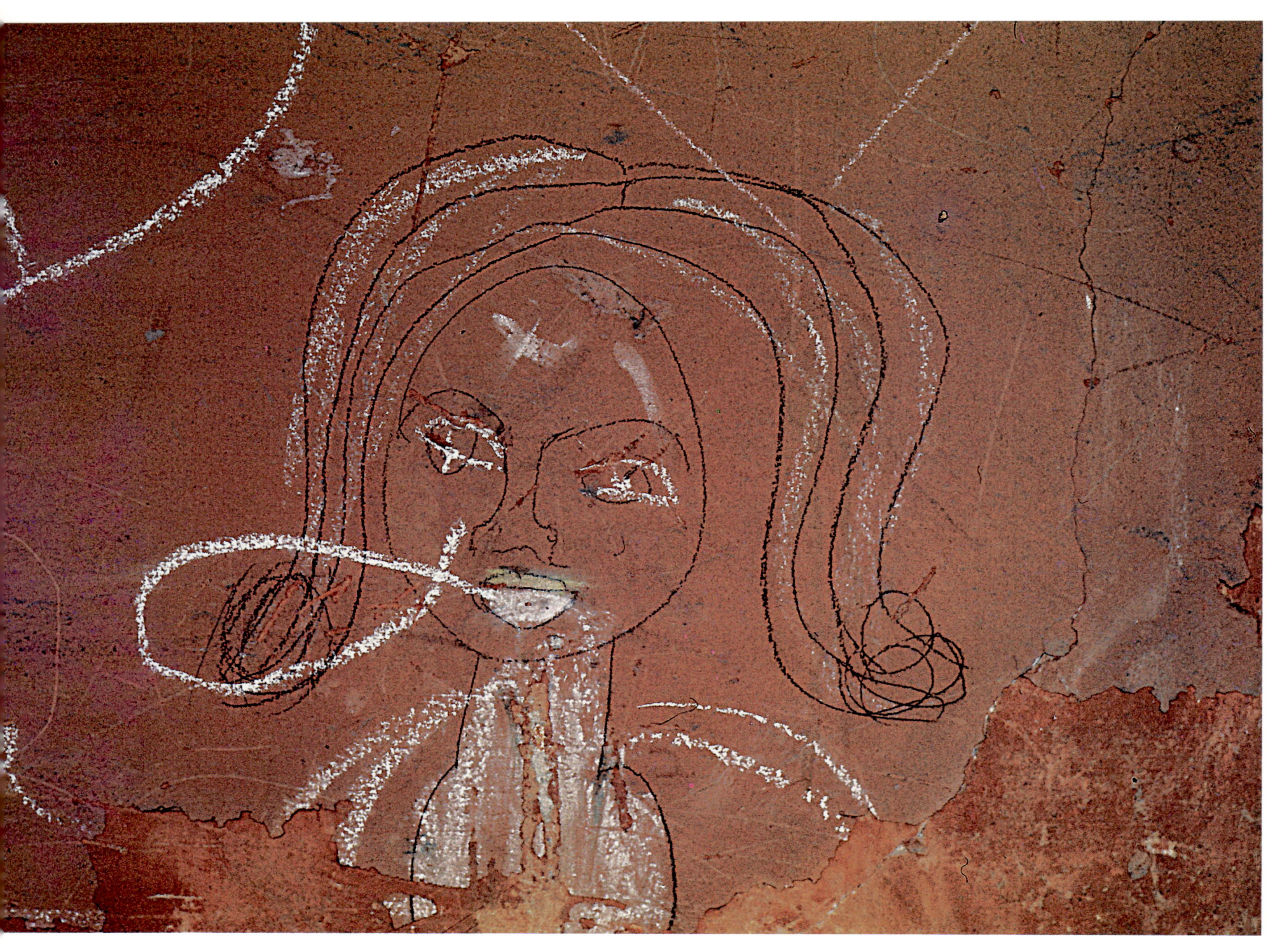

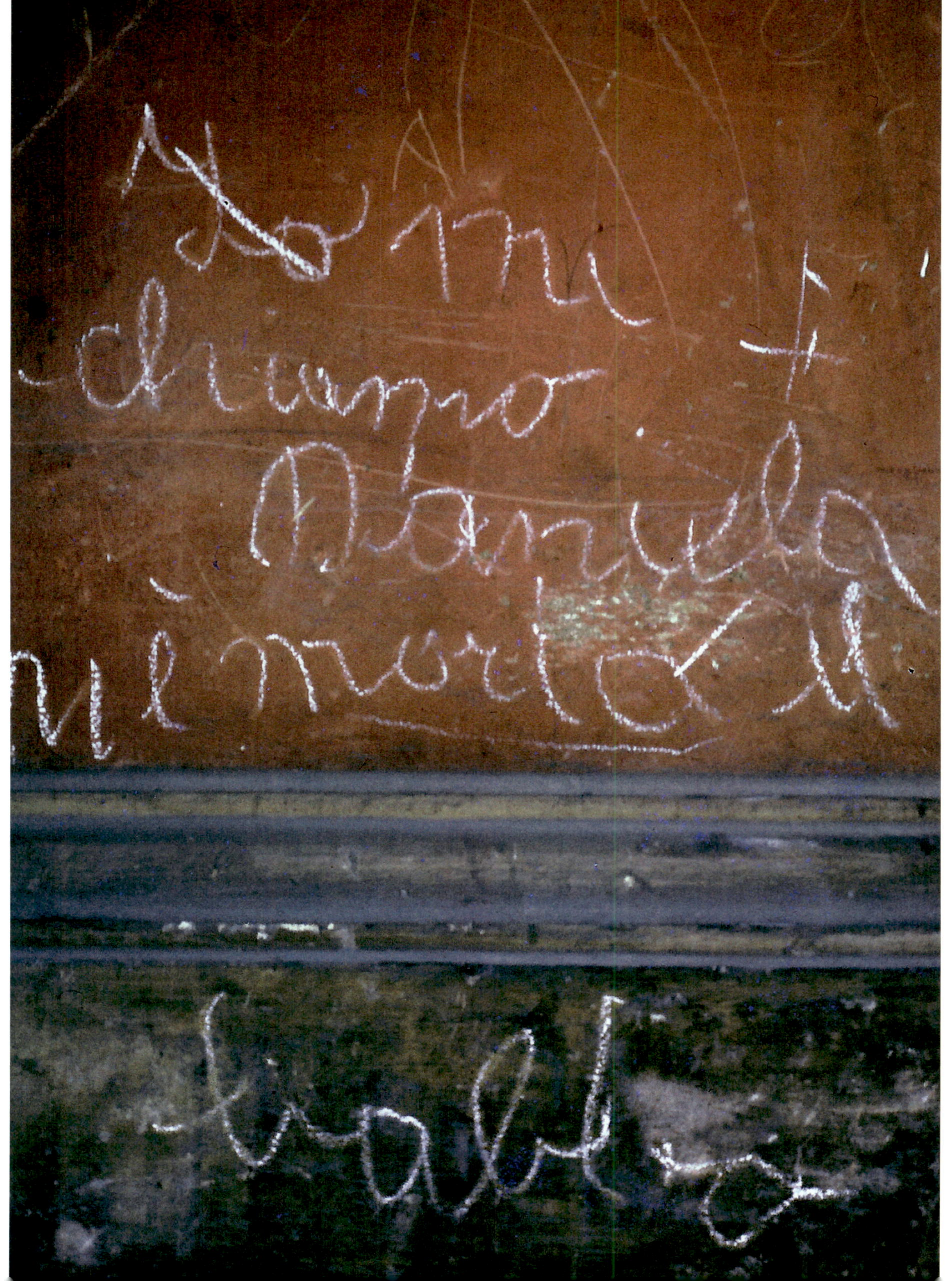
Io mi
chiamo †
Daniela
mi morta il
fiorela

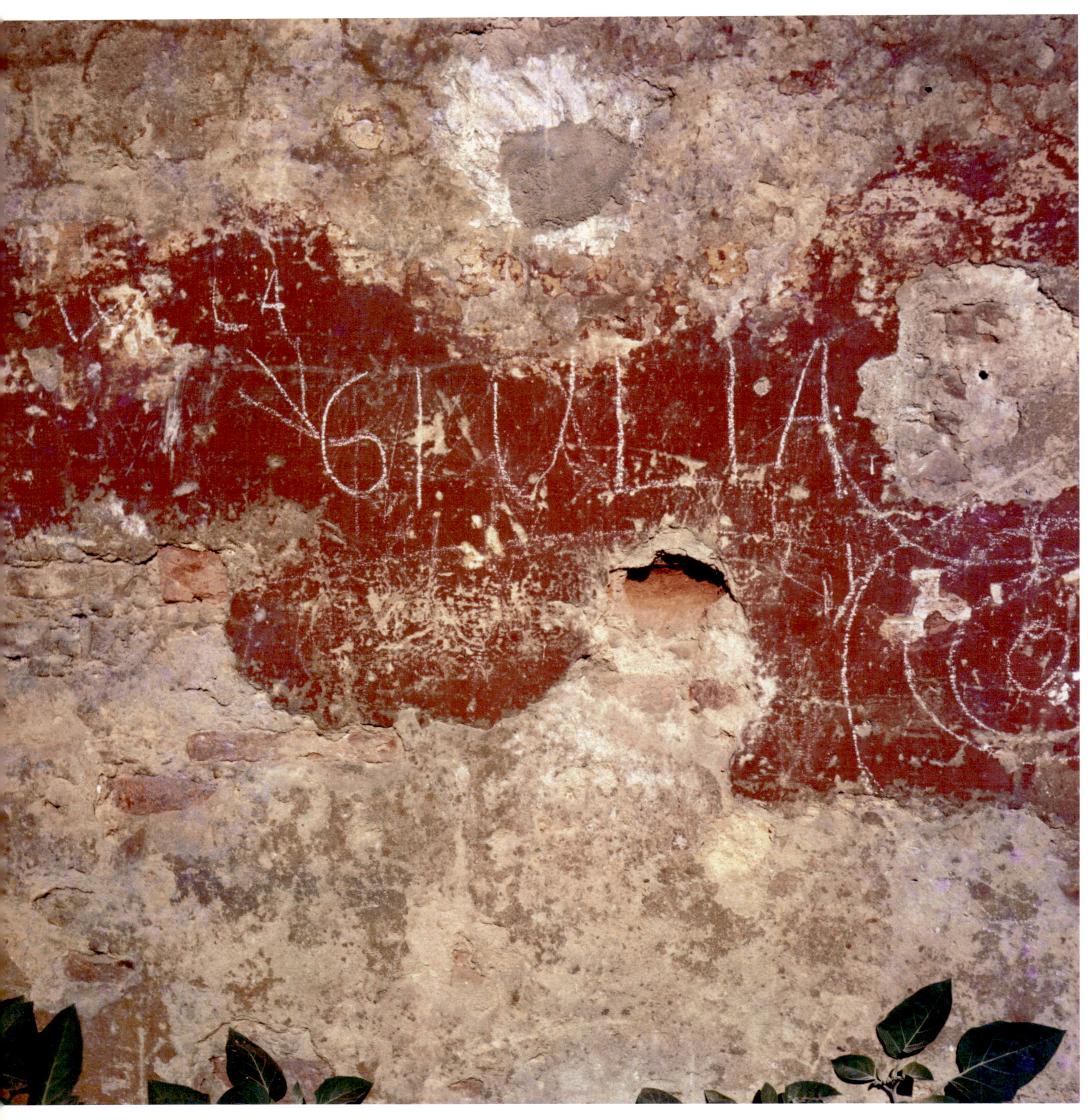
GIULIA

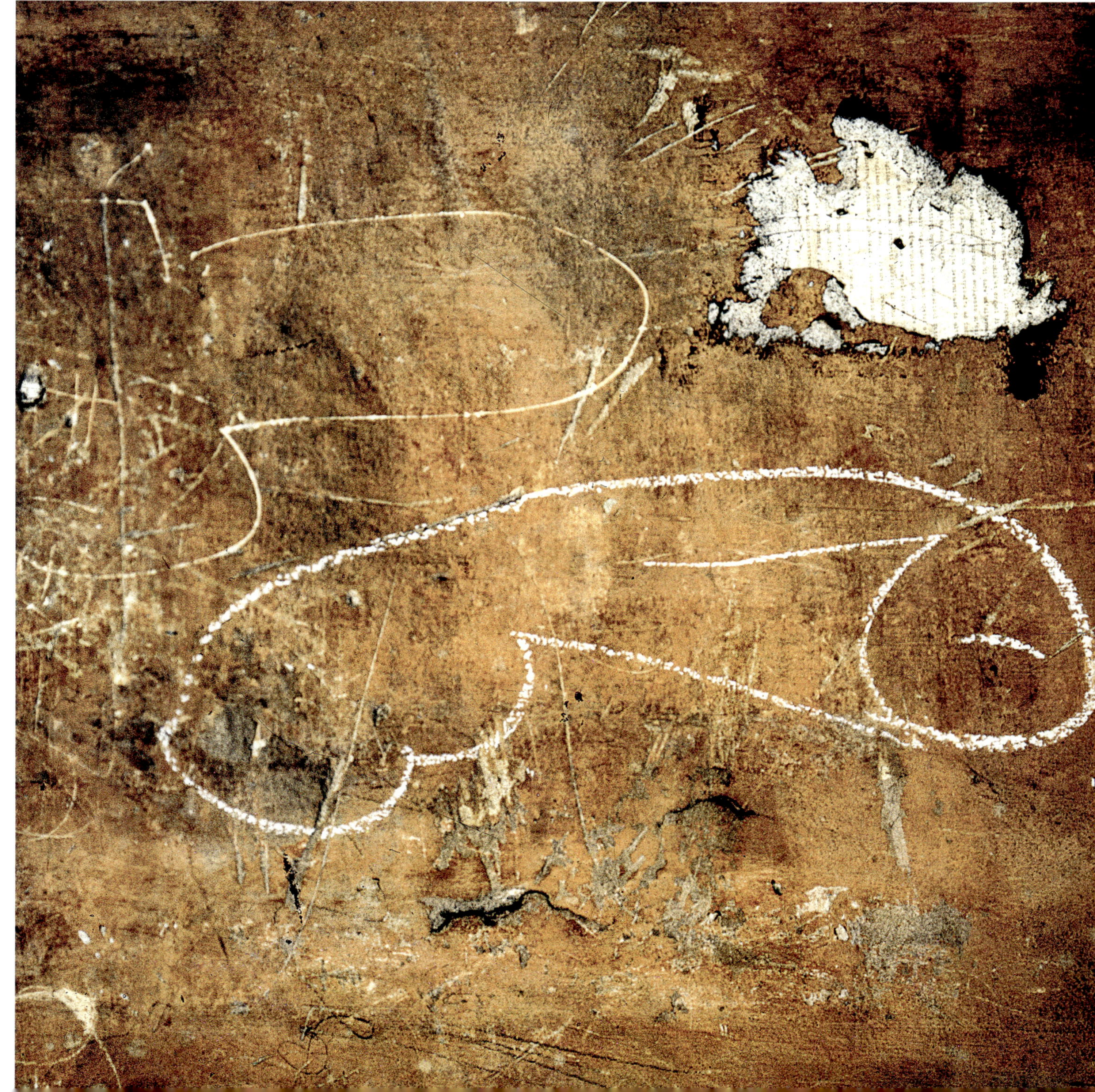

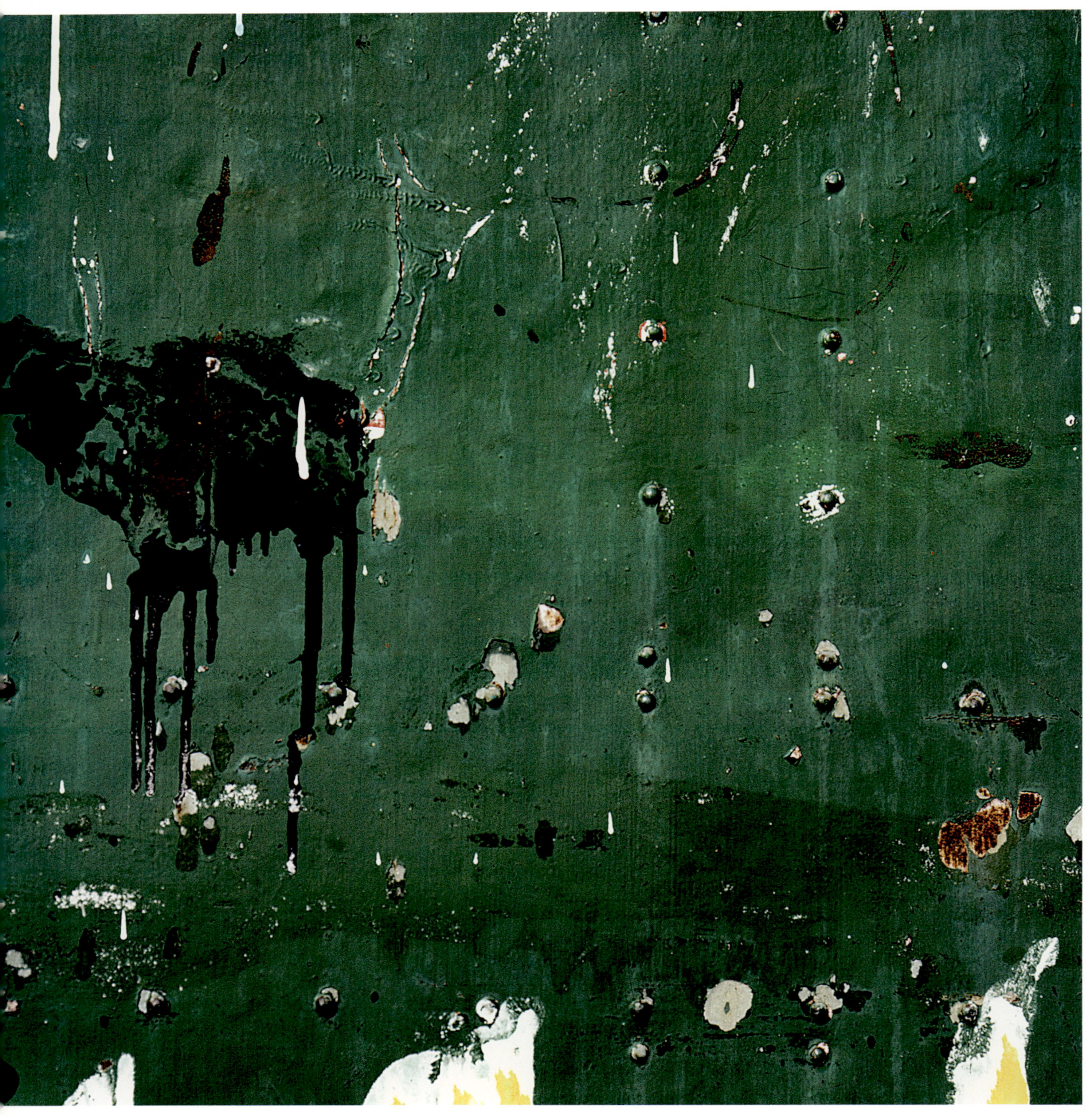

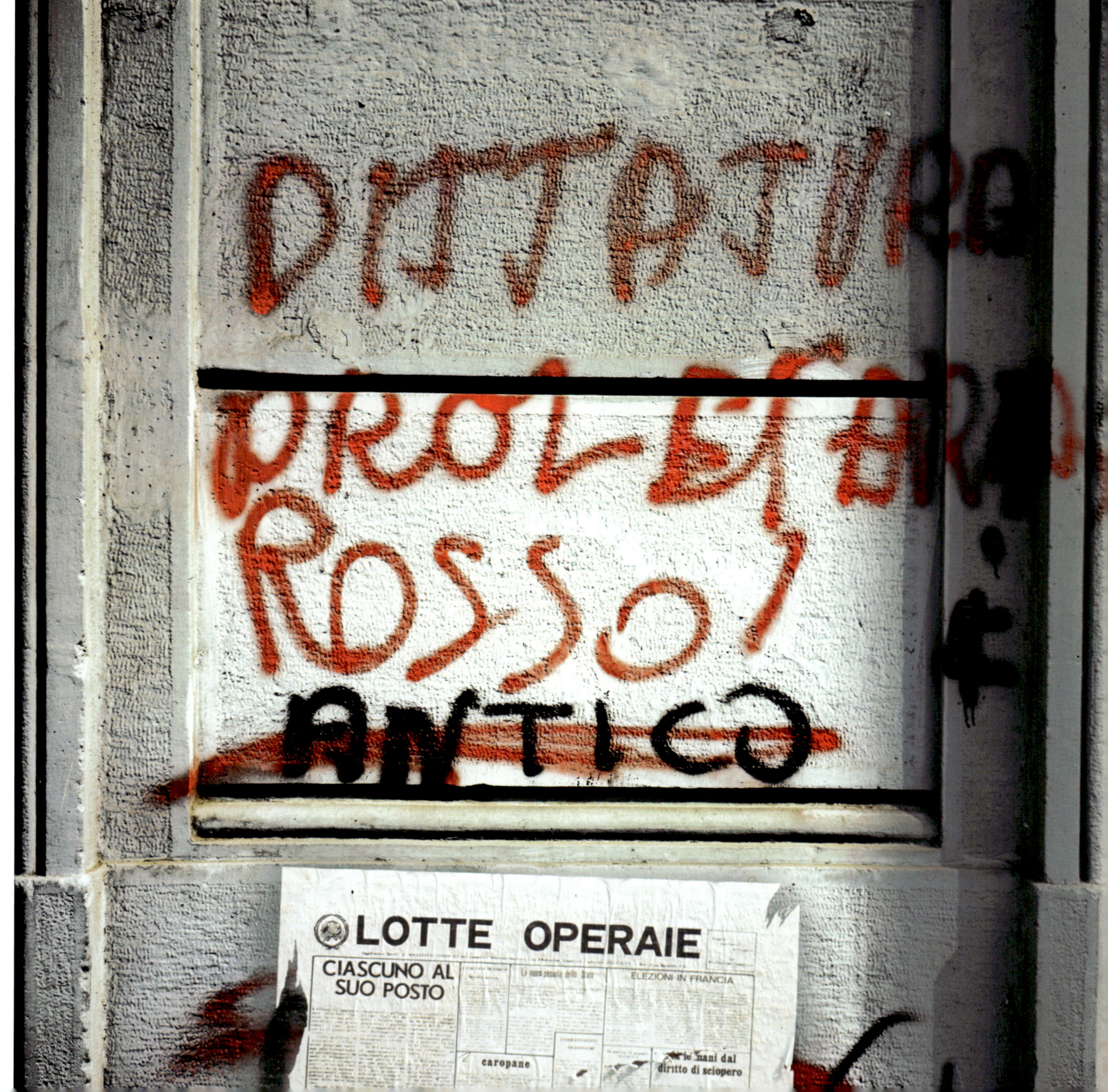
DITTATURA
PROLETARIA
ROSSO?
ANTICO
LOTTE OPERAIE
CIASCUNO AL
SUO POSTO
ELEZIONI IN FRANCIA
caropane
le mani dal
diritto di sciopero

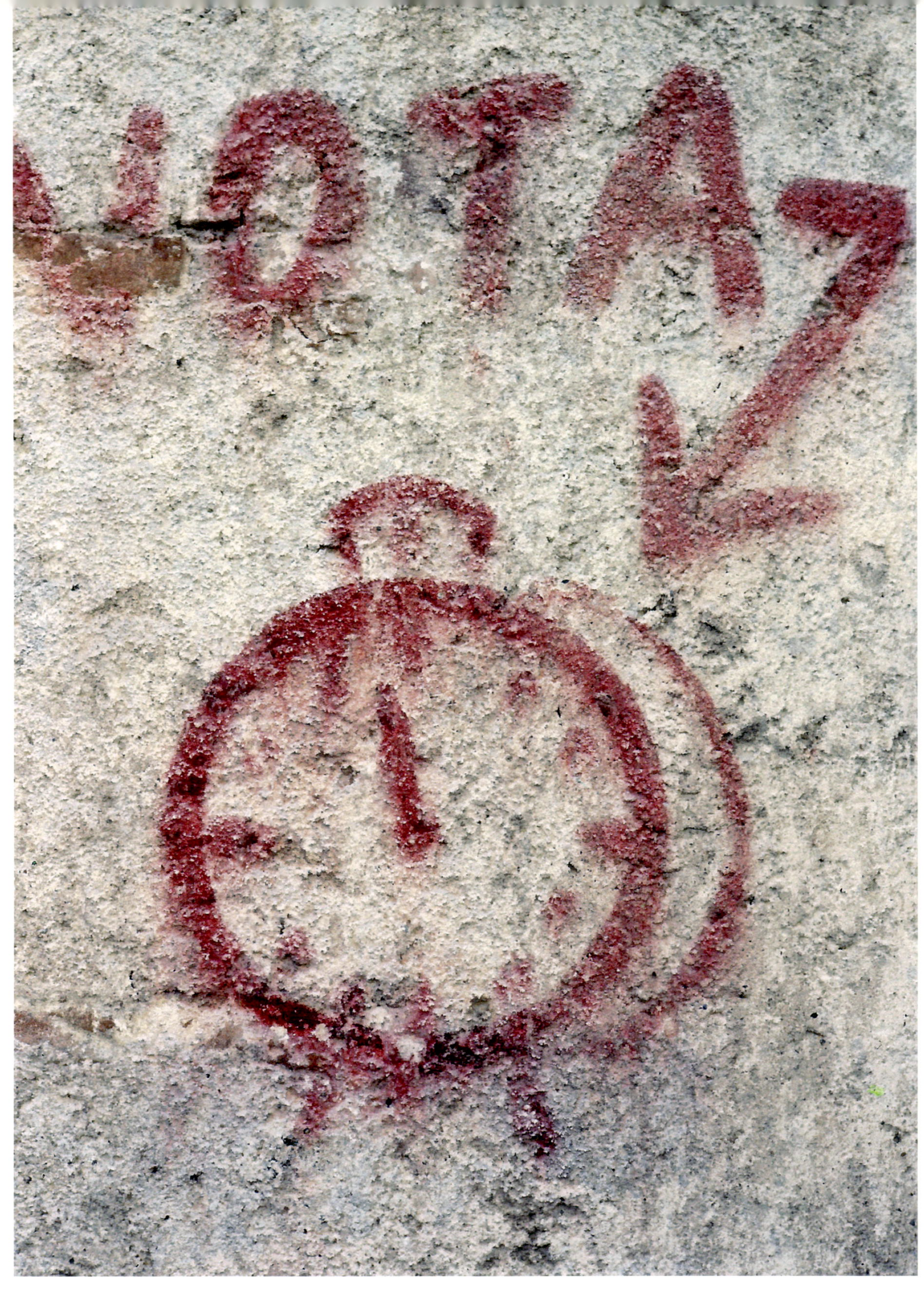

 da "MURI" anni '70

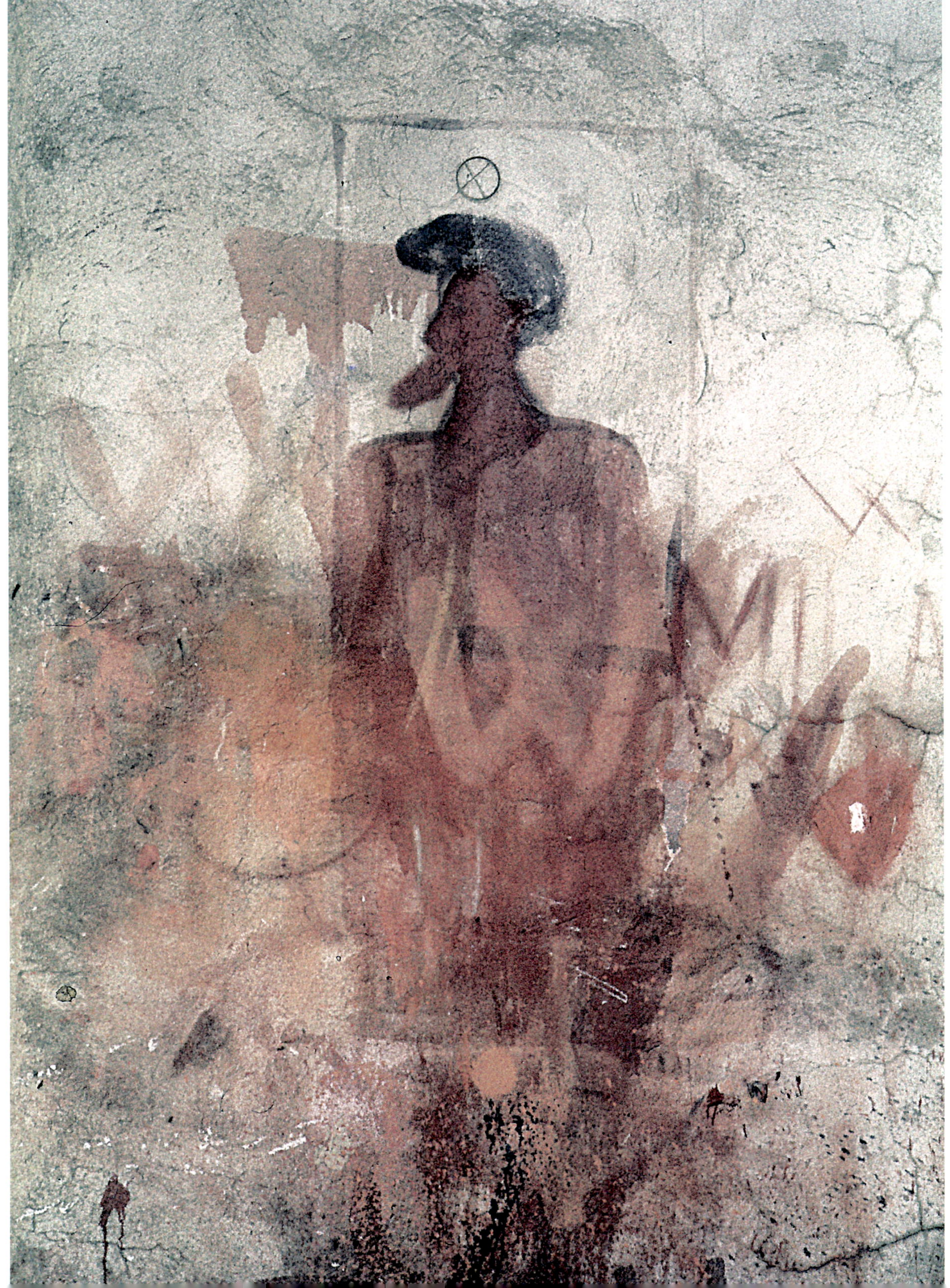

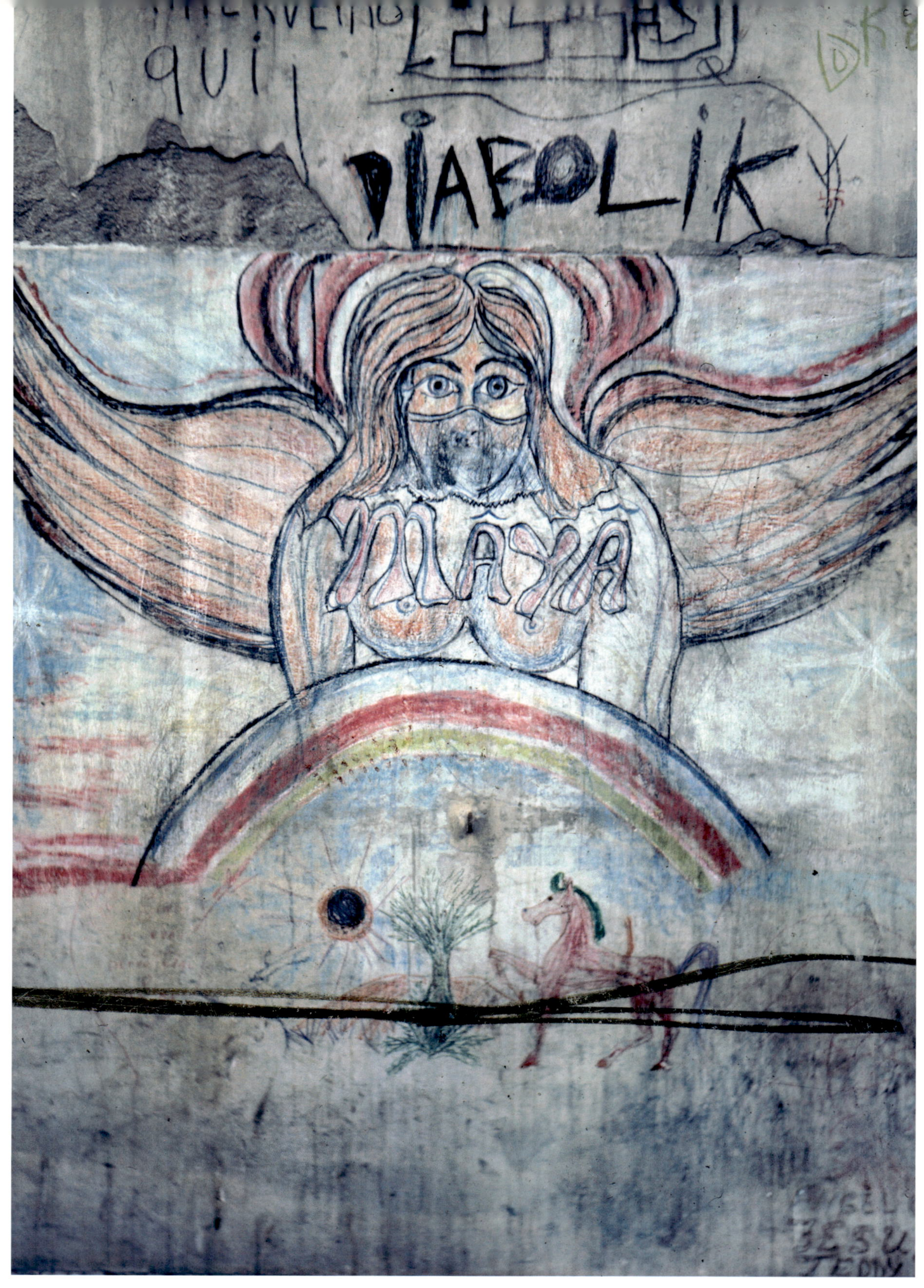
qui
DIABOLIK
MAYA

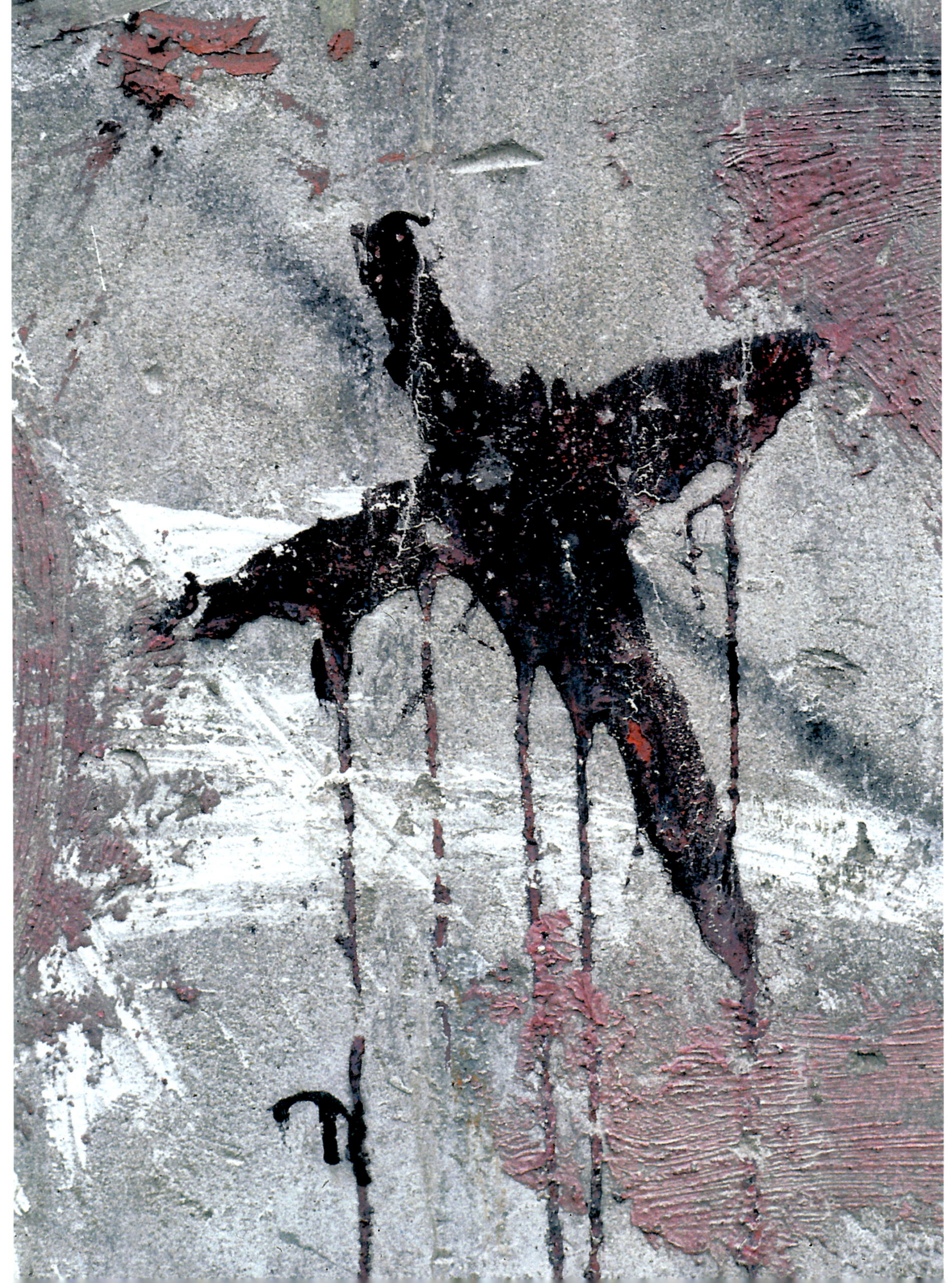

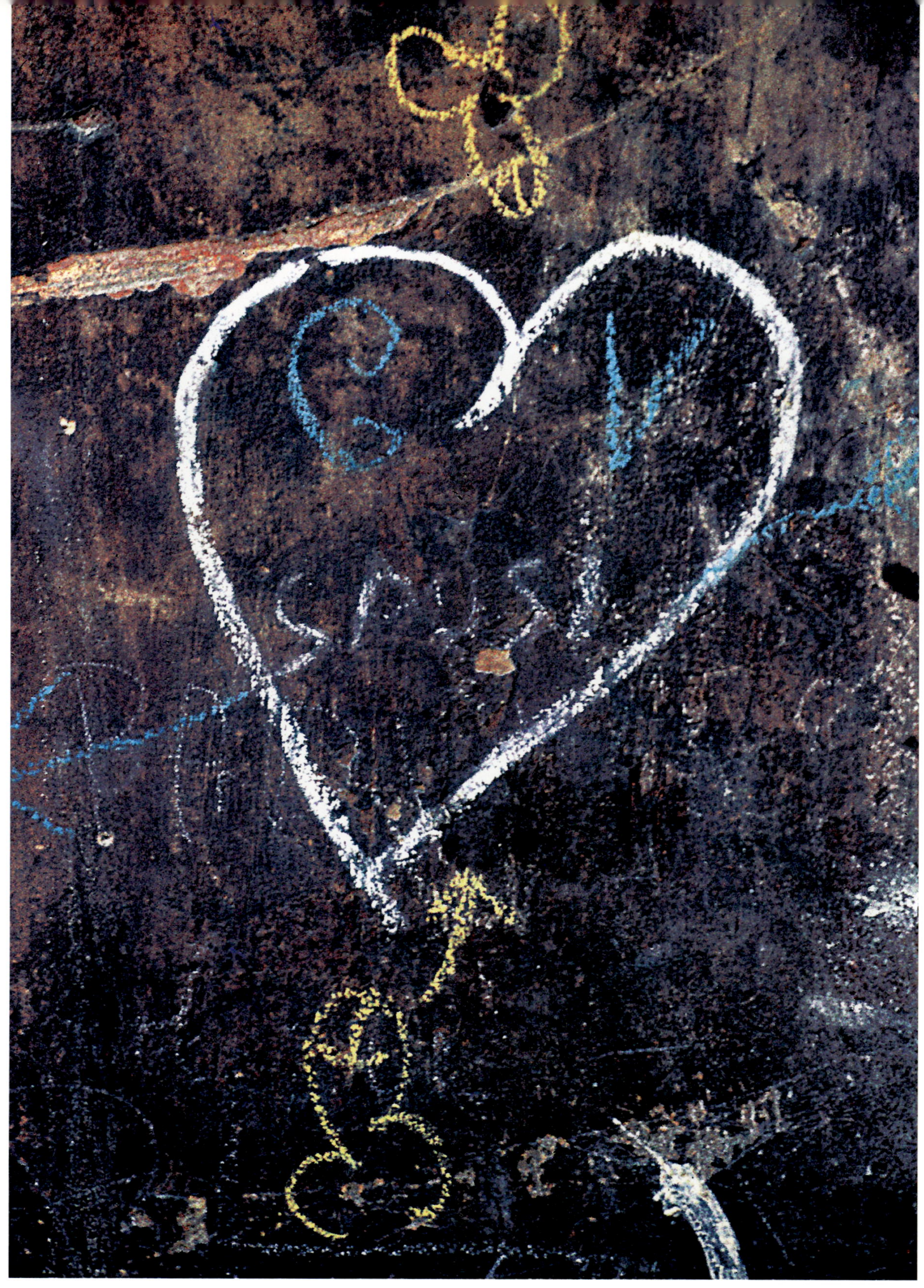

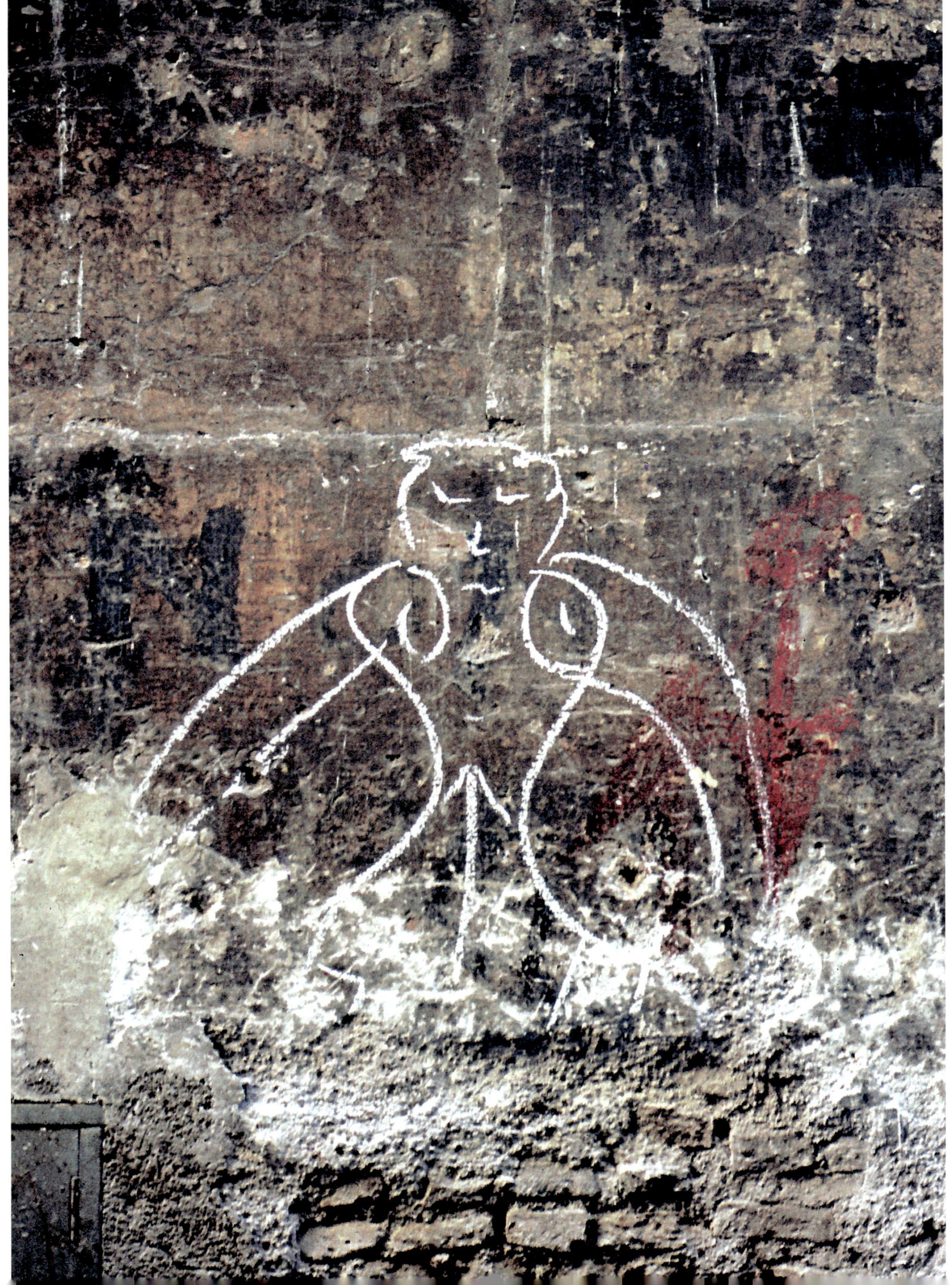

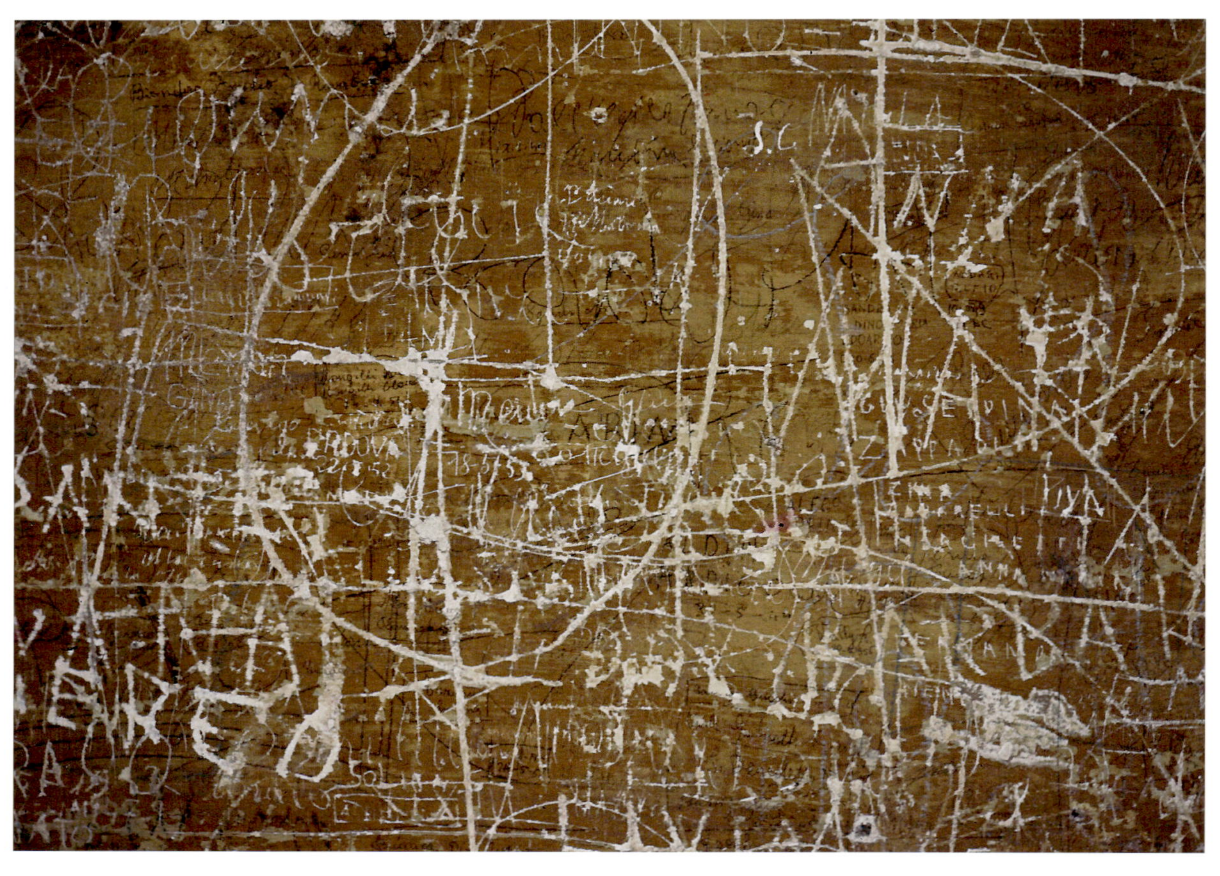

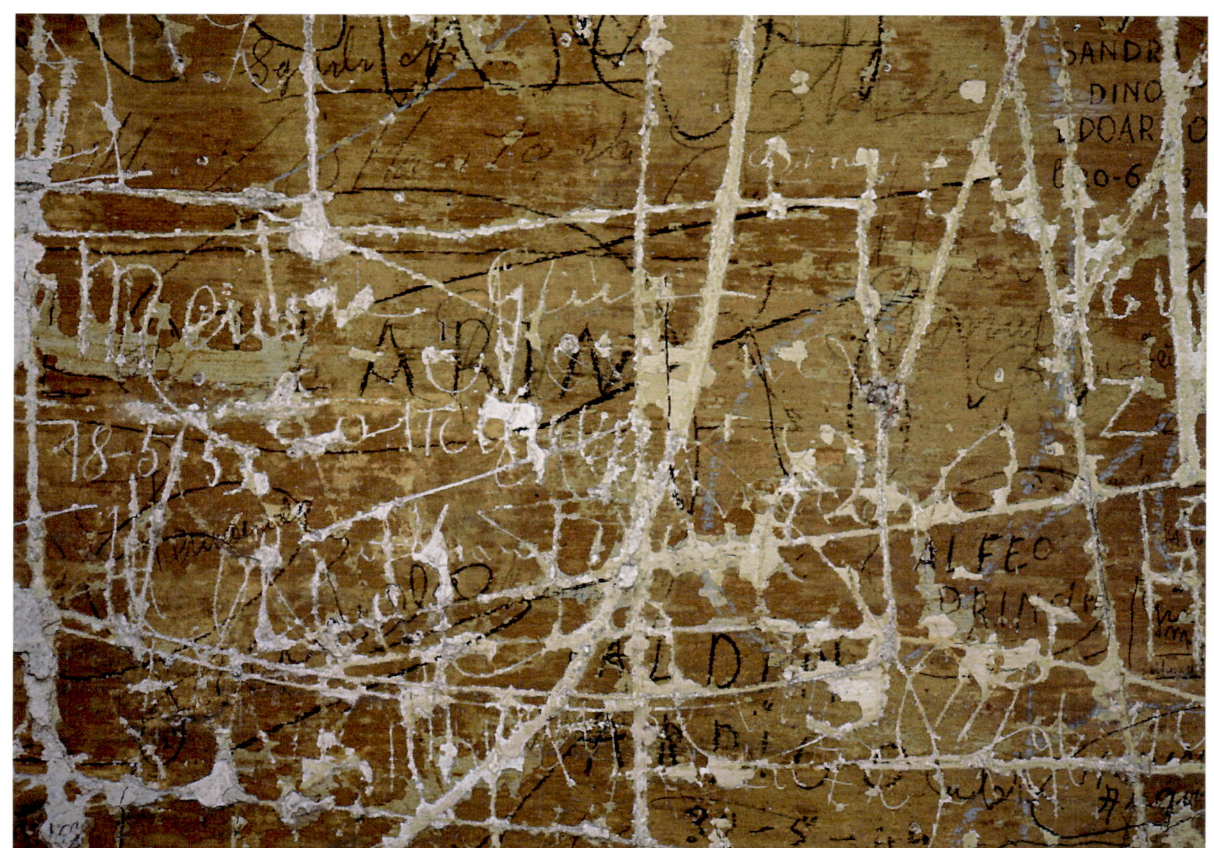

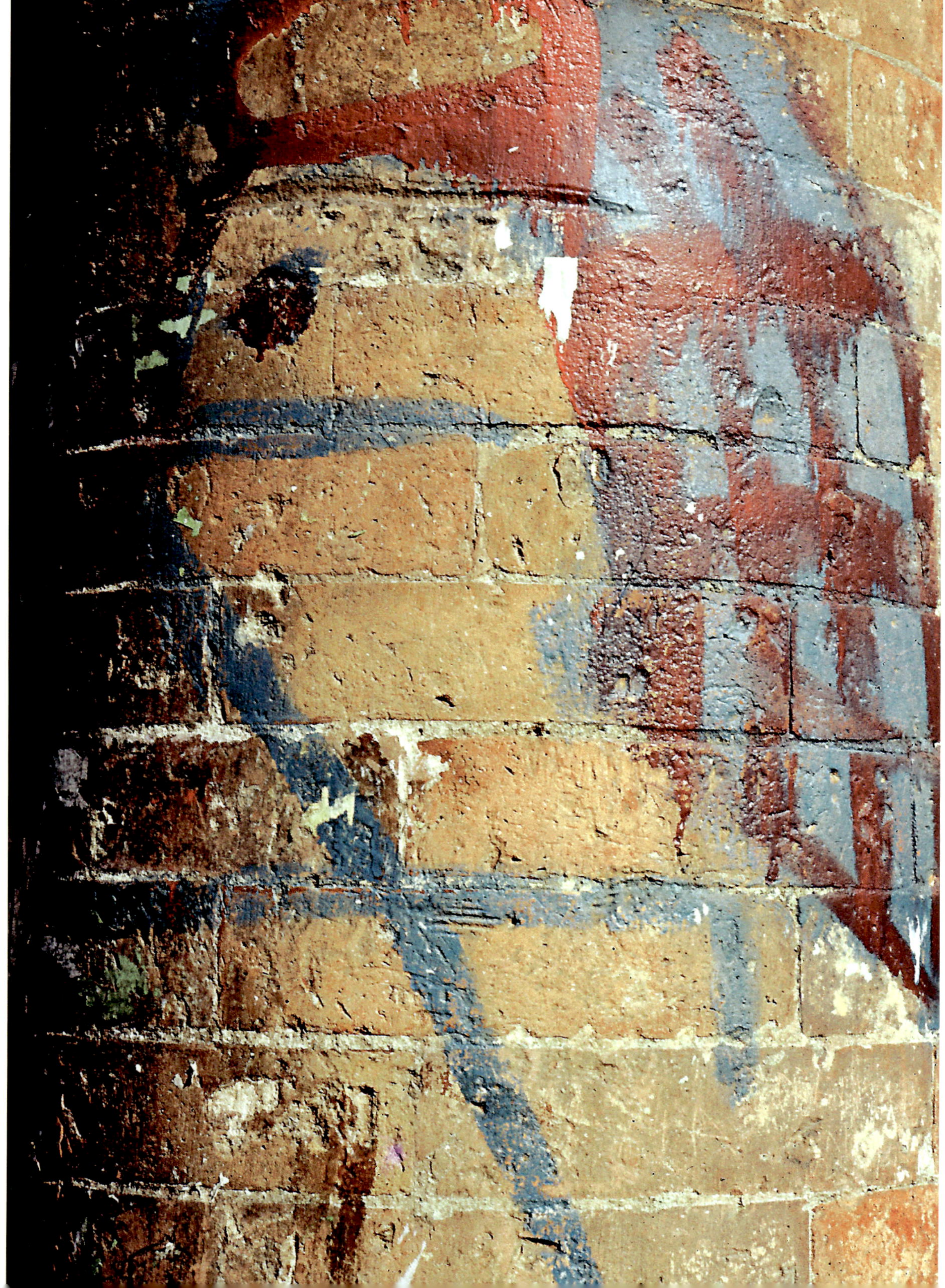

AMO
PIÑA

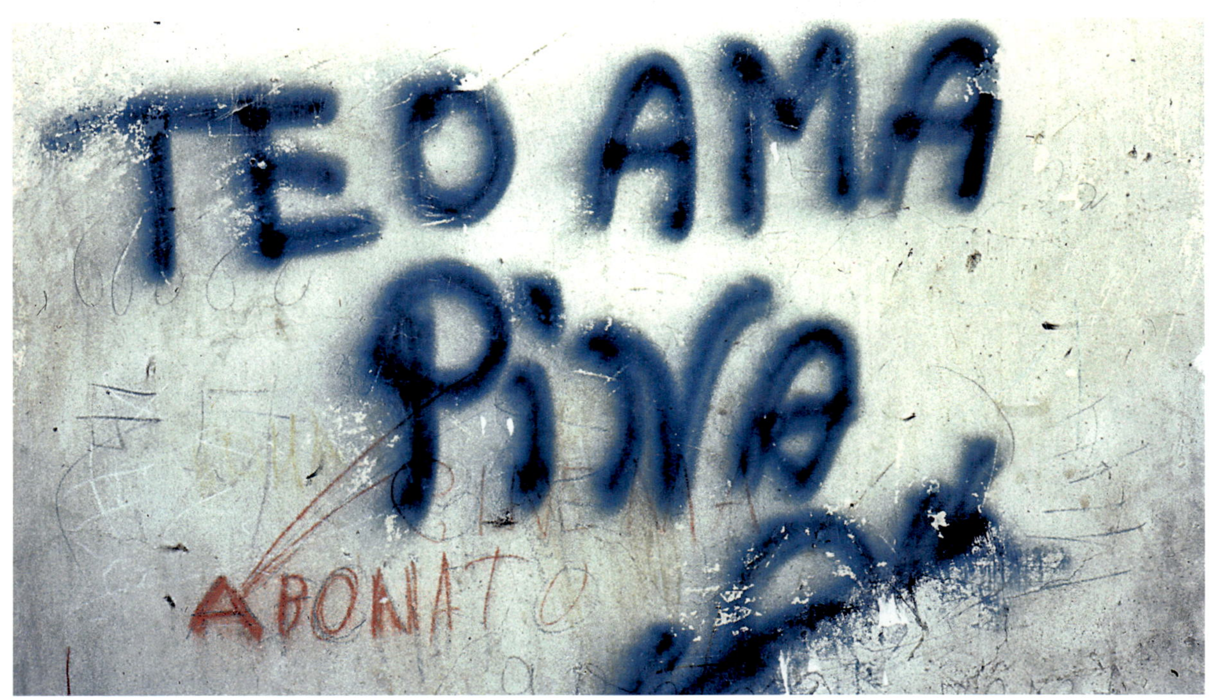

TEO AMA
PIÑA
ABONATO

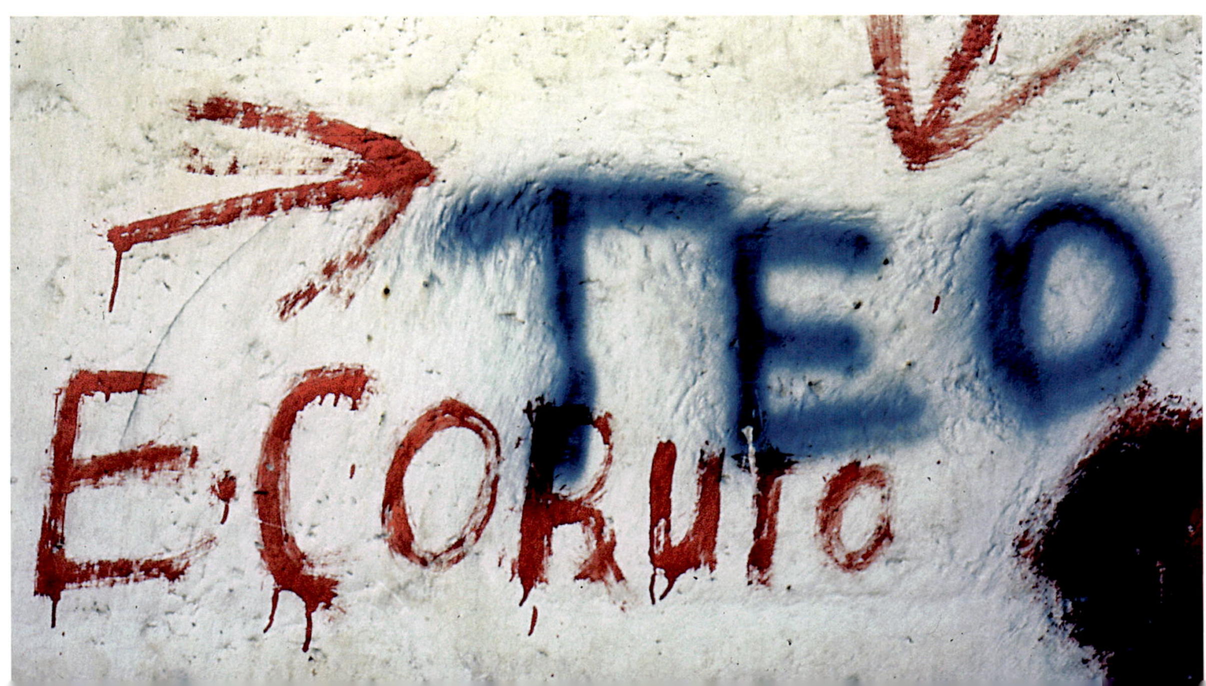

TEO
E CORUJO

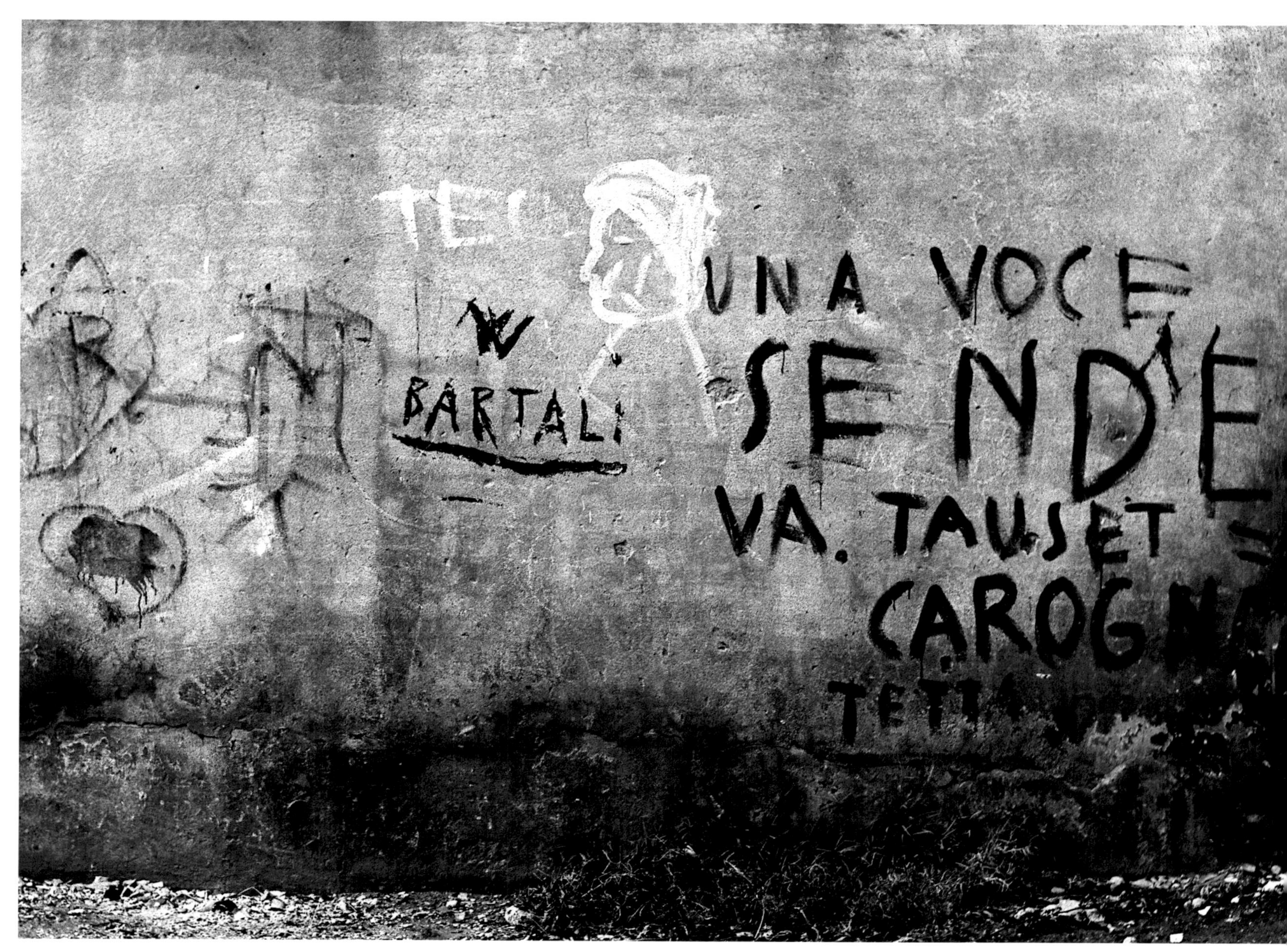
TE
UNA VOCE
W
BARTALI
SE NDE
VA. TAU S ET
CAROG
TETT

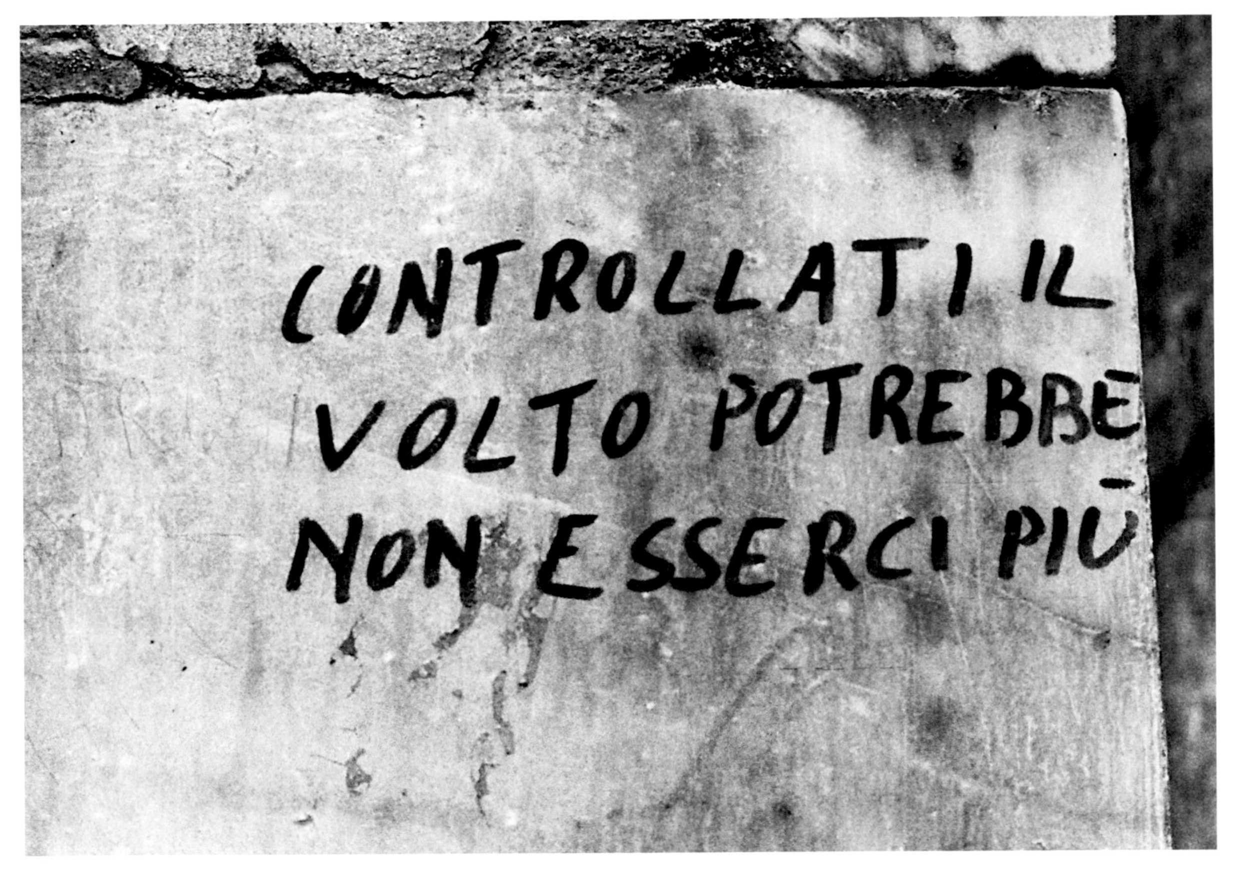

CONTROLLATI IL
VOLTO POTREBBE
NON ESSERCI PIÙ

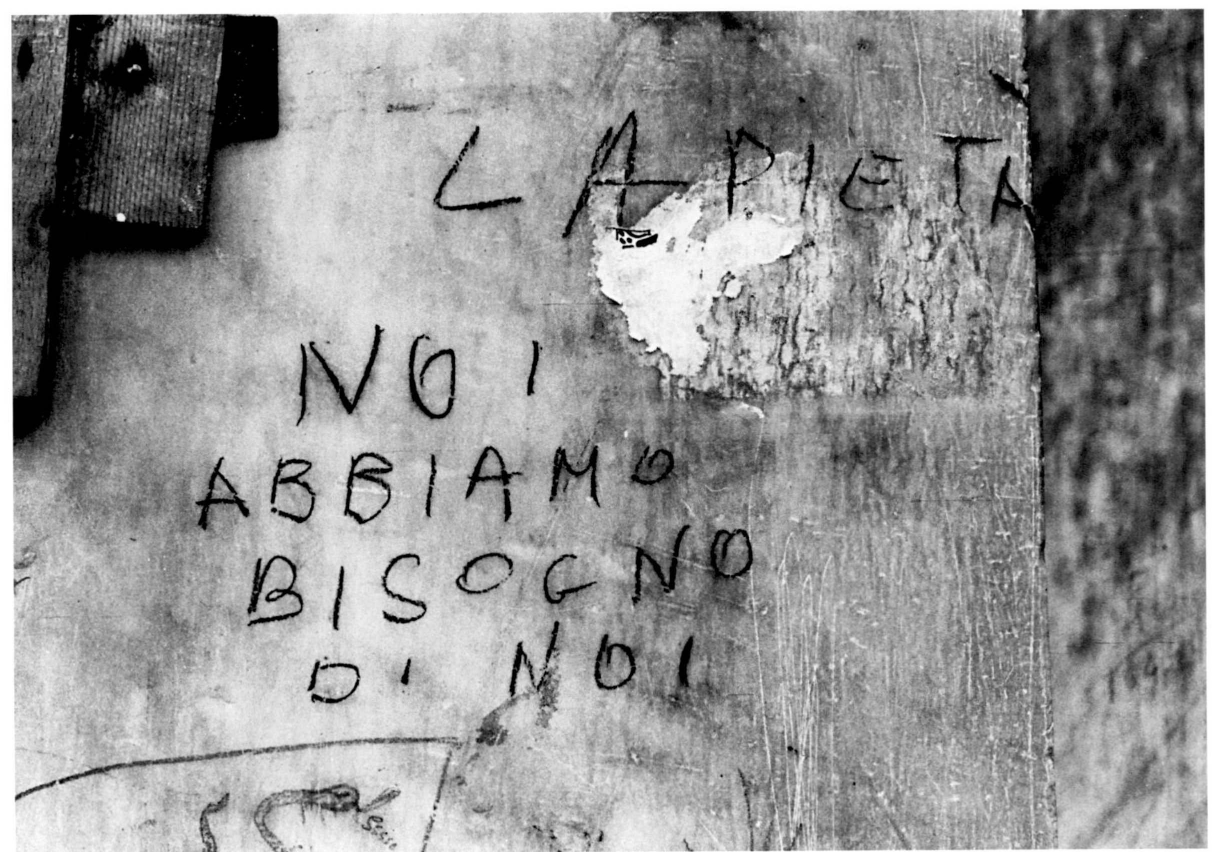

LA PIETA
NOI
ABBIAMO
BISOGNO
DI NOI

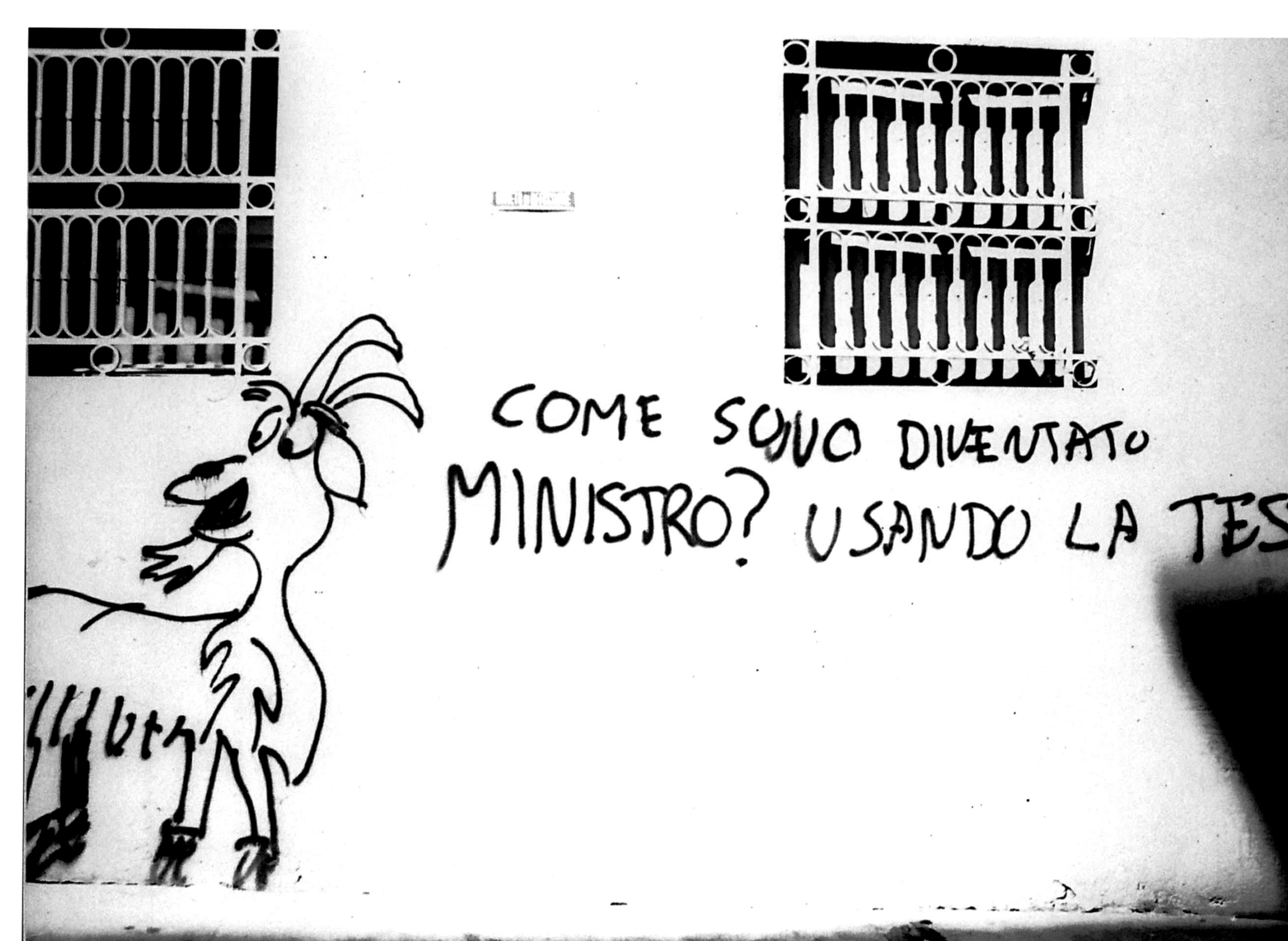
COME SONO DIVENTATO
MINISTRO? USANDO LA TES

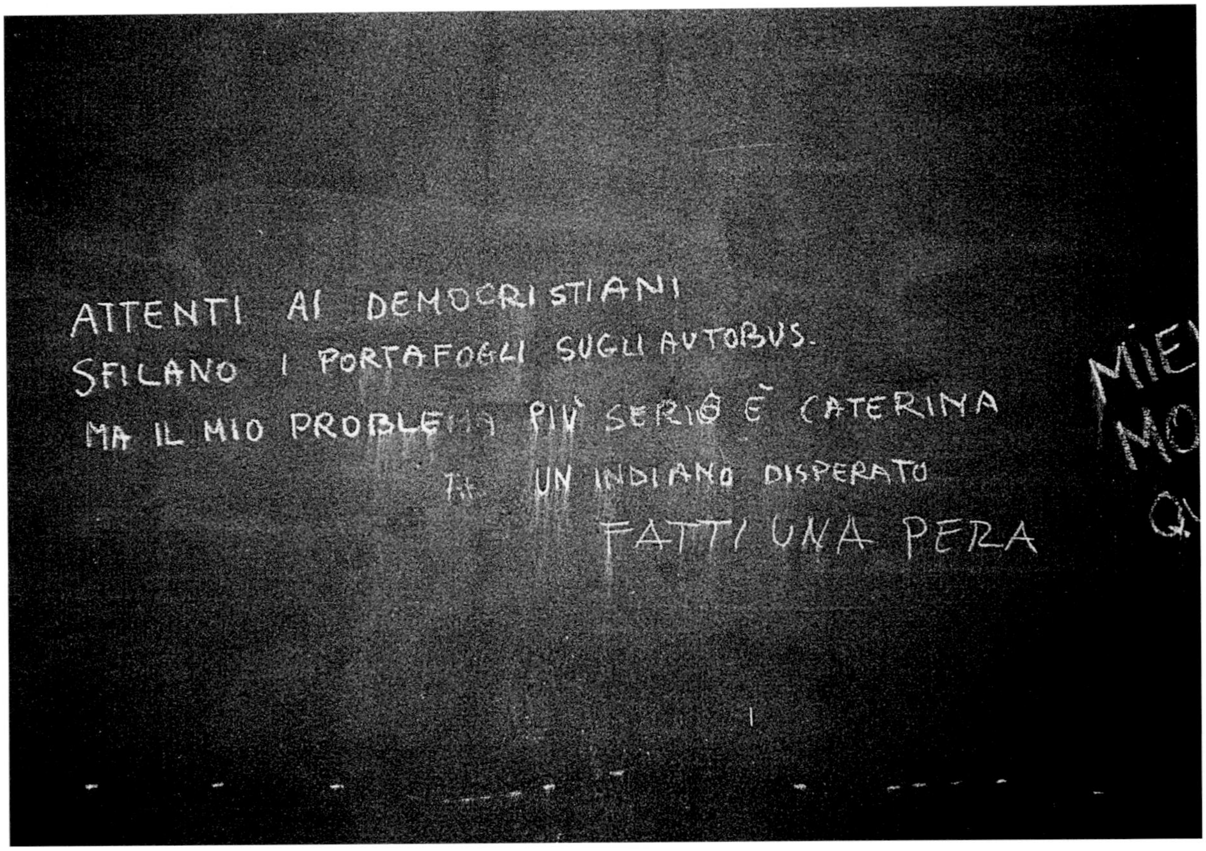

ATTENTI AI DEMOCRISTIANI
SFILANO I PORTAFOGLI SUGLI AUTOBUS.
MA IL MIO PROBLEMA PIÙ SERIO È CATERINA
F.to UN INDIANO DISPERATO
FATTI UNA PERA

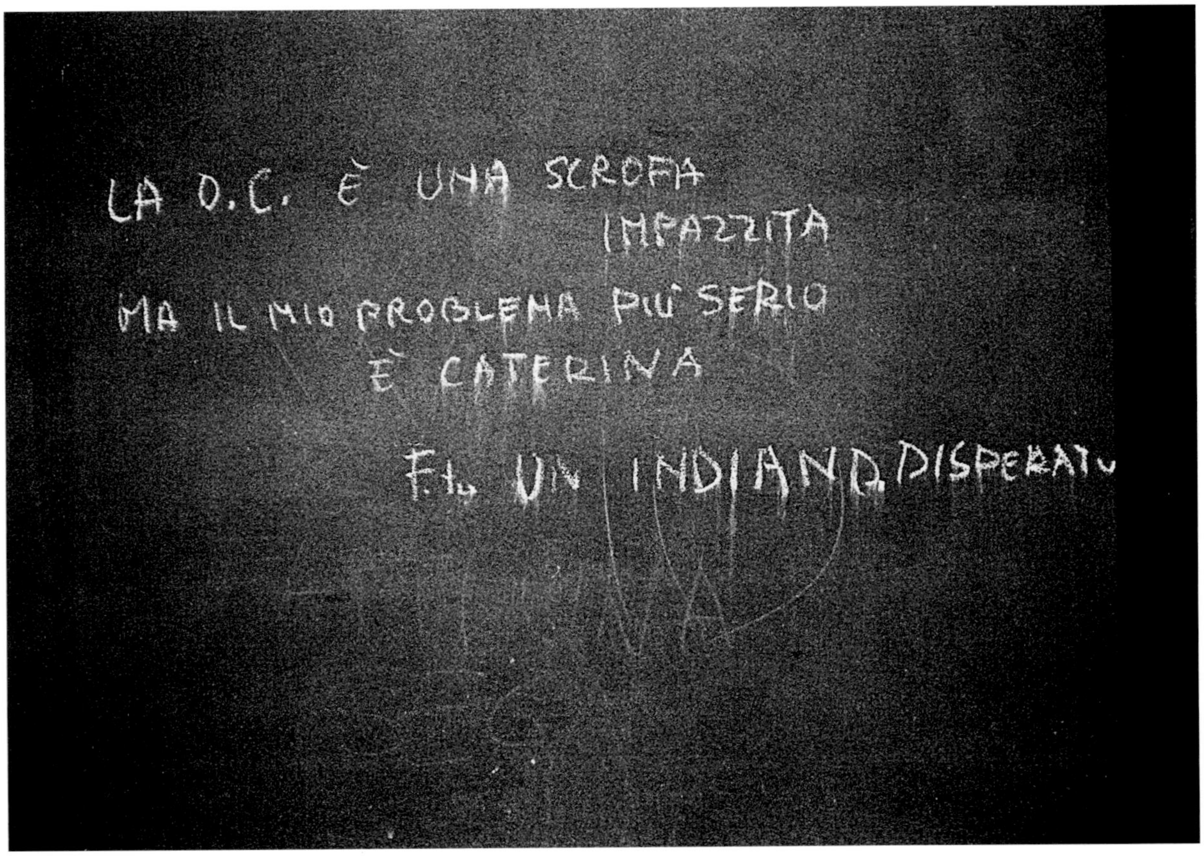

LA D.C. È UNA SCROFA
IMPAZZITA
MA IL MIO PROBLEMA PIÙ SERIO
È CATERINA

F.to UN INDIANO DISPERATO

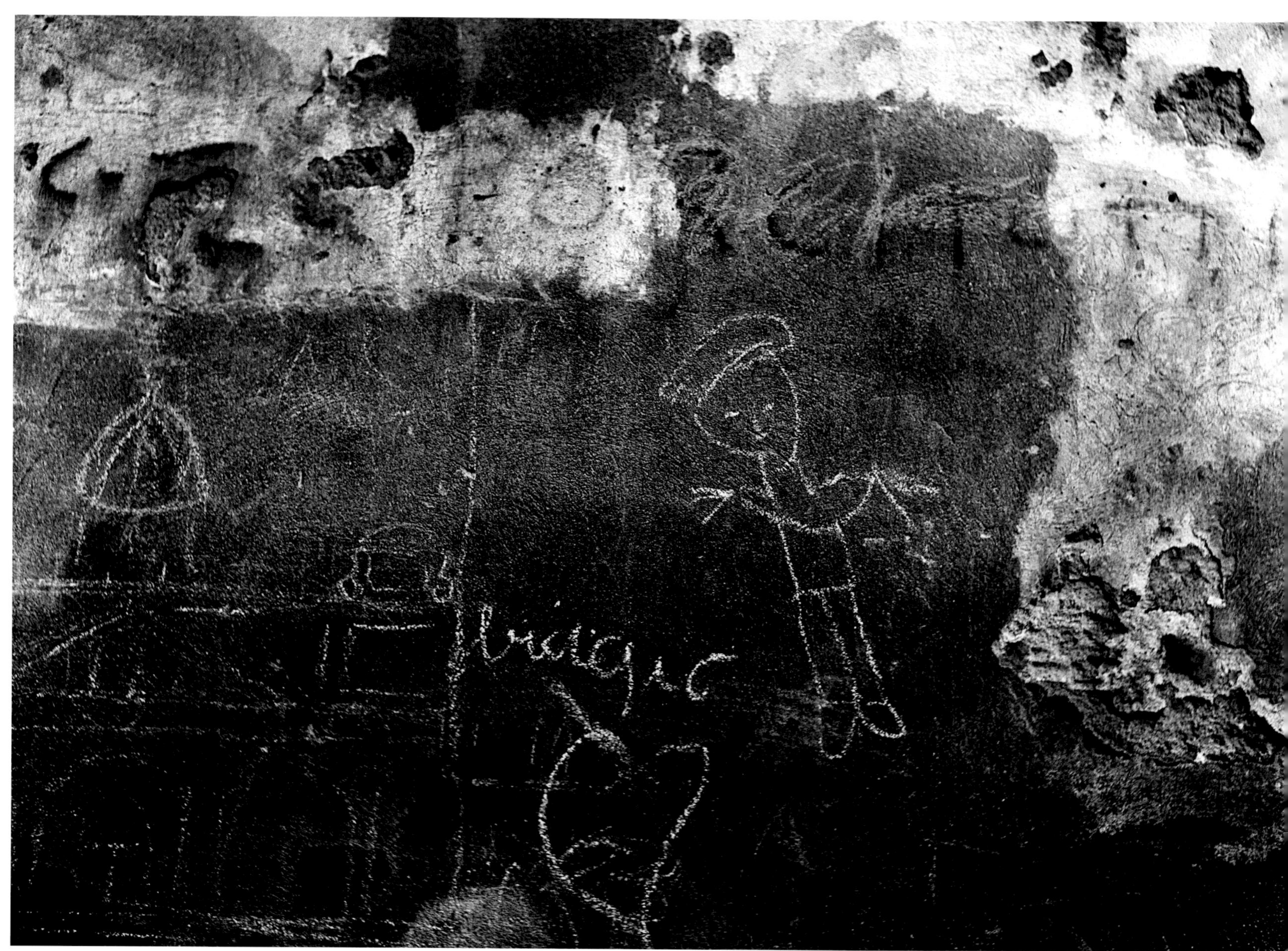

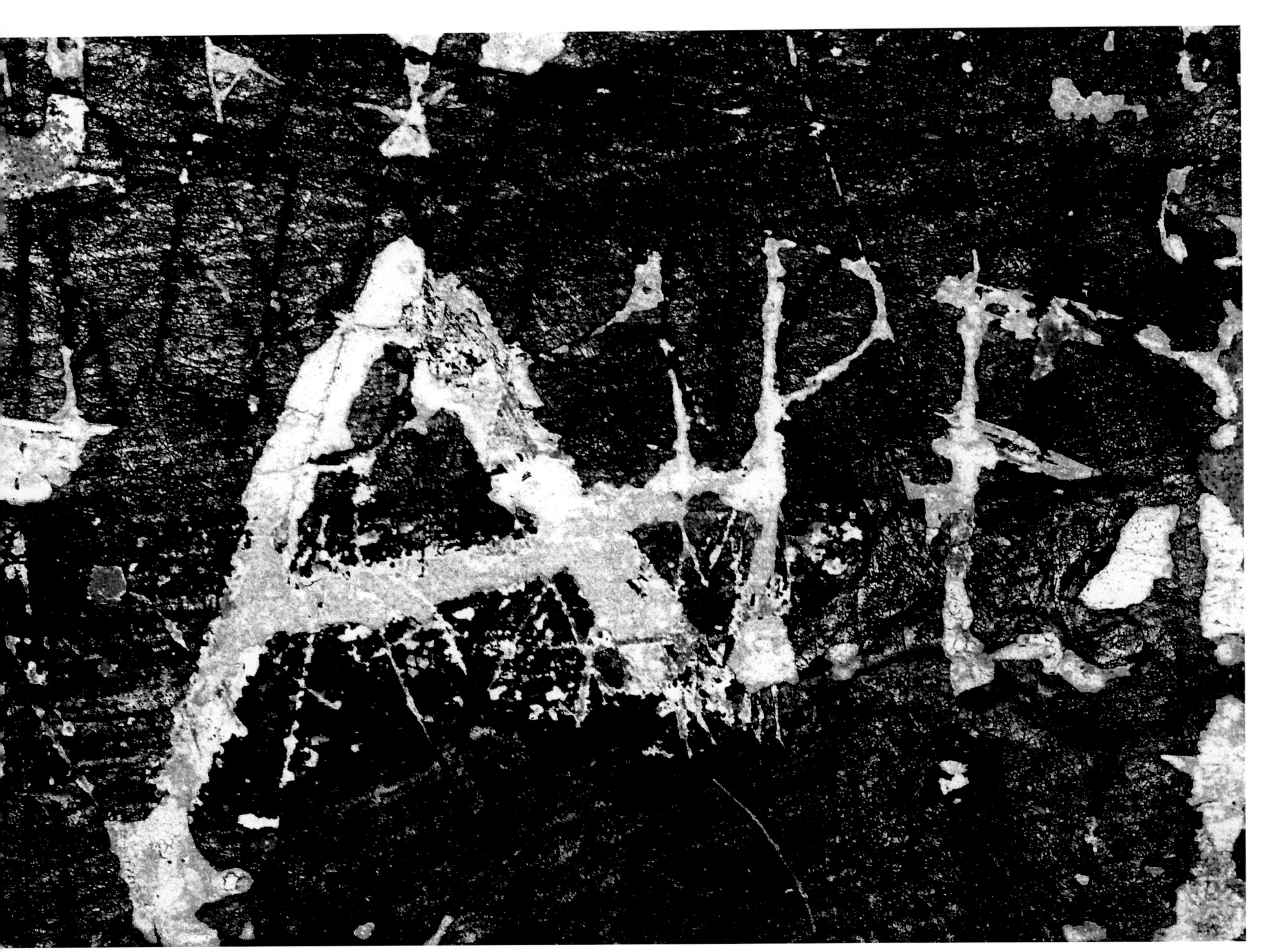

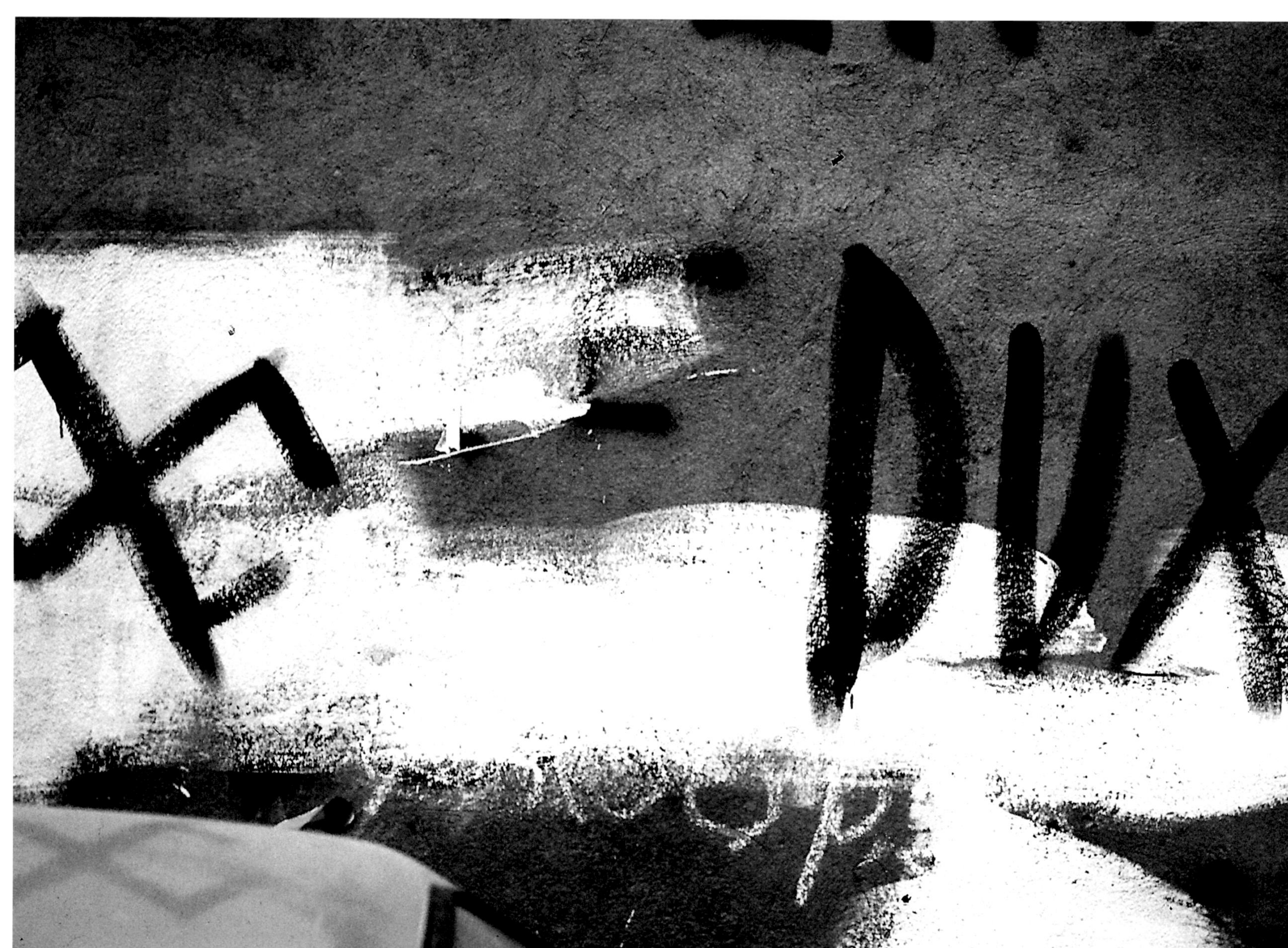

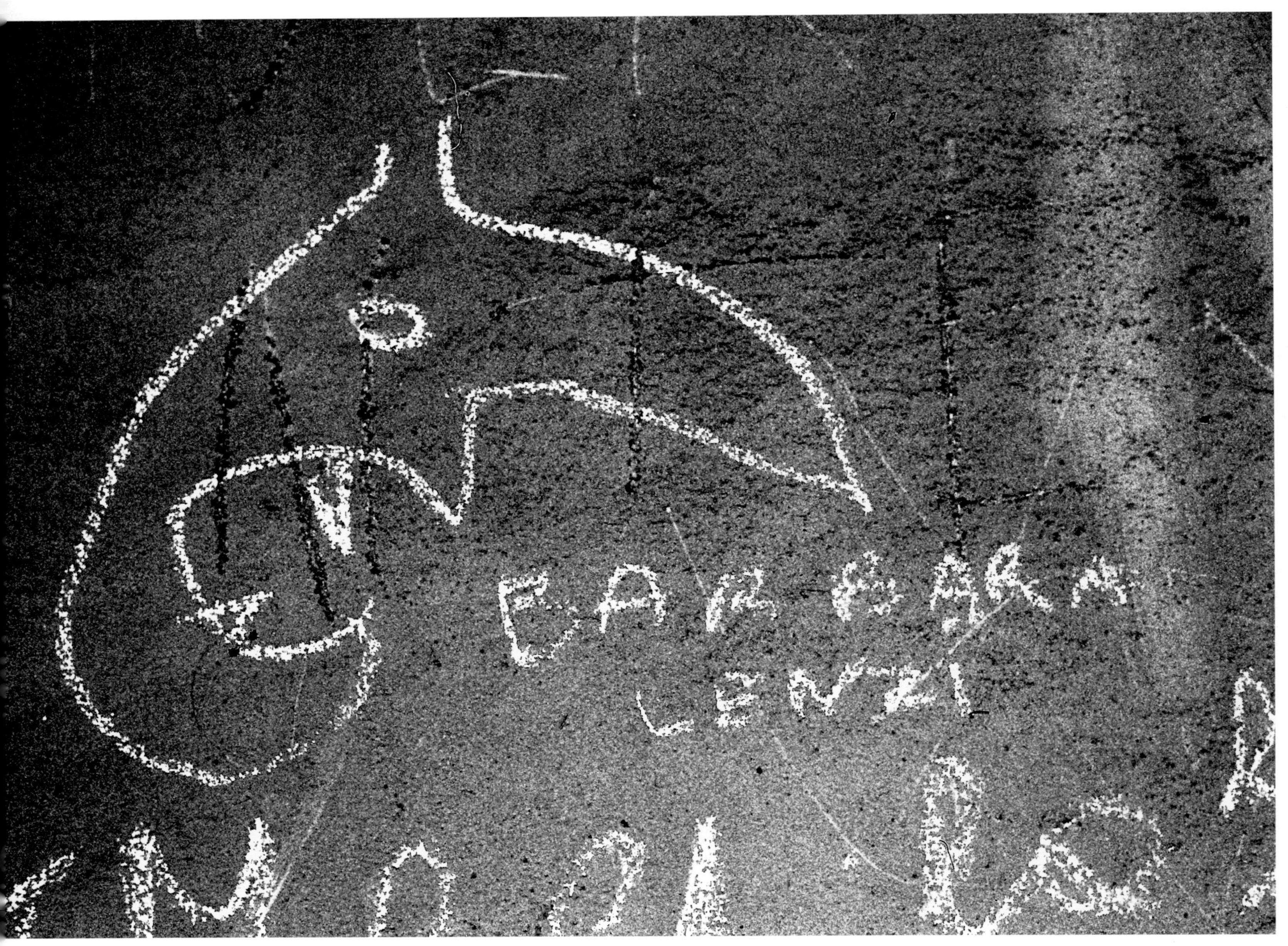

BARBARA
LENZI

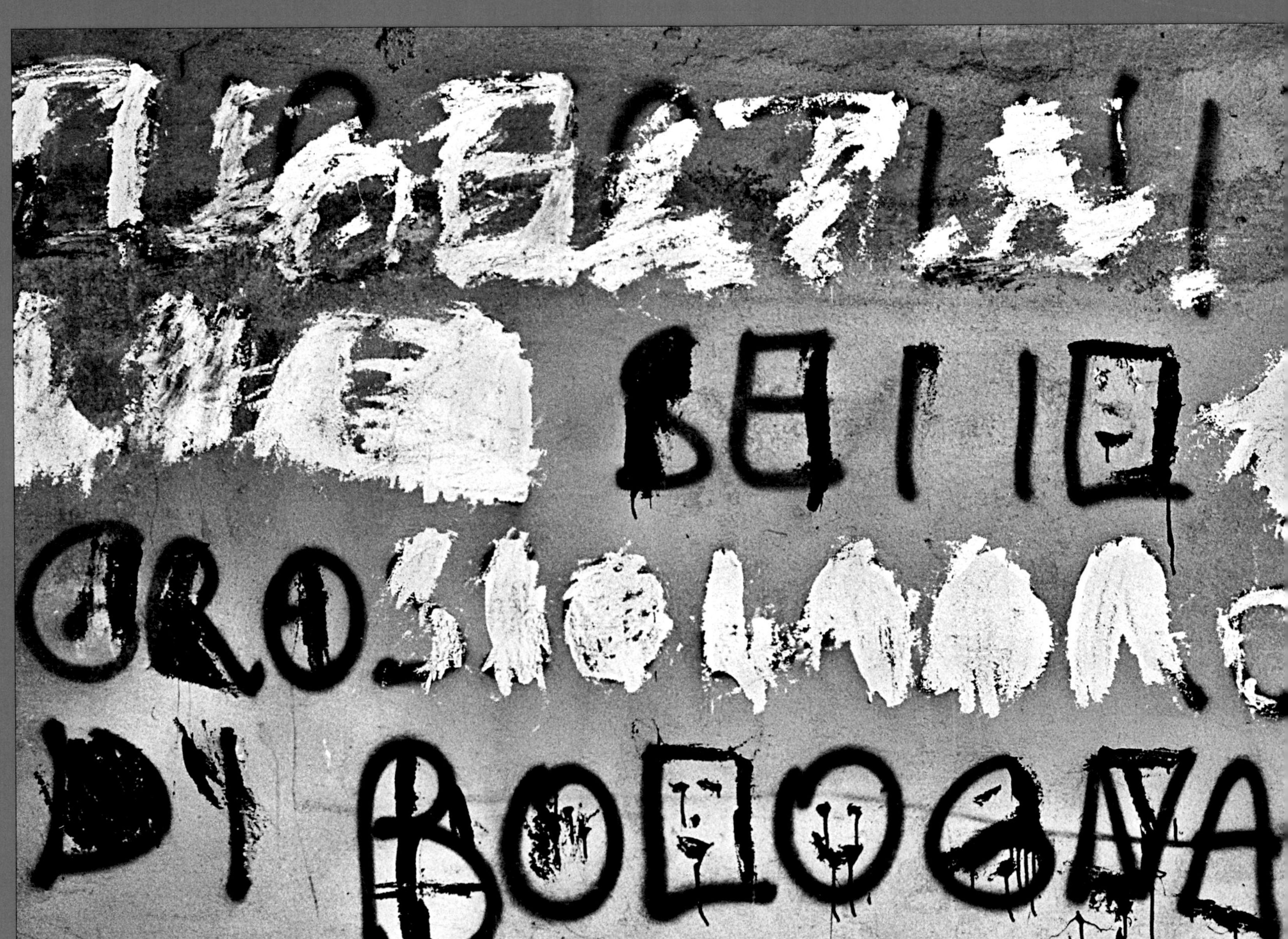
DI BOLOGNA

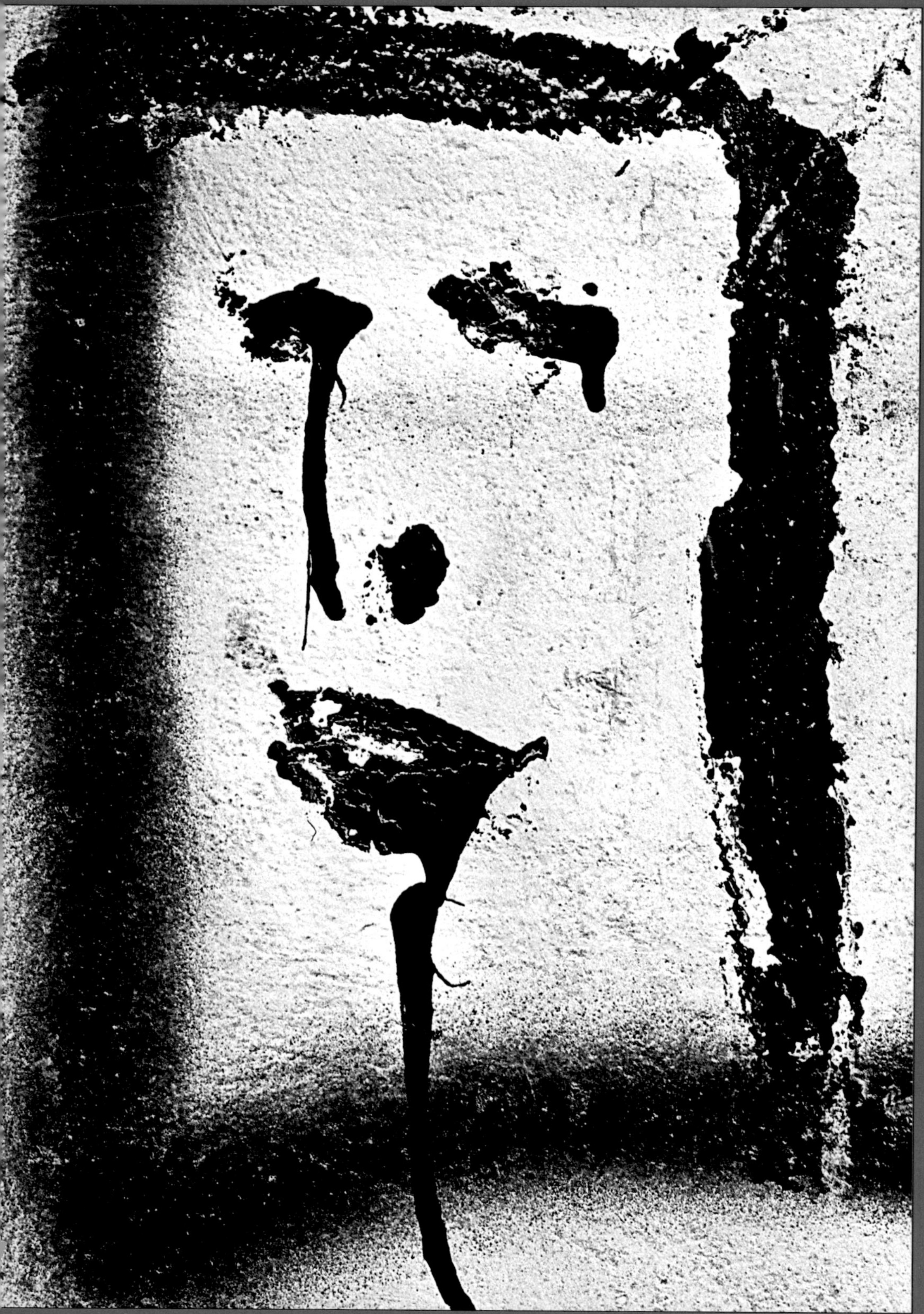

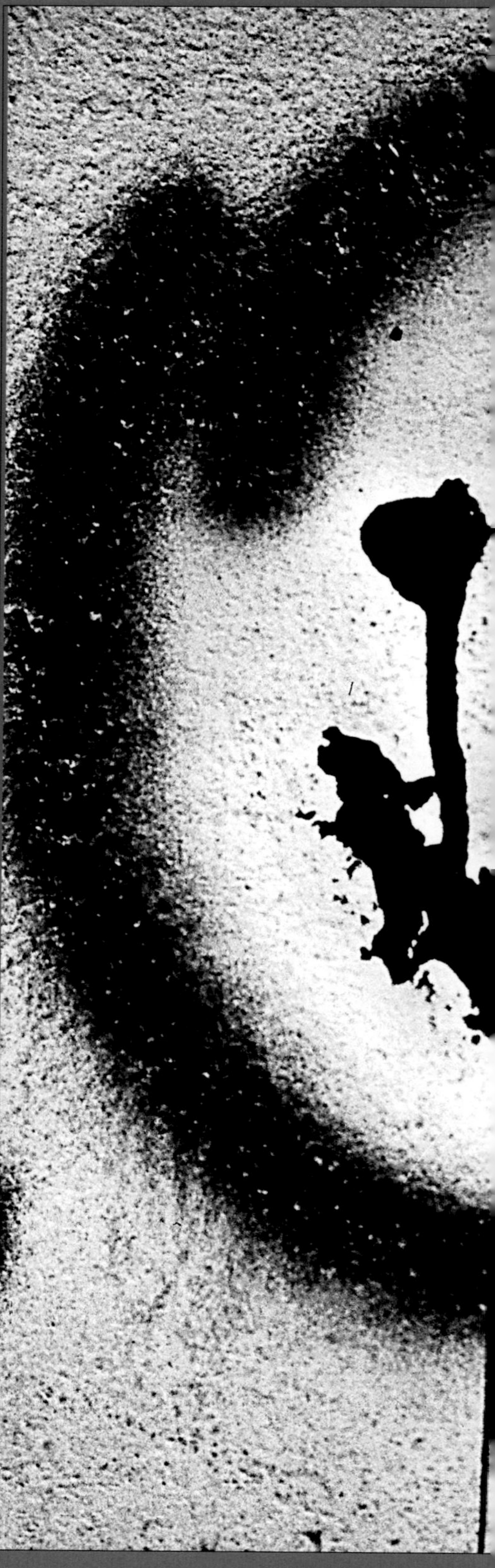

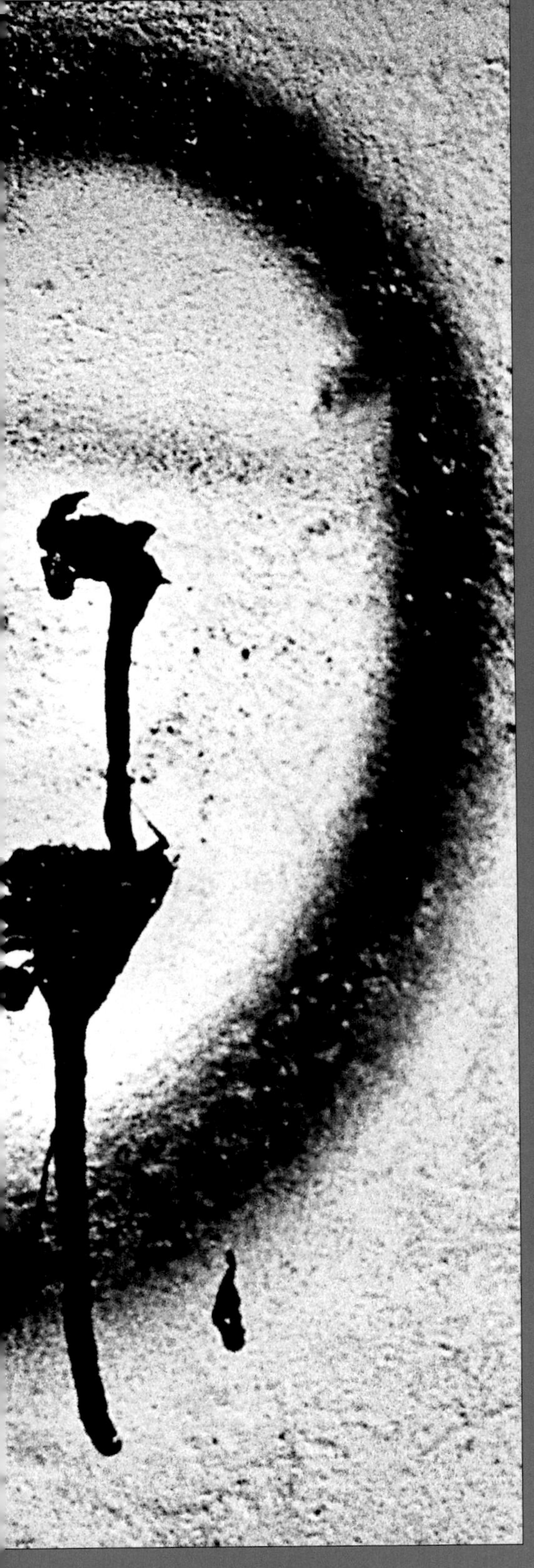

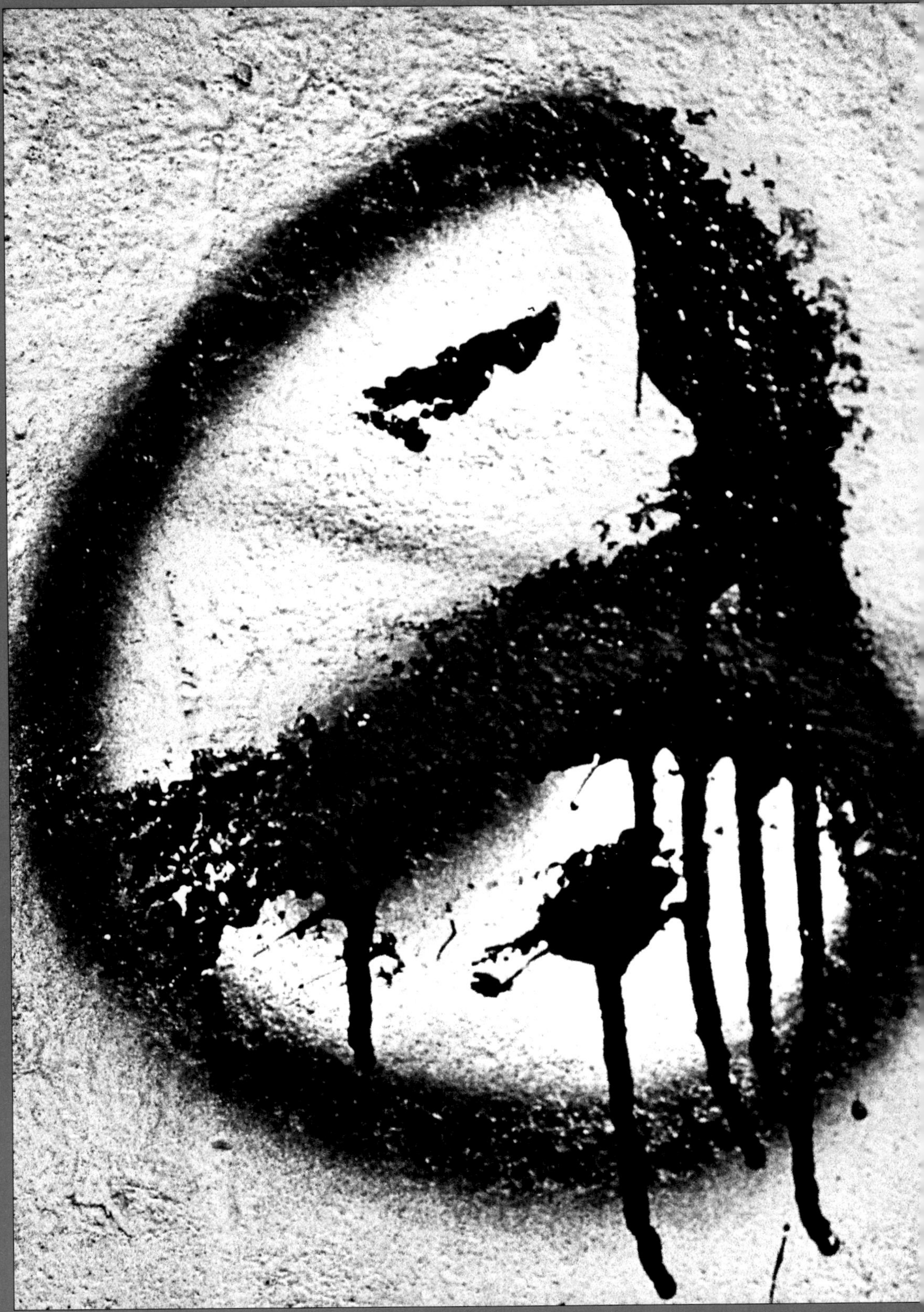

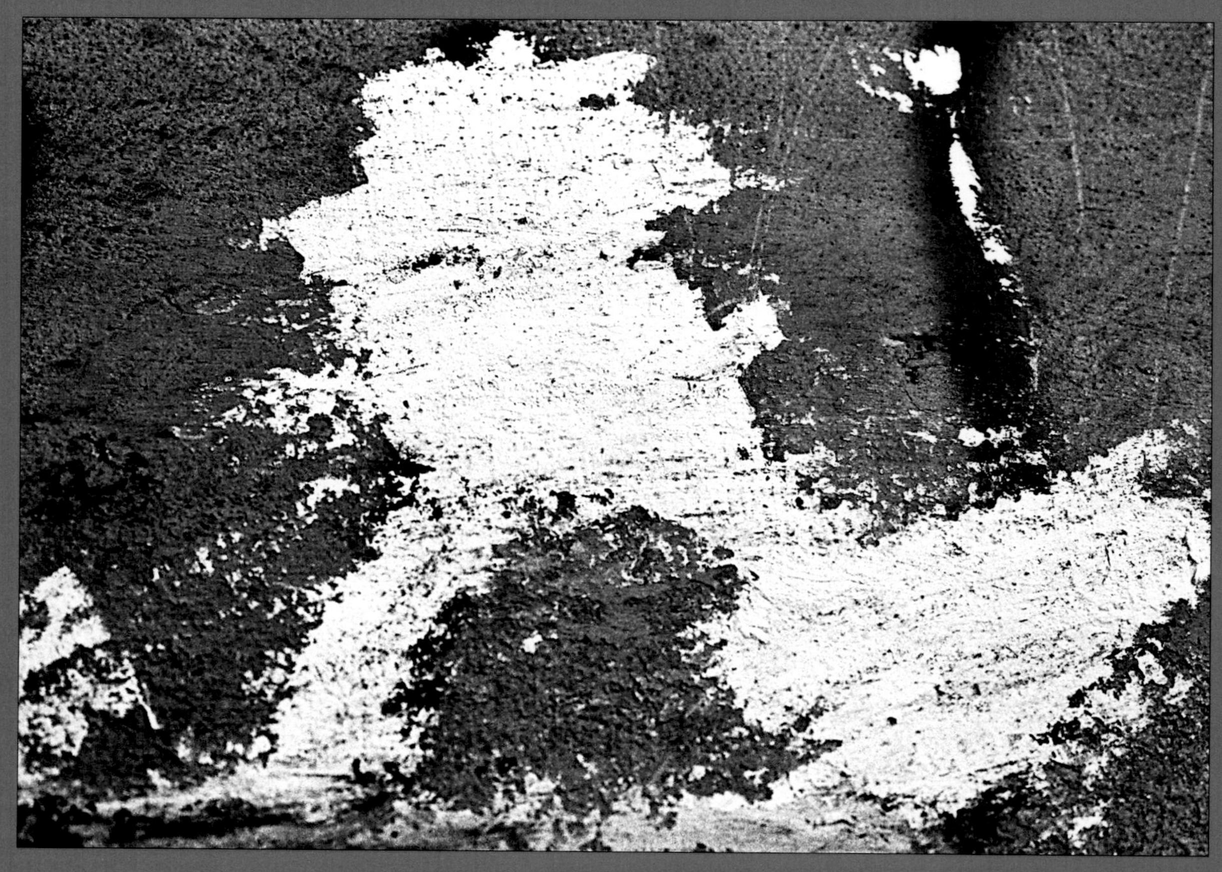

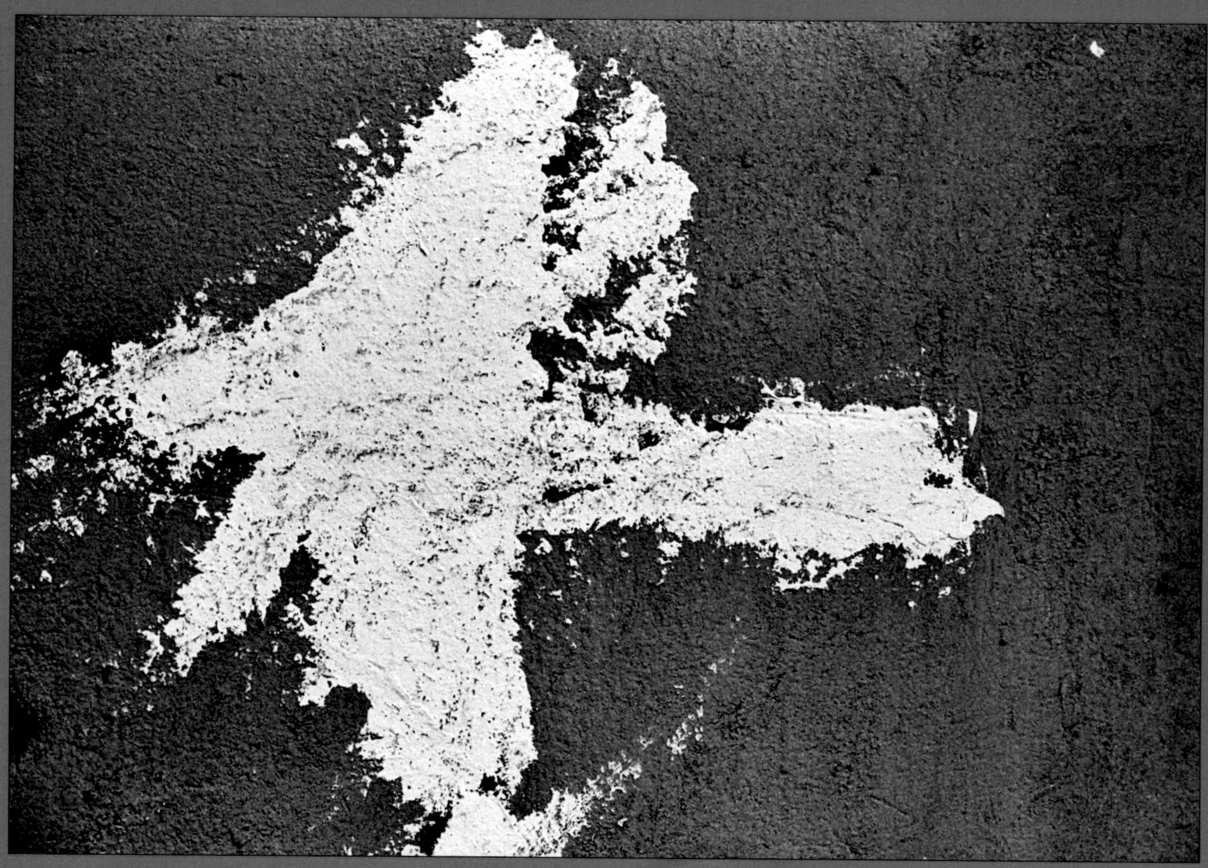

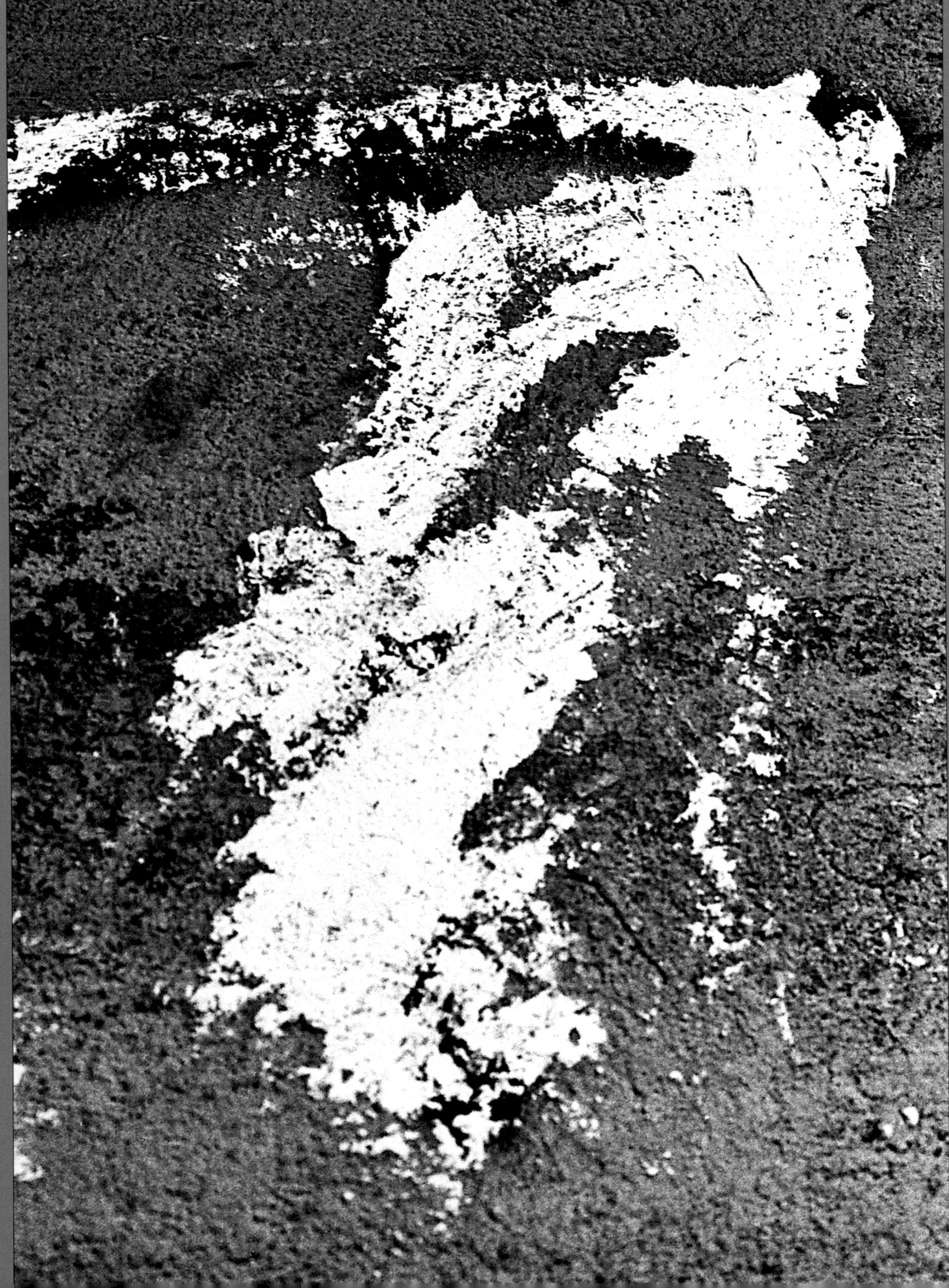

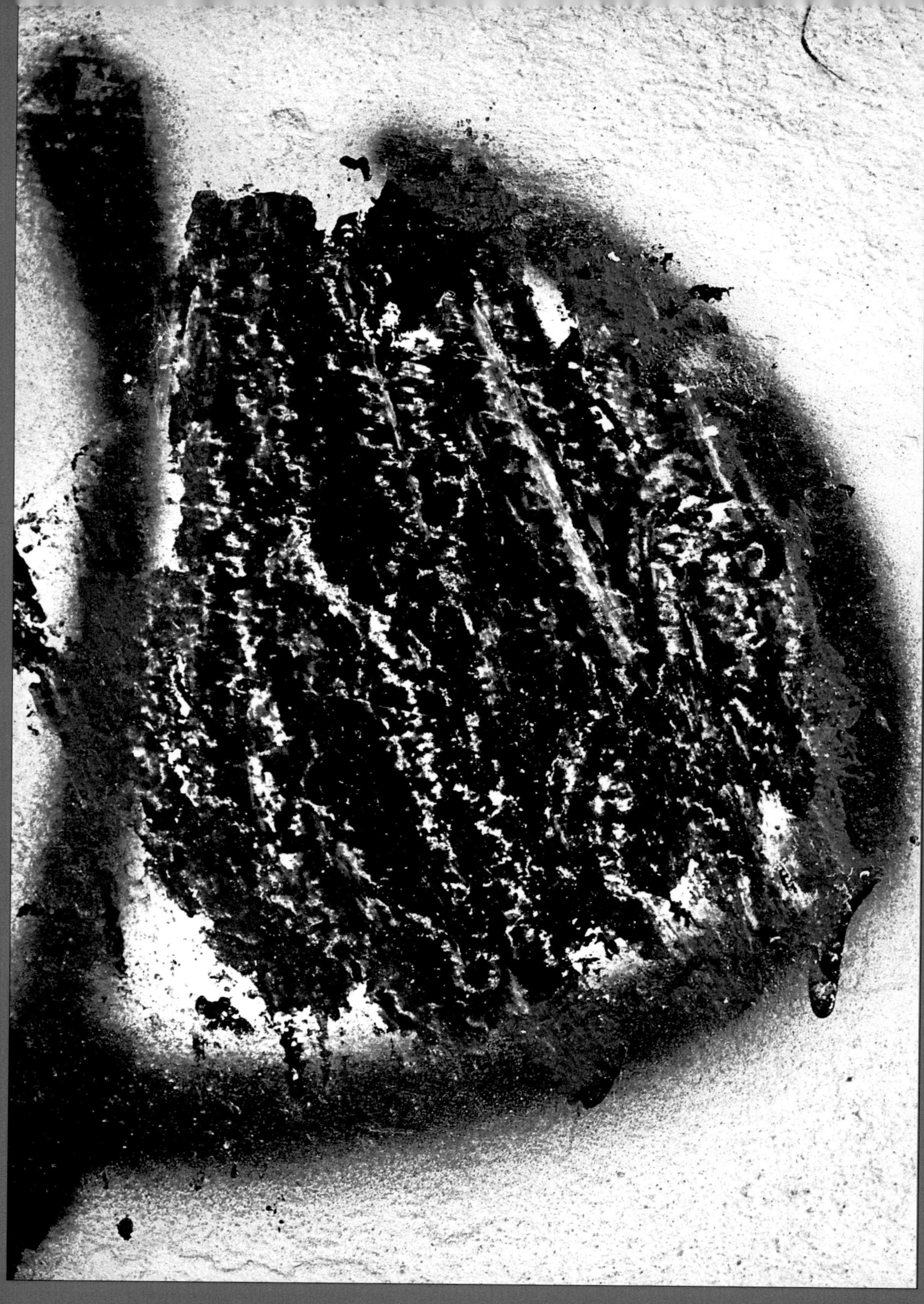

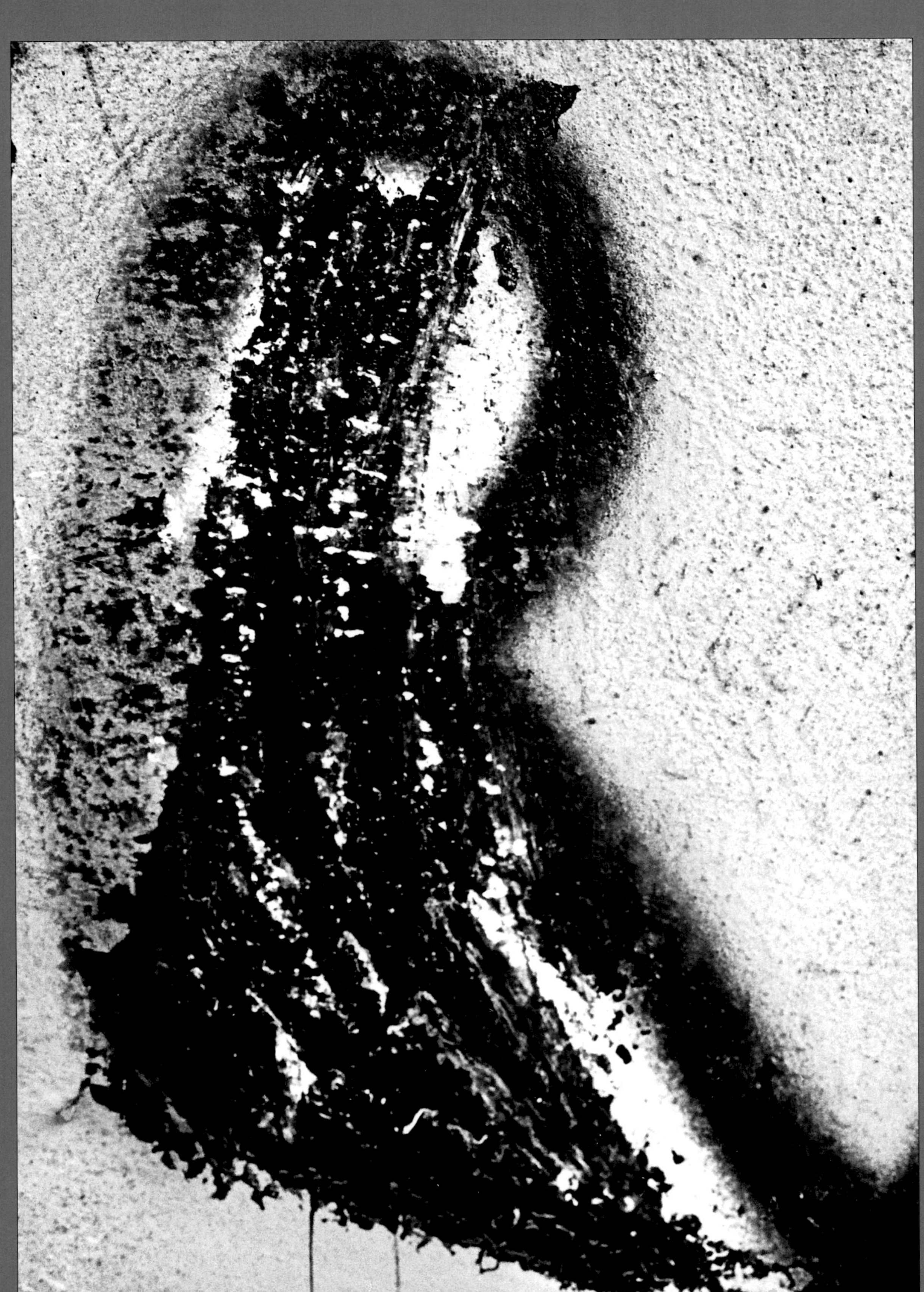

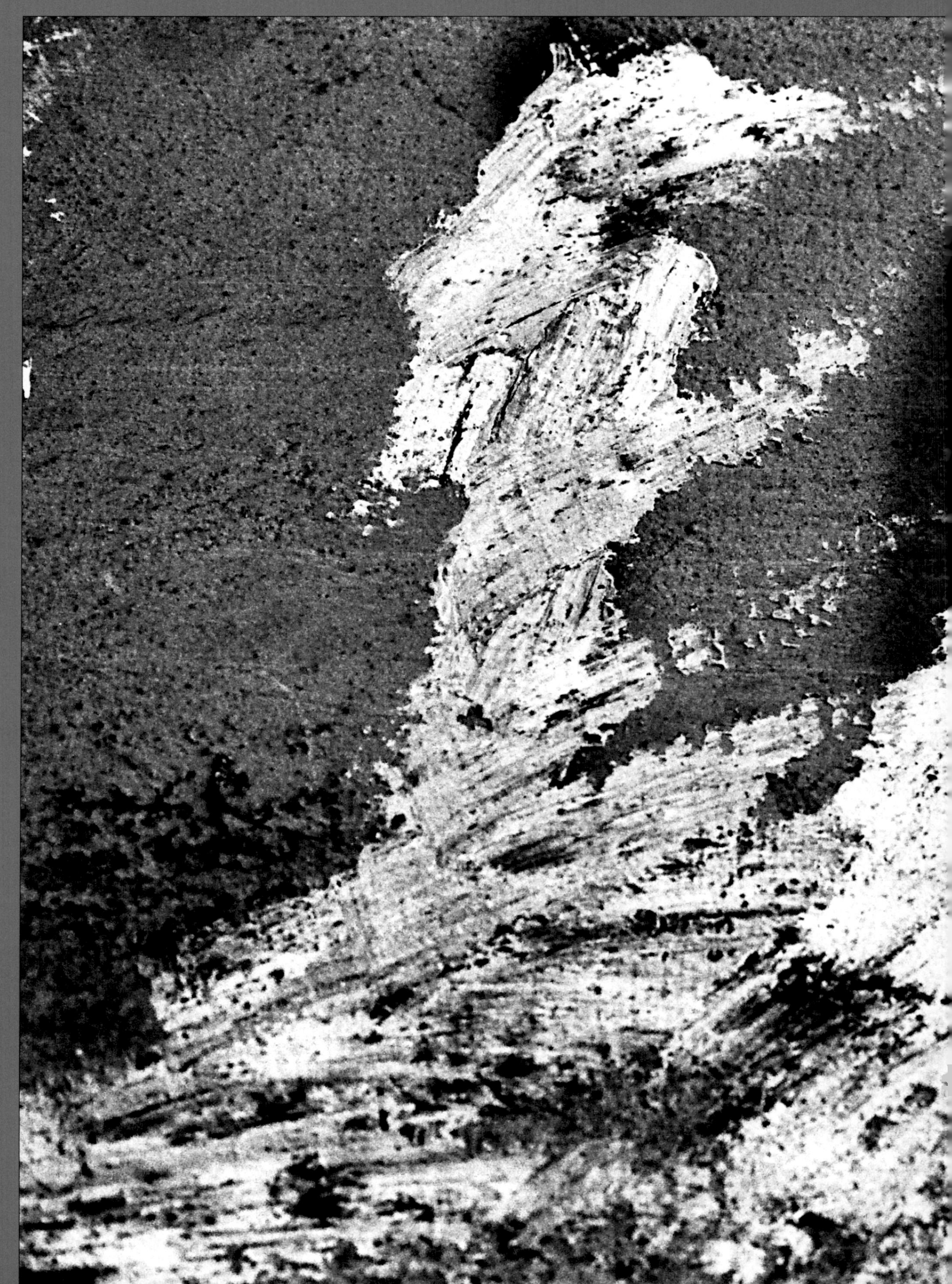

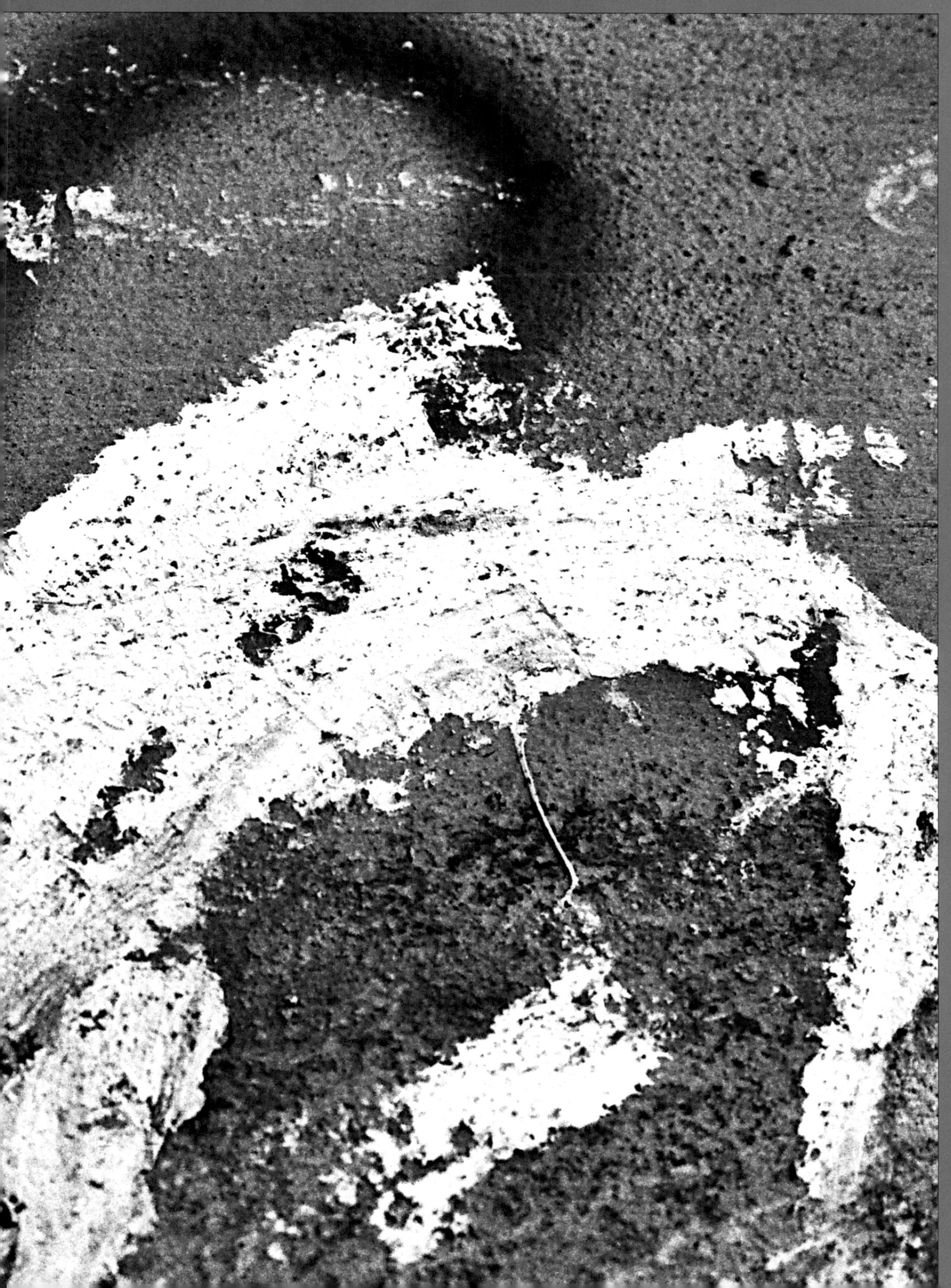

Forse Nino Migliori neppure lo sa; ma fra le non molte opere d'arte che circondavano Morandi nella sua casa di via Fondazza c'è anche una sua bella fotografia. S'è trovata infatti, fra le pagine d'un volume su Henry Cartier-Bresson (il solo libro di fotografia che Morandi teneva nella sua biblioteca) appunto una immagine di Migliori scattata nel 1958, ovviamente in bianco e nero; e raffigura, guarda caso, un brandello di muro, sbrecciato e consunto dal tempo e dalle intemperie. Somiglia, quell'intonaco sdrucito, a ciò che proprio in quegli anni non pochi pittori europei e americani evocavano nelle loro tele: da Burri a Tàpies, da Dubuffet a Fautrier, ed altri. Era, la loro, una ricerca sull'informe e sulla materia, perfino memore, chissà, delle considerazioni di Leonardo sulle fantasie che le irregolari casualità degli intonaci sui muri potevano suscitare, in tempi in cui s'apprezzava invece la mano precisa che traccia limiti e confini, guidata da una mente allenata alla geometria. E così ci è parso giusto, come primo passo della nostra fondazione, dar vita a ciò che Marilena Pasquali ha da tempo suggerito: e cioè una rassegna di muri; non dipinti, come quelli per cui la città di Dozza è divenuta a tutti nota, ma così come il caso li ha condotti sotto il nostro occhio. Certo, il nostro occhio neppure se ne sarebbe accorto, e non ci avrebbe proprio fatto caso, a quei muri; se i pittori non li avessero rievocati; ma questo è appunto, da sempre, il merito dei pittori: quello di aprirci gli occhi, e di attirare la nostra attenzione sui mille aspetti del mondo visibile, di cui neppure ci accorgeremmo. E anche la scelta di far iniziare questo percorso a Nino Migliori non è casuale. Migliori, infatti, è un fotografo: ma appunto per questo sa bene di essere l'erede di una millenaria tradizione figurativa, che dalle grotte di Lascaux si stende fino alle ninfee di Monet, e oltre, e che s'arresta per sempre proprio all'irrompere della civiltà industriale; quando cioè ogni usuale compito della pittura è sostituito dalla fotografia, dal cinema, e poi dalla tivù. Sa bene, cioè, che Picasso e Pollock non sono gli eredi e continuatori di Fidia e di Raffaello; i loro veri eredi sono Daguerre, Nadar, i fratelli Lumière, e così via: quelli che ancor oggi ci mostrano il volto del mondo, della nostra civiltà, e della nostra barbarie.
Ma Migliori, ecco, sente anche fortissima l'attrazione che il nuovo mondo dell'arte esercita tutt'attorno a sé; e quindi usa la macchina fotografica in modo inconsueto, e non solo per riprodurre il visibile; la pellicola e la carta sensibile, per lui, sono, come la tavolozza e la tela, strumenti di un'avventura dagli esiti imprevedibili, ove la fantasia si libera, e gioca con l'oggettività dell'obbiettivo fotografico, conducendolo perfino ad approdi opposti a quelli per cui è predisposta la macchina fotografica, con sorpresa di chi guarda.

Eugenio Riccòmini
Presidente
Fondazione Dozza Città d'Arte

> *"Platone nel Timeo asserisce che il 'fuoco sottile' che riscalda il corpo umano scorre fuor dagli occhi in un tenue torrente di luce. Così un ponte tangibile viene a stabilirsi tra l'osservatore e la cosa osservata e, sopra tale ponte, gli impulsi luminosi che emanano dall'oggetto viaggiano sino agli occhi e di lì all'anima"*
>
> Rudolf Arnheim, 1954[1]

> *"Se accettiamo la definizione per cui fotografia è scrittura di luce, e considerando che ho sempre cercato di fare qualcosa di simile alla scrittura usando la luce, posso allora definirmi fotografo"*
>
> Nino Migliori, 1997[2]

In un saggio fondamentale del 1977[3] Arturo Carlo Quintavalle pone le basi più salde per l'interpretazione del lavoro di Nino Migliori sui muri, una lettura imprescindibile per chiunque intenda affrontare ancora una volta questa che è certamente esperienza nodale e fondante nell'intera opera del fotografo bolognese, da tempo riconosciuto tra i protagonisti della fotografia non solo italiana.

Protratta per circa trent'anni[4], dai primi anni Cinquanta ai tardi anni Settanta, l'indagine di Migliori sui muri si rivela così ricca di interesse e di possibili stimoli visivi ed espressivi da fungere quasi da *fil rouge* per tutto il suo lavoro, in un coerente e costante sviluppo che va da una iniziale attenzione per gli affioramenti e l'espressività della materia stessa, osservata con sguardo libero dal giovane che pure respira l'aria dell'Informale, alla piena maturità della sua immagine fotografica, colta di preferenza nel gesto e nel segno che prendono ad abitare il muro e lo fanno parlare con il linguaggio della protesta, dell'ironia, dell'amore, perfino del sogno.

Quintavalle analizza le diverse fasi di questo lavoro approfondito ed appassionato in una ricerca che pare non avere fine, ma soprattutto ne indaga le ragioni teoriche e gli stimoli psicologico-percettivi, puntando la sua attenzione sulla categoria del tempo, in particolare sul concetto di durata, e sottolineando come nel discorso di Migliori "il punto centrale sta nella durata dell'immagine"[5].

Ma il senso del tempo di Migliori è davvero così "profondamente nuovo, rivoluzionario", e perché? Credo che una possibile risposta, evidentemente affermativa, stia nella sua singolare capacità di dare un corpo e un volto alla memoria, "fissando" un frammento del reale, astraendolo dal fluire del tempo, bloccandolo nell'apparente atemporalità dell'immagine e consegnandolo, appunto, alla durata. Ma, nel momento stesso in cui Migliori "salva" la porzione di vita che ha colpito la sua acuminata sensibilità di artista, ne riconosce anche la fine, la scomparsa come entità reale, come oggetto e vi sostituisce l'altrettanto intensa - e forse più affascinante - realtà dell'immagine.

Attratto ed ammaliato dalla stratificazione dei tempi degli uomini, da ciò che ora c'è e fra un attimo non sarà più - o, almeno, non sarà più così - il fotografo ne consegna una immagine, la sua, al tempo dell'opera che così diviene l'unica realtà, la trasposizione infedele e conturbante di ciò che è stato e non è più.

In tutto ciò si avverte anche la sua difficoltà, molto umana, di accettare la morte, quasi che individuare e selezionare brandelli di quotidiano, ciò che possiamo definire "fenomeno", e trasformarli in icona, valga a preservare anche il loro "salvatore", al quale l'opera garantisce una insostituibile possibilità di presenza, di durata, di vita.

Naturalmente questo non vale solo per Migliori né solo per i suoi *Muri*, ma è indubbio che il suo indagare senza sosta per quasi trent'anni questi palinsesti di vita, possa fornire un esempio tra i più autentici e convincenti della facoltà quasi medianica - scintilla divina della creazione, si diceva un tempo - che rende unici gli artisti e concede loro il dono di sconfiggere il tempo.

Non solo questo acuto senso dell'effimero ma anche il modo in cui Migliori lo affronta, e quindi il modo in cui egli "costruisce" l'immagine (uso volutamente questo termine per sottolineare la caratura dell'intervento dell'autore, il suo peso, la sua forza determinante) lo pongono fra coloro che nel dopoguerra per primi hanno saputo riconoscere ed interpretare l'inquietudine, il senso di angoscia esistenziale che la rinnovata consapevolezza della presenza del Male nel mondo aveva portato in dono a tutti con gli orrori della guerra e con i suoi infiniti strascichi di insicurezza, planetaria ed individuale. Scrive ancora Quintavalle che "la cronologia delle sue esperienze è assai 'alta' e i suoi tempi sono in perfetto parallelismo, se non antecedenti, a molto di quanto in pittura si viene elaborando" (chiaramente si riferisce ai *Décollages* di Mimmo Rotella, alle proposte di nuova materialità di Tàpies, a molte sperimentazioni informali dal *dripping* di Pollock agli assalti dissolventi alla forma del più vicino Vasco Bendini).

L'osservazione delle date dei *Muri* di Migliori è interessante non solo per l'inizio ma anche per la conclusione della sua ricerca: egli in pratica la abbandona verso la metà degli anni Settanta, allorchè lo scrivere sul muro e l'usarlo come supporto d'immagine diviene pratica artistica con il lavoro dei *Writers* e dei graffitisti americani (anche la maggior parte dei *Murales*, più o meno politici, più o meno artistici, nasce in quegli anni). Ma c'è una grande, fondamentale differenza concettuale tra il lavoro del writer o del graffitista e quella del fotografo: i primi compiono la loro opera, il loro intervento *sul* muro, *nel* corpo stesso del muro; il secondo si confronta con il muro e da questo porta fuori, astrae l'immagine, facendone cosa sua.

E' forse proprio da quando lo scrivere ed il dipingere i muri delle città sono ufficialmente entrati a far parte dei linguaggi artistici che Migliori ha smesso di creare immagini *dal* muro? E' forse perché non gli interessa fare opera da un'opera intenzionale, non spontanea ma programmata, linguisticamente orientata verso l'artisticità? Lasciamo la risposta all'artista - e Migliori mi perdonerà se mi viene naturale chiamarlo così, perché tale lo considero -. Una cosa mi pare però certa: i primi *Writers* a New York e sulla West Coast erano spontanei e autentici portatori di bisogni e richieste di una collettività marginalizzata (ed in quanto tali avrebbero potuto interessare Migliori), ma quando diventano scuola e vengono adottati dal mercato - *embedded*, si direbbe oggi -, quando si allineano ad un linguaggio più o meno codificato che diviene genere e poi maniera, allora escono decisamente dalla sua zona di interesse e di intervento. Tra le ultime opere del suo lungo ciclo figurano le immagini del *Muro dei drogati* scattate nel 1977, a Genova, ed in questo lavoro ben possiamo cogliere il discrimine fra materiale spontaneo che il fotografo interpreta e ricrea, da un lato, e l'ulteriore, possibile incontro tra due precise intenzionalità artistiche, dall'altro; ma fare immagine su un'immagine d'arte non è ciò che cerca Migliori nei muri metropolitani, altre sue ricerche andranno in tal senso[6], ma non ora e non qui, perché il muro per lui è innanzitutto racconto spontaneo di vita e di memoria.

Migliori si prende cura del muro, ne è "curioso" e lo fa con la sua naturale spontaneità gestuale, con la sua esuberanza di modi[7]. Come egli stesso sottolinea, il suo è un discorso linguistico, gestuale e semiologico che s'avvale di un metodo del tutto personale, ben preciso, definito nel rifiuto dei generi, degli ambiti, delle classificazioni per privilegiare due fasi del processo creativo: la percezione e la restituzione, in quella che Arnheim da par suo definisce "visione come esplorazione attiva"[8]. La percezione, in quanto presa di coscienza dell'esperienza sensibile, in lui è istintiva, immediata, acutissima perché, come tutti i veri artisti, egli è innanzitutto e soprattutto un "occhio" attraversato, vivificato dalla luce, quel "fuoco sottile" riconosciuto da Platone. Ma la percezione non basta, è necessaria con pari dignità anche la restituzione, cioè la capacità di tradurre in immagine autonoma lo stimolo visivo, il suggerimento sensoriale, l'accenno emotivo.

Si assiste dunque ad un doppio passaggio: dalla realtà, dalla personalità del muro, con la sua materia in costante trasformazione, i suoi gesti, le sue scritte, alla realtà e personalità del fotografo, che legge e interpreta ogni cosa come un traduttore infedele che sa diventare autore unico, fors'anche protagonista unico di quel riflesso del Sé che è l'immagine. Questo passaggio può ovviamente moltiplicarsi, aggiungendo segno a segno, gesto a gesto, in una catena di cancellazioni, di aggiunte e di ripristini e fusioni fra strato e strato che avrà fine soltanto con la distruzione totale del muro. Ciò che conta è che in tutto questo divenire l'unico punto fermo è rappresentato dall'occhio del fotografo, l'unica opera è la sua fotografia.

Quello di Migliori è dunque un approccio di tipo sostanzialmente gestaltico, cioè di forme e di rapporti tra le forme, di analogie e associazioni, di organizzazione ed orientamento dello spazio, quello spazio che egli definisce con nettezza, escludendo ogni disturbo visivo al di fuori della porzione di muro ritratta, ogni contestualizzazione, ogni cornice. Come acutamente osserva ancora Quintavalle, Migliori fotografa il muro, considerandolo come una superficie da incidere - e qui è la luce che lo fa, senza bisogno di punte né di morsure - perché, da fotografo, vuole vedere come quella pellicola, che è l'intonaco, sappia reagire al segno e all'intervento fotografico.

Per lui però il muro è anche una pagina di cui scegliere, coordinare e registrare i segni e i gesti di altri, unicamente di altri; una scrittura che poi, a ben guardare, non è altro che la sua stessa scrittura, cioè in filigrana la sua storia di uomo e di artista. Egli si comporta di fatto come il regista che si avvale della presenza attiva degli attori per un lavoro a più mani che porta in ogni caso la sua inconfondibile impronta; come il direttore d'orchestra che esegue la sua musica, la sua interpretazione attraverso l'azione dei professori strumentisti di cui indirizza e dirige ogni gesto.

Alcune osservazioni ancora mi premono, prima di esaminare più da vicino i *Muri* di Migliori, raggruppati in tre nuclei principali per data di esecuzione e per convenzione critica, anche se, proprio nell'analisi attenta delle singole fotografie e delle loro interrelazioni, si scopre che i confini non sono poi così netti e che nello stesso periodo la ricerca di Nino sulla memoria si incrocia con quella sul gesto e questa con le immagini in cui l'autore scopre un segno particolarmente evocativo. E mi sia concesso di rafforzare con il grassetto alcuni termini che considero parole-chiave per l'interpretazione del suo lavoro.

In primo luogo mi preme sottolineare la stretta, indispensabile e contraddittoria relazione che si instaura fra lo sguardo sempre disponibile - apprensivo e quasi famelico - di Nino e il **caso**. Non è necessario qui riprendere la *vexata quaestio* tra casualità e causalità, è piuttosto opportuno ricordare come questo fotografo, questo artista sappia cogliere l'occasione - anche la più imprevista e fortuita - e farla sua, dando un ordine a ciò che passa e va, come un demiurgo mutando il caos in cosmos. Tale atto di trasformazione e di appropriazione avviene attraverso lo strumento del **riconoscimento**, che è essenzialmente rapporto con il **visibile** (parola assai cara ai pittori, e penso anche ai fotografi), cioè con il fenomeno, la manifestazione della realtà, la sua apparenza ottica e sensoriale.

Oltre a ciò va sottolineata la **profondità** del *Muro* di Migliori, quella sua ricchezza di stratificazione e di presenza che lo rende inesauribile come fonte di stupore e di racconto. In esso si avverte con potenza che c'è qualche cosa d'altro oltre il primo piano, qualche cosa che preme per emergere, per guadagnare anch'essa la scena; e Nino non può non restare, lui per primo, affascinato da questa possibilità di andare al di là dell'apparenza, così da far emergere **il non detto, il non visto**, e dargli dignità d'immagine.

Unito al tema della profondità va considerato anche quello del **rapporto figura-sfondo**: attenzione infatti alle immagini di Migliori perché assai spesso, per la loro funambolica capacità metamorfica, in esse tale rapporto si ribalta e ciò che, come novella Cenerentola dovrebbe restare in ombra, esce invece in pieno sole. Ma poi, se si indaga ancora, si scopre che nel *Muro* di Nino **tutto è figura**, tutto è protagonista con pari diritti, dal momento che la scelta è stata fatta dall'autore a priori, nel taglio, nell'inquadratura, e quindi tutto nell'immagine è accettato, nulla resta in sordina di quanto egli ha voluto comprendervi.

Ed ecco infine un tema dall'artista toccato più volte, quello del **paesaggio**. Riconosce infatti Migliori in un testo pubblicato nel 1993, in occasione della XLV Biennale di Venezia[9] : " Per me il paesaggio è tutto, non solo la documentazione di ciò che vedo, è nella mente prima che negli oggetti che mi circondano; è quello che vedi, ti affascina, ti stimola. Non è solo il discorso naturalistico di riproduzione, è la cartolina illustrata, è la rivisitazione del costume della gente, è il selciato, è la strada che percorriamo, che varia da zona a zona, da clima a clima, che passa dal fango alla ghiaia, dalla ghiaia all'asfalto dell'autostrada".

E allora, guardando i suoi *Muri*, mi viene da accostarli anche concettualmente a quella che può esser vista come il loro *alter ego* e che è anche il loro palcoscenico, la loro dimensione quotidiana: la strada. Entrambi sono luoghi dell'incontro, cercato o casuale che sia, e come tali appaiono fortemente caratterizzati dalla presenza dell'uomo e si presentano come l'opposto - salvifico, necessario - di quei terrificanti, disumanizzanti non-luoghi studiati dall'odierna sociologia per denunciarne la pericolosità: gli aeroporti, i supermercati, le autostrade e tutto ciò che è progettato e realizzato per appiattire le differenze e, con queste, l'umanità stessa dell'uomo.

Al contrario - e, vorrei aggiungere, per fortuna - i *Muri* di Migliori sono luoghi dell'umano e, al tempo stesso, sono paesaggi interiori, riunendo in un unico atto, che è del cuore e della mente prima ancora che dello sguardo e della mano, quel processo di identificazione fra uomo e natura, fra uomo e ambiente, che solo consente al primo di riconoscere e amare ciò che lo circonda, di farsene dimora e di trasformarlo in spazio per ogni più arrischiata avventura, per ogni ripresa del cammino, per ogni nuovo inizio.

In questa strada comune, che Migliori percorre attraverso la sua immagine, non c'è un tipo di muro che lo attragga più di altri: certamente il prescelto, quello che in un raptus immediato dello sguardo lo ferma e lo invita alla sfida dello scatto fotografico, deve essere un muro "vissuto", di segno intenso, ma ciò che gli importa veramente è, per usare un'espressione assai felice che appartiene ai mondi paralleli della psicologia e della pedagogia[10], "dare un nome alle nuvole", procedere per analogie, echi e rimandi, "inventare" il muro nel senso originale del verbo, da invenio, cioè trovo.
Nei primi anni Cinquanta la sua attenzione è concentrata sulle tracce del tempo, sulla memoria negletta che il muro conserva e ostende, sul volto inconscio, rimosso della città[11]. E qui tutto lo interessa: la porzione di muro rigonfia di materia, che nello sfaldarsi progressivo degli intonaci diviene "figura" (penso in particolare al volto da incubo, di fantasma minaccioso, che affiora per sottrazione in una fotografia in bianco e nero del 1950) come la superficie fittamente, ossessivamente incisa in cui ogni graffito, ogni segno aggiunto - o, forse, sottratto- non fanno altro che aumentare l'impressione di un andamento a onde, quasi da scrittura musicale dell'insieme; il *Muro* su cui il gioco è tutto del colore, anche molto aggressivo come accade in quello verde del 1950, in cui il colore vivace del fondo piuttosto che alleggerire accentua la drammaticità di una macchia nera che pare ancora colare come sangue rappreso sul muro di una fucilazione (ma, con le sue borchie piantate nel verde e ormai corrose, il frammento potrebbe anche essere metafora metropolitana del legno della Croce); il muro su cui compare un nitido segno bianco sulla pelle vellutata del nero, le prime scritte, i primi disegnini – l'uomo con i palloncini, un volto da faunetto appena schizzato, due sagome di bimbi che si tengono per mano come nei girotondi ritagliati con le forbici nella carta -, in cui si avverte con chiarezza l'amore di Nino per le figure in continua metamorfosi di Paul Klee, come lui affascinato dal disegno infantile, matrice di ogni pensiero visivo, sorgente inesauribile di scoperte; le superfici da cui affiorano muffe o su cui fioriscono escrescenze e quelle tutte corrose e bucherellate dalle cadute di intonaco, certamente le più "informali" tra le opere di Migliori, ottenute grazie ad un processo di addizione e sottrazione che in una tessitura complessa di vuoto e pieno unisce alla trama di crepe, buchi ed erosioni un ordito di crateri, rigonfiamenti ed esplosioni di materia.
Ma non basta ancora, perché è immagine di un tempo troppo spesso negato anche la superficie "mangiata" da un'ombra nera che la invade come una lebbra infuocata (e qui non si può non pensare alle coeve esperienze *off-camera* di Migliori ed ai suoi *Pirogrammi*), e le figure di elementare, contratta poeticità che emergono ritagliandosi dallo sfondo fino a diventare icona, come il "re" e la "regina" scoperti da Migliori nei primissimi anni Cinquanta su un rosso muro bolognese di via Fondazza e da lui donati a Giorgio Morandi, durante uno degli incontri in cui, superando tutte le barriere di età, differenze culturali e scelte estetiche, il vecchio maestro e il giovane fotografo parlano di fotografia, di cinema, di pittura: cioè semplicemente di immagine.

Si approfondisce in seguito la ricerca sul gesto e sui "manifesti strappati" - e siamo tra gli anni Cinquanta e la ripresa del tema nei primi anni Settanta -, forse il momento più chiassoso, da periferia metropolitana e quindi più disperato, dell'intero lavoro sui *Muri.* Che le foto siano in bianco e nero o a colori poco importa, ciò che conta è l'incontro-scontro dei colori timbrici che aggrediscono il nostro sguardo, quasi la sensazione di un lacerarsi troppo rumoroso della carta che assedia senza possibilità di riparo il nostro orecchio interiore: provocazioni visive e auditive che stanno lì, nella foto, come prove concrete e tangibili dell'inanità di ogni messaggio pubblicitario, della vacuità di ogni promessa mediatica di cui si scopre il balbettìo insensato, la ripetizione indifferente, la sostanziale falsità e inutilità.

Ma, al di là di un discorso propriamente politico-sociale, ciò che qui viene messo in discussione è il linguaggio, la capacità umana di scambiarsi parole per comunicare e, utopia delle utopie, magari per comprendersi. In questa torre di Babele di lettere perdute, parole incomplete e frasi smozzicate che si sovrappongono freneticamente per mangiarsi e annullarsi l'un l'altra, regna sovrana una sensazione di precarietà, di inquietudine, di perdita del senso. Forse ciò che resta, ciò che anzi assume identità e vigore in questa deriva di gesti distruttivi, è proprio il vuoto, il frammento di spazio libero, la nuova forma che si crea negli interstizi tra le forme non più significanti.

E poi, a volte, nei *Muri* di Migliori questa strapazzata, calpestata, rifiutata immagine di massa riesce a trasformarsi e a divenire qualche cosa di unico: mi hanno infatti particolarmente colpito quattro foto, tutte accomunate dalla stessa magia, quella dello sguardo che riesce a rompere il bozzolo delle parole rifiutate per rivolgersi intatto al passante casuale ed al fotografo-cacciatore, in un gioco di rimandi e di richieste perentorie di attenzione, in un *panopticon* come dimensione visiva in cui non si sa più chi sia l'osservato e chi l'osservatore ma che certamente costruisce una possibilità di dialogo. Nelle prime due immagini sono gli occhioni ammiccanti di personaggi dei fumetti dell'epoca a trapassare gli strati di carta per guardarci diritti in faccia; nella terza foto è lo sguardo imperioso dell'unico occhio di Moshe Dayan che esce dalla penombra di un manifesto illeggibile per pretendere attenzione; nella quarta emerge dal rosso sangue della stupidità e malvagità umane lo sguardo consapevole e, nonostante tutto, sereno di Antonio Gramsci.

All'aprirsi degli anni Settanta la ricerca di Migliori concentra l'attenzione, con un approccio fortemente motivato, alle scritte sui muri, ai segni - questi sì, colmi di significato - che gli uomini, i singoli uomini lasciano sui muri della città per raccontarsi, affermarsi, confrontarsi.
In queste opere non si avverte il senso di solitudine che prende alla gola nei "manifesti strappati" ed anzi pare di assistere e di partecipare ad un discorso a più voci, ad un coro in cui le individualità si sfidano, si rincorrono, si corteggiano, si rifiutano.
Nino è regista e interprete di tutto: dei messaggi politici, veri e propri palinsesti di segni ove i colori giocano un ruolo fondamentale ed ancor più importante appare il bianco pesante della cancellazione che consente l'inizio di un nuovo round; della scritta decodificata in trenta ideogrammi della complessa operazione del 1975, *In immagin abile - Lessico distratto*; delle grandi, persino solenni icone di *PACE GUERRA E POI PACE* e di *EUROPA LIBERA*, che sono diventate per molti di noi autentici paradigmi visivi di richieste irrinunciabili, oggi più che mai attuali e urgenti.
Un po' dappertutto ed in particolare sul rosso affocato di tanti muri bolognesi, Migliori trova anche e fa proprie le immagini degli altri, da quelle sfumate e approssimative come le sagome elementari tracciate da mani inesperte - un profilo di donna, una silhouette barbuta, una profetica sveglia "elettorale" che trent'anni più tardi riprenderà a suonare - ai simboli inquietanti del terrore, la stella a cinque punte marchiata a fuoco nella carne nera del muro, un pugnale scuro che è anche croce ed insieme aeroplano e che si abbatte in picchiata lasciando nere scie di morte, fino ai "diavoletti" cornuti (pupazzi grotteschi nati dalla trasformazione di un'ascia bipenne, maschere dalle lunghe orecchie e dagli occhi allucinati) che parlano di sofferenza e di degrado ma anche di fantasia sbrigliata e di innata capacità di alleggerire il vivere anche più duro con uno sberleffo.

E, in ultimo come perle nella polvere, Migliori incontra le immagini della tenerezza: i "Ti Amo" ripetuti e ingranditi in un gesto ossessivo che è grido di liberazione; un "indiano disperato" che parla didascalicamente di politica, usando il muro come una lavagna di scuola elementare, per poi riconoscere sconsolato che sempre e soltanto di amore si tratta; la confessione struggente di "Io mi chiamo Daniela. Mi è morto il babbo", così stringata e totale nella sua dolorosa semplicità. L'artista ne è toccato, ma non per questo rinuncia all'attenzione per la pulizia della forma che sta a lui imprimere come una firma nell'immagine, isolandola e astraendola dal contesto.

E poi, infine, c'è un incontro particolare, forse unico per aura poetica e nitidezza dell'immagine, in cui la sua natura d'esteta incontra un segno raffinato che pare già di per sé opera, tanto che gli basta coglierlo con il suo sguardo esperto per offrirlo a tutti come un dono: è il *Fiore del muro rosa*, nato dall'incontro spontaneo fra la forma a calice di sei fori aperti nella parete e la creatività di un ignoto, certamente un animo giovane. Con la stessa, intatta giovinezza, oggi Migliori ce lo dona.

Marilena Pasquali

---

1) *Rudolf Arnheim, Arte e percezione visiva, Milano, Feltrinelli, 1984, p.56.*

2) *Paolo Barbaro, Conversazione con Nino Migliori, in Luci e Tracce, Cavezzo, 1997.*

3) *Arturo Carlo Quintavalle, Muri, in catalogo della mostra Antonio Migliori, Parma, Salone dei Contrafforti, 1977, p. 30-33.*

4) *Ibidem, p. 30. " Fotografavo i muri perché mi interessava l'uomo, è l'unica documentazione del passato dell'uomo, dalle grotte di Altamira fino ai graffiti o alle pitture sui muri di Pompei. L'uomo davanti ai muri si disinibisce, sia che adoperi una moneta, una chiave per graffiare o un pezzo di gesso o una bomboletta spray, libera il suo inconscio, la sua gestualità ed è se stesso. Ecco perché la ricerca sul muro, ia macchia, l'informe, le muffe, l'umidità, le tracce. Soprattutto i muri dove vi sono interventi successivi di decine di persone hanno un fascino particolare per ché documentano il passaggio del mondo. Morandi era molto attento alla fotografia, gli piacevano molto i miei muri e qualcuno, che avevo fatto in via Fondazza, se lo teneva in studio, come quello dove si vedono un paio di figure informali che lui chiamava il re e la regina. Fu lui che mi parlò di Brassaï, e mi fece vedere lui, appunto, Brassaï ; aveva anche libri di Cartier-Bresson, di Bishof, di Capa; ma a Morandi piaceva Bresson. Discutevo con lui di queste fotografie. La linea di ricerca di Brassaï, il suo libro sui " Graffiti", che ho visto di sfuggita, in fondo fa una ricerca su questo tema che però è al di fuori della sua fotografia che invece esce tutta da Bresson e dalla sua concezione dell'immagine rapita; si tratta di un documento su Parigi, molto attento al segno, al segno appunto graffito e quindi alla storia di Parigi; mi pare che il discorso che ho portato avanti io sia diverso. Quanto alla tecnica è semplice, parto da una diapositiva a colori, oppure da un negativo in bianco e nero e tendo ad avvicinarmi molto per isolare il solo particolare; quasi mai, salvo pochissimi casi appunto, scelgo l'insieme. Ho sempre cercato di estrarre la scena dall'ambiente. "*

5) *Ibidem, p. 31.*

6) *Ricordo la sua interessantissima indagine, Segnificazione, su un'incisione del Guercino, letta come traduttore "infedele" nei suoi particolari di scrittura e presentata nell'ambito della indimenticabile mostra di Franco Solmi, Metafisica del Quotidiano, organizzata nell'estate 1978 alla Galleria d'arte moderna di Bologna.*

7) *Devo queste felici definizioni a Claretta Stefanelli Spatzer, la quale nel 1992 propone un interessante confronto fra la fotografia off- camera di Luigi Veronesi, da lei definito "apollinea", e quella "dionisiaca" di Nino Migliori.*

8) *Rudolf Arnheim, cit., p.55.*

9) *Cfr. Arturo Carlo Quintavalle, Muri di carta, Fotografia e paesaggio dopo le avanguardie, Milano, Electa, 1993, p.91.*

10) *Migliori è certamente un maestro nell'educazione all'immagine per i giovani, e da anni si dedica con passione alle iniziative che possono favorire l'ingresso della conoscenza della fotografia nella scuola, collaborando con distretti e istituti scolastici come con facoltà universitarie e con assessorati all'istruzione.*

11) *Vale, a questo proposito, riportare un'altra illuminante riflessione di Quintavalle (cit., 1977, p. 32): "L'idea che l'intonaco sia graffito, che sia fiorito di muffe, scolato di colori sbavati, che sia gonfio di umidità o polverulento per il calore del sole d'estate, che sia addensato di manifesti strappati o scolorito, fa parte della storia urbana, anzi della percezione della città. Per adesso nessuno lo ha ancora fatto ma verrà un giorno che metà delle analisi degli urbanisti sulle città, sulle città come strumenti di comunicazione, saranno proprio sulle pavimentazioni, sugli intonaci, sulle pareti scrostate, sulle scritte". E chiunque intenda farlo, aggiungo io, non potrà prescindere dal lavoro di Nino Migliori.*

"Facevo i *Muri* perché mi interessava l'uomo, è l'unica documentazione del passato dell'uomo dalle grotte di Altamira fino ai graffiti o alle pitture sui muri di Pompei. L'uomo davanti ai muri si disinibisce, sia che adoperi una moneta, una chiave per graffiare o un pezzo di gesso o una bomboletta spray, libera il suo inconscio, la sua gestualità ed è se stesso"; questa dichiarazione di Migliori - tratta dalla monografia di A. C. Quintavalle[1] del 1977 - risulta preziosa perché consente di afferrare esattamente quale fosse l'interesse principale del nostro autore. Qui infatti noi possiamo osservare un ricco repertorio di testimonianze nelle quali l'opera di documentazione che è implicita alla nozione stessa di servizio giornalistico viene piegata ad un'esigenza nuova: quella di fermare nel tempo, celebrandoli, un complesso di interventi umani costitutivamente votati all'effimero e all'irrilevanza pratica, che possono venire decifrati come altrettanti modelli di reazione psicologica nei confronti dell'ambiente dispersivo e spesso opprimente della metropoli.

L'azione di Migliori non è di prelevamento e ricollocazione dadaista, come pure venne interpretata, e neppure gli interessa astrarre particolari che possano assumere una soddisfacente valenza di ordine compositivo, nello stile formalistico di un Cavalli: in questo caso, piuttosto, "il fotografo avvicina il muro come una grande lavagna, su cui natura e uomini hanno lasciato una impronta che è soprattutto quella del *tempo*"[2].

Ci imbattiamo dunque nel tema della temporalità che non viene evocata come campionatura dell'istante, ma al contrario le muffe, le scialbature sbucciate, le cancellature o le correzioni di precedenti scritte inducono un senso di consumazione, di lenta e inarrestabile dissoluzione che molto più tardi, nel 1976, Migliori ha saputo esprimere anche in riferimento a sé nella celebre sequenza di autoritratti dove il suo volto cede progressivamente i lineamenti alla sagoma di un teschio.

Spesso queste immagini fuggono da ogni ricercatezza, il muro non è ispezionato al fine precipuo di ricavarne una composizione astratta, informale o di "nuova scrittura": esse si limitano a registrare la sedimentazione progressiva di tracce grafiche o scritturali che rinviano ad anonime presenze umane, in una forma comparativamente non dissimile, sotto il profilo etologico, dalla emissione di tracce biologiche praticata da alcune specie animali al fine di marcare l'appartenenza del territorio.

Occorre rilevare che il numero di fotografi almeno episodicamente interessati a questo tema fu tale da suscitare anche la curiosità di uno studioso come Umberto Eco, che pubblicò un breve saggio sull'argomento nel 1961[3] . Esaminando alcuni aspetti della produzione di altri fotografi sul medesimo soggetto ci occuperemo pertanto del francese Brassaï e dello statunitense Aaron Siskind.

Parlando di Brassaï, il quale già negli anni Trenta aveva realizzato una celebre serie fotografica dedicata ai *Graffiti parisiens*, risulta abbastanza comprensibile il motivo per il quale egli sia stato spesso considerato un referente, seppur inconsapevole, del lavoro di Migliori: le analogie sono precise, ma una volta di più l'analisi non può arrestarsi ad un livello di semplice grammatica della visione.

Anzitutto, esaminando un insieme più ampio di immagini che presentano il medesimo soggetto si può verificare la sussistenza di una "storia delle scritte", così come è stata prefigurata da Quintavalle[4] e idonea per riconoscere una cronologia delle tecniche, dei temi o dei movimenti di varia natura. Sotto questo profilo, ad esempio, potremmo difficilmente aspettarci una scritta a spray, o la presenza di particolari slogan politici in una foto dell'autore francese, ma questo ci induce ad allargare ulteriormente l'orizzonte di osservazione.

Riflettendo sul complesso delle rispettive produzioni potremmo allora ricordare che "la poetica di Brassaï è quella di Bresson e dell'idealismo bergsoniano della cultura francese: il fotografo deve essere un testimone che si nasconde davanti all'evento, deve cogliere la immagine e portarla ad altri, e l'immagine deve essere racconto"[5] . Il suo è dunque un discorso sulla città, sugli episodi rilevanti o irrilevanti del quotidiano, su personaggi e scorci osservati con ironia disincantata e purtuttavia non priva di una screziatura di nostalgia; una cronaca, in definitiva, che vuole subito farsi storia perché consapevole di valorizzare aspetti fugaci di una città in rapida trasformazione.

Ben diverso, come si può intuire, è l'ambiente culturale di Migliori nonché il suo atteggiamento di fondo nei confronti della fotografia. Si potrebbe intanto sottolineare che la scelta di mantenere attiva questa produzione per molti anni è stata accompagnata da un progressivo slittamento del suo nucleo d'interesse precipuo, non rintracciabile nell'autore francese. Parole recenti di Migliori chiariscono in merito che tutto il lavoro "forse lo si può dividere in due o tre periodi. Inizialmente sono stato spinto dalla curiosità per i segni sui muri, poi l'interesse per le macchie e le muffe, l'informale riletto attraverso il muro, e per finire viene il discorso delle scritte sui muri. È un periodo in cui considero il muro come supporto di scrittura, di comunicazione, di gestualità"[6]. Partizioni, queste, di entità peraltro flessibile dal momento che egli stesso conferma di aver "sempre affrontato i muri in modo abbastanza istintivo", senza obbligarsi a "pensare per percorsi predisposti"[7] .

Se d'altro canto si inquadra anche questa produzione in un ambito più generale, comprensivo delle parallele ricerche in camera oscura di Migliori, possiamo notare che si evidenzia una persistente ricerca sulle possibilità e le forme della scrittura fotografica in quanto tale. Da questo punto di vista possiamo dunque collocare questa investigazione su altre scritture - ideografiche, gestuali o alfabetiche - in una zona liminare tra i due mondi dell'*in* e dell'*off-camera*, che si affianca e talvolta si sovrappone alla precedente. Molti negativi realizzati con l'apparecchio fotografico diverranno infatti pretesto grafico per una serie di successivi trattamenti sotto l'ingranditore.

Diversamente da Brassaï, che si è interessato ai muri solo in un momento preciso della propria attività, per il newyorkese Aaron Siskind la scelta di isolare con l'obbiettivo porzioni minime di realtà ha assunto nel tempo una cifra stilistica inconfondibile.

Per comprenderne il significato, in questo caso è necessario ripercorrere brevemente l'itinerario professionale del fotografo, che principia negli anni Trenta con la realizzazione di alcuni reportage per la "Film & Photo League"; *Harlem document* e altri lavori, peraltro, si distinguono subito per l'estrema raffinatezza delle immagini, dimostrando come "anche nella fase di maggiore dedizione documentaristica Siskind non abbia mai perso di vista i valori della composizione"[8] .

L'insoddisfazione per questo tipo di attività si manifesta però qualche anno più tardi, quando l'autore - nell'estate del 1944 - giunge ad una determinazione che segnerà il corso dell'intera produzione successiva; Siskind, infatti, si accorge che "for the first time in my life, subject matter (...) has ceased to be of primary importance. Instead, I found myself involved in the relationships of these objects, so much so that these pictures turned out to be deeply moving and personal experiences"[9]. In questa direzione risultano interessanti altre affermazioni di registro espressionista, come "the interior drama is the meaning of the exterior event"[10], oppure riguardo una concezione della fotografia "shifted from what the world looks like to what we feel about the world and what we want the world to mean"[11]. Questo atteggiamento di fondo lo porterà necessariamente ad avvicinarsi all'ambiente dell'*action painting*, che proprio nella città di New York trovò un luogo d'elezione, attraverso una serie di rapporti abbastanza stretti, benché non sempre lineari, con i suoi principali esponenti[12]. Presto il tema del muro - prevalentemente reso con tonalità fortemente contrastate di bianco e nero - verrà sempre più frequentato sino a diventare pressoché esclusivo, in esito della presumibile esigenza di fermare su una superficie bidimensionale alcuni frammenti delle proprie proiezioni psichiche. Quest'ipotesi è confermata da altre dichiarazioni dell'autore, laddove confessa che "these photographs are psychological in character"[13], in quanto[14] "the reason I'm making pictures is out of a necessity to order the world, which is really ordering myself" .

Anticipando un raffronto con l'informale pittorico che dovremo subito recuperare più ampiamente, possiamo intanto rilevare che mentre nell'espressionismo astratto troviamo una continua ricerca di spontaneità istintiva e la compiutezza formale dell'opera generalmente deriva dalla reiterata pratica dell'automatismo psichico che tende ad annullare la tecnica pittorica, o piuttosto a renderla "trasparente", nel caso specifico di Siskind, al contrario, la estrema perfezione tecnica capovolge questo rapporto, raggrumando il gesto in piccoli cristalli iconici, pur sublimi ed affascinanti nel loro algore. Ciò evidentemente trova spiegazione nelle impeccabili procedure di ripresa, che risentono ancora fortemente della perizia acquisita negli anni di tirocinio fotogiornalistico e che - malgrado le apparenze - dispongono questa operazione perfettamente in linea con la mentalità oggettivante del Bauhaus, a cui sopra abbiamo accennato. Non dobbiamo infatti dimenticare che questo autore insegnò ed in seguito diresse per lungo tempo il Dipartimento di Fotografia dell'Insitute of Design, fondato nel 1944 dallo stesso Moholy-Nagy a Chicago.

I muri del fotografo americano, pertanto, rappresentano il frutto di un'attività documentaristica che si è evoluta in un ricerca di sé e della propria interiorità attraverso il soggetto ripreso: da questo punto di osservazione Migliori appare lontano. In definitiva però noi stiamo esaminando in entrambi gli autori una produzione talvolta molto simile esteriormente, che pur collocandosi all'interno di percorsi assai differenti ritrova poi elementi di accordo anche in una concezione generale della fotografia intesa, sempre nelle parole di Siskind, come "transformation or transfiguration" [15] di eventi e oggetti della realtà.

Se valutiamo invece questa produzione secondo una prospettiva più ampia, che coinvolga gli orientamenti maturati nel mondo delle arti visive durante gli anni Cinquanta, non è certamente possibile ignorare le forti analogie che questi lavori presentano sul piano visuale con alcune realizzazioni dell'informale, tali da giustificare il loro inserimento all'interno di rassegne artistiche ad esso dedicate[16] .

Il problema dunque, ancora una volta, insiste sul margine di accettabilità del confronto dialettico che accompagna l'intera storia della fotografia sin dalle origini, e che la critica in questo caso ha riferito ad autori italiani come Burri, Schifano o ai *décollages* di Rotella, oltre che a Wols, Dubuffet, Twombly e Tàpies.

Esaminando parallelamente sotto il profilo pittorico e fotografico il significato dei due soggetti che risultano qui predominanti, il segno e la materia, potremo compiere alcune osservazioni che ci aiuteranno a definire nel merito una posizione più precisa, senza peraltro dimenticare che Migliori ha avviato questa ricerca in forma assolutamente autonoma, talvolta in anticipo rispetto alle opere informali cui molte sue realizzazioni potrebbero eventualmente essere confrontate e comunque senza conoscere direttamente i protagonisti di questa corrente.

Anzitutto si può notare che la tecnica impiegata in questo caso da Migliori è quella convenzionalmente trasmessa, che prevede l'impiego dell'apparecchio fotografico e nei confronti della quale non vengono operate trasgressioni all'infuori di un ribaltamento del tradizionale rapporto figura/sfondo, o meglio di una loro sostanziale identificazione. Sotto questo aspetto non sembrerebbe giustificabile per questi lavori il riconoscimento di un differente statuto critico: potremmo dunque recuperare le stesse considerazioni valide per un paesaggio fotografico dell'Ottocento nei confronti di una analoga pittura ad olio, ma la nostra ricerca è diretta altrove. Procedendo, l'analisi del segno nella poetica informale coinvolge l'artista in una relazione particolarmente forte: esso si qualifica come qualcosa di intimamente personale e privato, talvolta orientato in senso regressivo all'infanzia o alla patologia, mentre al contrario queste fotografie, spogliate di ogni eventuale potenzialità proiettiva, raccolgono impronte altrui. Non casualmente, il segno tracciato in un quadro è destinato ad una vita più ritirata, entro i locali dell'atelier o della galleria e al cospetto di un pubblico selezionato; nelle immagini di Migliori il segno è pubblico, alla mercé di chiunque e solo eccezionalmente di addetti ai lavori. Tale segno, inoltre, non viene solitamente attuato con finalità artistiche: in caso contrario, al di là di approssimative rassomiglianze, esso raramente possiede il grado di consapevolezza che generalmente accompagna l'attività dell'artista professionista. Se è possibile interpretare la caducità come termine medio tra l'atto che produce il graffito e lo stesso gesto del fotografare, in quanto entrambe le operazioni si confrontano con materiali - l'intonaco e la pellicola fotosensibile - strutturalmente fragili e votati all'autodistruzione, la materia fisica del quadro e, per conseguenza, la memoria in essa custodita accolgono con sicurezza ben maggiore la sfida del tempo. Esaminando ulteriormente questo secondo termine, è del tutto evidente che nella fotografia la materia viene semplicemente rappresentata attraverso due dimensioni e spesso due tonalità, il bianco e nero, mentre la materia pittorica è reale, tridimensionale al punto di revocare spesso il confine con le stesse discipline plastiche. In una stampa fotografica la materia è parte di un insieme funzionale, poiché si tratta pur sempre di edifici che assolvono la propria funzione indipendentemente dalle muffe o dalle scritture che possono comparirvi: da mere sovrastrutture biologiche o culturali quali sono, questi elementi si trasfigurano solo agli occhi di chi li studia o li ammira. Diversamente la materia informale, combusta, entropizzata oppure al contrario primigenia, germinale e palingenetica non risulta in ogni caso funzionale, all'infuori dei termini espressivi entro i quali si trova collocata. Le dimensioni o la fisicità complessiva di molti interventi pittorici, infine, alle quali non è peraltro estraneo il carico di riflessi empatici suscitati dall'elemento cromatico, determinano un poderoso impatto percettivo che non può venire surrogato in alcun modo dal cartoncino fotografico.

Da ultimo ed in riferimento ad un accenno dello stesso Migliori, contenuto nella frase riportata in apertura del presente intervento, ricorderemo brevemente anche una lettura in chiave psicoanalitica di questa produzione, pur essendo consapevoli del fatto che all'epoca l'autore, per sua stessa ammissione, non conosceva quell'ambito di ricerca introspettiva. Sicuramente scritte e graffiti rappresentano per chi li traccia un "momento liberatorio dell'angoscia, della passione, della libidine"[17] , mentre nello stesso tempo "se fotografi un muro che ha una storia, un muro dove molti hanno lasciato traccia del proprio passaggio, conduci sulla città un'operazione profondamente rivoluzionaria perché poni l'accento proprio su quanto è stato rimosso, sul "vecchio", su tutto ciò, insomma, che non può essere venduto, spacciato, ritenuto insomma "antico" "[18] .

In questo atteggiamento è peraltro individuabile una ragione del grande successo che queste fotografie incontrarono, esprimendo una sensibilità diffusa nel secondo dopoguerra.

Flavio Eugenio Marelli

[1]   A.C. Quintavalle, Antonio Migliori, catalogo della mostra, C.S.A.C. Dipartimento fotografia, Parma, 1977.

[2]   Vedi A. Colombo, Nino Migliori, in "Progresso fotografico", novembre 1977, p. 55.

[3]   Vedi U. Eco, Di foto fatte sui muri, in "Il Verri" n°4, Milano, 1961.

[4]   Vedi A.C. Quintavalle (a cura di), Enciclopedia pratica per fotografare, Fabbri, Milano, 1979, pp. 1434 e 1436.

[5]   Ivi, p. 1432.

[6]   Vedi P. Barbaro, C. Cavatorta, N. Migliori, Luci e tracce, Assessorato alla Cultura di Cavezzo, Cavezzo, 1997, p. 9.

[7]   Ibidem.

[8]   Vedi L. Ballerini, Le meraviglie del mondo screziato, o la canzone d'amore di Aaron Siskind, in G. Scimè (a cura di), Aaron Siskind. Cinquant'anni di fotografia 1931 - 1981, Selezione d Immagini, Milano, 1984, p.13.

[9]   Vedi J. Green, American Photography. A critical history 1945 to the present, Harry N. Abrams Inc., New York, 1984, p. 53.

[10]   Ibidem.

[11]   Ivi, p. 55.

[12]   Sull'argomento apprendiamo infatti da James Enyeart, Direttore del Center for Creative Photography dell'Università dell'Arizona, che nonostante il primo libro fotografico di Aaron Siskind fosse stato parzialmente finanziato dalla vendita di un dipinto di Franz Kline e presentato da Harold Rosenberg, critico e sostenitore del movimento, pur tuttavia il lavoro del fotografo venne solo in parte accettato dagli artisti (vedi G. Scimè , 1984, p. 7).

[13]   Vedi J. Green, 1984, p. 53.

[14]   Ivi, p. 55.

[15]   Ibidem.

[16]   Vedi l'esposizione su L'informale in Italia, a cura di Renato Barilli e Franco Solmi, svoltasi presso la Galleria d'Arte Moderna di Bologna nel 1983, che dedicò una sezione alla "fotografia informale" nella quale furono esposte immagini di Nino Migliori, Paolo Monti, Emilio Vedova e Luca Patella.

[17]   Vedi Migliori al Diaframma, in "Progresso fotografico", Milano, aprile 1974, p. 8.

[18]   Vedi A. C. Quintavalle , 1977, p. 31.

MOSTRE PERSONALI SELEZIONATE

1955
Antonio Migliori, Salone del Podestà, Bologna,
1-22 giugno.

1975
Trois photographes italiens – Nino Migliori,
Fnac Etoile, Paris, 1 settembre – 11 ottobre.

1977
Nino Migliori, Palazzo della Pilotta, CSAC,
Università di Parma, 1-27 marzo.

1982
Photographemi, Studio Marconi, Milano,
novembre.

1985
Carte ossidate, Palazzo Massari, Ferrara, 16
marzo-18 aprile.

1999
Instant, Palazzo Ducale, Galleria d'Arte
Contemporanea, Pavullo, 26 settembre-
24 ottobre.

Il neorealismo di Nino Migliori, Palazzo delle
Nazioni, Fiera di Padova, 30 ottobre -1 novembre

2000
Nino Migliori, Premio Internazionale Guglielmo
Marconi, Galleria Paolo Nanni, Bologna, 15
aprile-10 maggio.

Trasfigurazioni, Villa Gori-Stiava, Lucca, 8 luglio-
6 agosto.

2001
Neorealismo – Scenes of life in post-war Italy,
Keith de Lellis Gallery, New York, 12 gennaio –
3 marzo.

Neorealismo, ArtScan Gallery, Houston, 15
marzo - 23 aprile.

2002
Nino Migliori. Le Avanguardie e il Realismo,
Galleria Fiaf, Torino, 7 febbraio-15 marzo.

Nino Migliori. Ombre di Luce-50 anni di ricerca
sul potere della visione, Fondazione Italiana per
la Fotografia, Torino, 7 febbraio-24 marzo.

Nino Migliori. Materie e memorie nelle scritture
fotografiche, Galleria d' Arte Modena e
Contemporanea, Torino, 9 febbraio-14 aprile.

2003
Nino Migliori. Pop up, Museo Ken Damy di
Fotografia Contemporanea, Brescia,
10 maggio -7 settembre

MOSTRE COLLETTIVE SELEZIONATE

1954
VI e Salon International d'Art Photographique,
Bordeaux, febbraio.

1955
5e Esposition Internationale de Photographie,
Palais du Conservatoire, Lyon, 18 giugno- 10
luglio.

1956
The Danish Salon of Photography, Marienlyst-
Helsingor, 2-9 maggio.

Photokina – Internationale Photo und Kino
Ausstellung, Koln, 29 settembre – 7 ottobre.

1974
I Migliori, Galleria Il Diaframma, Milano, 2-13
aprile.

1975
Alle origini dell'arte, Galleria d'Arte Moderna,
Bologna, giugno.

1978
Metafisica del quotidiano, Galleria d'Arte
Moderna, Bologna, giugno.

1979
Venezia '79. La fotografia, Magazzini del Sale,
La Biennale di Venezia ,17 giugno-16 settembre.

1980
Fotografia e immagine dell'architettura, Galleria
d'Arte Moderna, Bologna, gennaio-febbraio.

1981
Linee della ricerca artistica in Italia 1960-1980,
Palazzo delle Esposizioni, Roma, febbraio-aprile.

1983
Fotogramme, Fotokunst Museum im Munchner
Staad Museum, 22 aprile-3 luglio.

L'Informale in Italia, Galleria d'Arte Moderna,
Bologna, giugno-settembre.

1985
The European Iceberg, The Art Gallery of
Ontario, Toronto, 8 febbraio-7 aprile.

1989
L'insistenza dello sguardo, Palazzo Fortuny,
Venezia, 25 marzo-2 luglio.

1990
Photogramme und die Kunst, Kunsthaus,
Zurigo, 31 marzo-27 maggio.

1993
Muri di carta, Padiglione Italia, XLV Biennale,
Venezia, 13 giugno-10 ottobre.

1994
The Italian Metamorphosis,1943-1968 Solomon
R. Guggenheim Museum, New York, 7 ottobre
1994-22 gennaio 1995;

1995
L' io e il suo doppio. Un secolo di ritratto
fotografico in Italia,1895-1995,
Padiglione Italia, XLVI Biennale, Venezia, 11
giugno-15 ottobre;

1996
Europa de postguerra 1945-1965. Art depres
del diluvi, Sala Catalunya, "La Caixa",
Barcellona, 12 maggio-30 luglio.

1997
Fotografia italiana per una collezione,
Fondazione italiana per la fotografia,Torino,
6 settembre-18 ottobre.

Un paese unico-Italia, fotografia 1900-2000,
Palazzo Medici-Riccardi, Firenze,
24 settembre-2 novembre.

1998
I Maestri, Castello di Venaria Reale, Torino,
2- 17 maggio.

1999
El neorrealismo en la fotografia italiana, Centro
Cultural del Conde Duque, Galeria del 98,
Madrid, 18 giugno-29 agosto.

Il Rosso e il Nero, Palazzo della Pilotta, Salone
delle Scuderie, Parma,
28 novembre 1999-13 febbraio 2000.

2000
Sport Illustrated, Jane Corkin Gallery , Toronto,
Canada,13 luglio-26 agosto.
Amen Fotografia, Villa Savorgnan, Lestans,
15 luglio-17 settembre.

2001
Esercizi di stile, Palazzina delle Arti, La Spezia,
26 gennaio – 25 febbraio.

Italian Neorealism, Fotofest, Houston, 15 marzo
- 23 aprile.

I fotografi e Morandi, Museo Morandi, Bologna,
1 aprile – 31 agosto.

Lo sperimentalismo fotografico in Italia, 1970 –
2000, Villa Savorgnan, Lestans, 14 luglio –
16 settembre.

Gli anni del Neorealismo. Tendenze della
fotografia italiana, Cassero, Prato
22 luglio – 16 agosto.

2002
Postwar Italian Photography, Museum of Fine
Arts, Houston, Texas, 2 febbraio – 28 aprile.

Collezione Permanente. Nuove Acquisizioni,
Centro per l'arte Contemporanea Luigi Pecci,
Prato. 10 luglio – 8 settembre.

2003
Mamme d'Italia, Stazione Centrale, Milano. 7 –
30 marzo Stazione Termini- Spazio espositivo,
Roma. 15 aprile – 4 maggio.

April showers – May flowers, Keith de Lellis
Gallery, New York.10 aprile – 13 giugno.

Flash: swimsuits and sports, Jackson Fine Art
Gallery, Atlanta, 11 luglio – 30 agosto.

Gli Anni della Dolce Vita. Tendenze della fotografia italiana, Museo dell'Automobile, Torino
6 dicembre 2003 – 1 febbraio 2004.

2004
Il museo, le collezioni,Museo di Fotografia
Contemporanea Villa Ghirlanda,
Cinisello Balsamo 3 aprile – 27 giugno.
Voolare, Palazzina delle Arti, La Spezia,
6 maggio – 4 luglio.

MONOGRAFIE E CATALOGHI
DI MOSTRE PERSONALI

1977
Antonio Migliori, CSAC, Quaderni n.36,
Università di Parma, catalogo della mostra.
Testo di A.C.Quintavalle.

1978
Segnificazione, Grafis Edizioni, Bologna. Testo di
A.C. Quintavalle.

1979
Fotografia gestuale di Nino Migliori, Quaderni
del Verri, n.2, Bologna. Testo di C. Gentili.

1982
Nino Migliori, Gruppo Editoriale Fabbri,
Milano. Testi di M.Capobussi, G.Celli,
A. Colombo.

1997
Nino Migliori in "Fotomagazine", n.5, Milano.
Testi di E.Prando, M.N.Truant.

1999
Instant, Galleria d'Arte Contemporanea-Pavullo,
catalogo della mostra. Testo di P. Barbaro.

Gente-Anni Cinquanta, L'Artiere Edizionitalia,
Bologna. Testo di A. Colombo.

2000
Nino Migliori, Fondazione Guglielmo Marconi,
Bologna. Testo di C. Cerritelli.

Nino Migliori. Trasfigurazioni, Edizioni
Caleidoscopio, Lucca, catalogo della mostra.
Testo di Gyonata Bonvicini.

Trasfigurazioni, Circolo Culturale Mario Cosci,
Stiava. Testo di P.E. Antognoli

2001
Neorealismo – Scenes of life in post-war Italy,
Keith de Lellis Gallery, New York, catalogo della
mostra. Testo di A.C.Quintavalle.

2002
Nino Migliori. Le Avanguardie e il Realismo,
Fiaf, Torino, catalogo della mostra. Testi di A.C.
Quintavalle e C. Pastrone.

Nino Migliori. Ombre di Luce-50 anni di ricerca
sul potere della visione, Fondazione Italiana per
la Fotografia, Torino, catalogo della mostra.
Testi di D. Curti e M. N. Truant.

Nino Migliori. Materie e memorie nelle scritture
fotografiche,Edizioni GAM, Torino, catalogo
della mostra. Testo di L. Miodini.

2003
Checked- One year under control, Ken Damy
Edizioni del Museo. Testo di M. Vescovo

Pop up. Tesi off camera, Ken Damy Edizioni del
Museo. Testi di P. Binante, P. Giarretta,
F.E. Marelli.

CATALOGHI DI MOSTRE COLLETTIVE E
PUBBLICAZIONI SELEZIONATI

1955
Fotografia italiana, Fantoni, Venezia.

1975
Grafica grafica I : I , Calcografia Nazionale,
Roma.

1978
Metafisica del quotidiano, Galleria d'Arte
Moderna, Bologna.

1979
Venezia '79. La Fotografia, Electa, Milano.

1980
Fotografia e immagine dell'architettura, Grafis,
Bologna.

1981
Linee della ricerca artistica in Italia 1960/80,
De Luca, Roma.

1983
L'Informale in Italia, Galleria d'Arte Moderna.
Bologna.

1985
Il dopoguerra dei fotografi, Grafis, Bologra.

The European Iceberg, Mazzotta, Milano.

1989
L'insistenza dello sguardo, Alinari, Firenze.

1990
Das Photogramme in der Kunst des 20 Jahrhunderts,
DuMont, Colonia.

Effemeride, Alinari, Firenze.

1993
Muri di carta, Electa, Milano.

1994
The Italian Metamorphosis, 1943-1968,Solomon
Guggenheim Museum, New York.

1995
L' io e il suo doppio. Un secolo di ritratto fotografico in Italia 1895-1995, Alinari, Firenze.

Europa de postguerra 1945-1965. Art despres
del diluvi, Fundacio "La Caixa", Barcellona.

1997
Fotografia italiana per una collezione, Neos
edizioni, Torino.

Un paese unico. Italia, fotografie 1900-2000,
Alinari, Firenze.

1998
Nove maestri, Monografie Fiaf, 16 , Torino.1999
El neorrealismo en la fotografia italiana,
Ed.Photoespana, Madrid.

Il rosso e il nero, Electa, Milano.

2000
Amen fotografia, Istituto Superiore per la Storia
della Fotografia, Skirà, Milano.
Fotoalchimie, Museo Pecci, Prato

2001
Esercizi di stile, Palazzina delle Arti La Spezia–
Le Mostre n. 6, SilavanaEditoriale.

Sperimentalismo fotografico in Italia, 1970
2000, Craf n°7,Lestans.

Gli anni del Neorealismo .Tendenze della fotografia italiana, Edizioni Fiaf, Torino.

2002
En plein air dopo Duchamp, Re Enzo editrice,
Bologna.

Collezione Permanente – Nuove Acquisizioni,
Museo Pecci Prato – Gli Ori, Prato.

2003
Mamme d' Italia, Mazzotta fotografia, Milano.

Gli Anni della Dolce Vita. Tendenze della fotografia italiana. Edizioni Fiaf, Torino.

2004
Il museo, le collezioni, Museo Fotografia
Contemporanea Villa Ghirlanda, Tranchida,
Milano.

Storia d'Italia. L'immagine fotografica 1945-
2000. Annali 20. Giulio Einaudi Editore, Torino.

Printed in Italy, june 2004
by Grafiche Damiani - Bologna
www.grafichedamiani.it